THOSE WHO SERVED

~~~

THOSE WHO WAITED

WWII Experiences as Told by the Veterans and Civilians of Brewster/Southeast New York

Compiled by
Dolores Beal Stephens

HERITAGE BOOKS
2008

HERITAGE BOOKS
AN IMPRINT OF HERITAGE BOOKS, INC.

Books, CDs, and more—Worldwide

For our listing of thousands of titles see our website
at
www.HeritageBooks.com

Published 2008 by
HERITAGE BOOKS, INC.
Publishing Division
100 Railroad Ave. #104
Westminster, Maryland 21157

Cover: Mayor Henry H. Wells was the chairman of the Selective Service Board and faithfully stood at the railroad station holding a large American flag, wishing farewell to the recruits as they were leaving home for military service. Cover photograph of Brewster railroad station courtesy Denis Castilli.

International Standard Book Numbers
Paperbound: 978-0-7884-2484-7
Clothbound: 978-0-7884-7586-3

This book is dedicated with appreciation to

those of Brewster/Southeast, N.Y. who gave their

lives in service to their country during WWII and to

those veterans who honorably served and returned

home.

Acknowledgements

The list of those who helped in the production of this book kept growing.

There was Robert Palmer on whom I came to depend more and more. He provided me with the honor roll list of Brewster/Southeast and another list on which he had circled the names of surviving veterans. We would exchange information as addresses changed – as knowledge of the whereabouts of veterans became known. When I found a correct spelling or an address, I would pass it along to Bob, because as an active member of the veterans' affairs through the VFW, I knew the corrections would be made.

Larry Molahan, a Korean War veteran from Carmel, N.Y. worked on the list of those killed in action in the town of Southeast. Seventeen was the final count. Many thanks to Larry for the corrected list.

There were those who supplied me with addresses, information or were helpful in other ways. Some of them follow:

Malcolm Beal	Joan Larkin
Gertrude Brennan	Muriel Pinckney Richards
Millie Buck	Willis H. Stephens
Beatrice Green	Charlotte Tuttle
Fran Edwards	Virginia Dutcher Ward
Robert Heinchon	H. Crosby Wells

George Carlone sent me copies of The Brewster Standard articles relating to many service men and women. These included many snapshots. Larry L. Woodard, author of *Before the First Wave – the Third Armored Amphibian Tractor Battalion* gave me permission to quote from his book and wished me well. A friend and neighbor in Tuftonboro, N.H. Docie McCormick came to my home and helped with problems, which arose with the computer. As I neared the stage of coordinating the book, Larry McCormick offered his help and experience in getting the pages together for the publisher. I learned much about what the computer can do. I also learned that I did some things the hard way. I am very appreciative to the McCormicks for their unselfish aid.

My thanks to Henry H. Maxfield, a Wolfeboro, N.H. neighbor who published a book about his experiences in the CIA and has written two novels, for his advice. And to Elisa Wright of the Wright Museum who volunteered to work with me on cleaning up the manuscript on the computer, my many thanks. My husband Mallory accepted my project, understanding not only how important it was to me but with a growing appreciation of what it was meaning to our living Brewster veterans and their families. He was always there when I wanted to discuss an issue.

There were numerous ends to tie up in the manuscript, and for this I asked a recent graduate of Clarkson University, John Thornton for help. Although he was the only person remunerated, I want to thank him for all the hours he spent at the computer. John was extremely helpful.

When I reached the point of talking with the editor of Heritage Books, I found Corinne Wills to be very helpful in explaining exactly what was required of me, and I appreciated that.

My thanks to all of the above people who made the course of this project much easier. And to the veterans and family members as well as home front contributors who let me interview them and follow up with questions by telephone and letter with patience and encouragement, my many thanks.   D.B.S.

Table of Contents

Introduction

My interest in the subject enclosed within these covers probably dates back to when I was three or four years old walking hand in hand with my mother in the Decoration Day parades in Brewster, N.Y. The men wore American Legion uniforms, and the women wore navy blue capes. There were also children in the junior auxiliary. The men's faces were filled with pride, and there must have been an air of reflection. They had been through "the war to end all wars", World War I.

As a teenager I played in the Brewster High School Band marching in the parades of every May 30th. When I finally moved up to the place of solo trumpet, it was my duty to play taps at the Electro-zone Field where there was a war monument and where the older men played baseball. It was a day of fun and a day out of school. But in 1944 when I graduated from high school, World War II was going full throttle, yet I didn't, even then, know what my friends, schoolmates and other Brewster servicemen and women were experiencing. Without the daily impact of television pictures, we only knew what was broadcast on the radio and what was written in the newspapers. We saw movies with war themes, with the music we were dancing to, with handsome pilots and Marines, tough sergeants, and glamorous leading ladies smoking cigarettes. They told us that everyone was behind the war effort, and we were going to win the war, but friends were being killed.

My father joined the Army Corps.of Engineers, and early in my junior year of high school he was in a convoy headed for the North African Campaign. In my senior year he was in Sicily. I cried into my pillow many nights. My mother was a rock, taking care of the myriad household responsibilities including the newly added coal stove in the basement that heated the water, caring for her children and working for the Red Cross three or four days a week.

Time passes - WWII finally ends and not long afterward there was the Korean War, then the Vietnam War. I was starting to understand the importance of homeland support when our citizens were in uniform and fighting. Today this is even more clear.

Many times I have been asked when I started to think about doing this book, and what made me want to do it. It was in the year 1997 when my husband, Mallory, and I were living in Mount Kisco, N. Y. Our son and daughter were out of the nest, and I had been taking courses at Pace University. The thought came to me, and I had never had a thought affect me as that did. But never having tackled anything as complex as putting a book together, it would slip to the back of my mind. Every now and then the thought would emerge with the same excitement and urgency.

We were talking about retirement and started looking far afield for a place to live starting in New York State, then Vermont and finally New Hampshire. Our son by then had gone to Wells, Maine and we started focusing within an hour of his residence. And so it was that we finally found a house in Tuftonboro, N.H., four miles north of Wolfeboro. Our daughter had by then moved to New Hampshire.

After settling our house, I started volunteering in the year 2000 at the Wright Museum in Wolfeboro. This is a World War II museum with not only a military building but also a home front building where looking at all the artifacts and displays one is taken back to the late 1930's and 1940's. This must have been the catalyst, as my interest in a book about the veterans of the Town of Southeast (Brewster) took hold for good. Having received an initial list of addresses in 2000, I sent out my first letter explaining my project saying that it did not matter what job the serviceman or woman was assigned to or whether he was in combat. Every job was important! Without the backup jobs or stateside duty, the front line servicemen couldn't function. There was no response. After a couple of months, I decided I must contact each one by telephone. They weren't going to make it easy for me. Almost every veteran with whom I spoke said, "sure, Dodie, I'll sit down and talk with you", or I was told he would write up his story and send it to me, but "I didn't do anything very important." I was off and running. But there were more contacts to make and more addresses to find.

From the beginning I wanted a section in the book containing stories of wives, brothers and sisters, students, and defense workers - those Brewster people who were saying good-bye as their serviceman or servicewoman went off to serve. They worked making airplane parts, had to deal with rationing, wrote V-mail letters and received the dreaded letters from the government. I wanted a voice from those who waited. I wanted not only the military histories but also the recollections of those young military men about Brewster and what life was like before their lives were irrevocably changed by war. The stories of the young women who worked in defense factories merely substantiate our knowledge of what women across America did for the war effort during WWII.

Robert Palmer, a Brewster veteran, supplied me with the Southeast Honor Roll list, and we both started locating veterans and addresses. He is an active VFW member and has great interest in all veterans. It is he who watches over the graves of veterans in the Southeast cemeteries, placing flags starting a month before Memorial Day. We met several times going over the Honor Roll list and talking about who was where. Bob has been a great support and believer in my collection of veterans' stories. I could not have proceeded without him. Part way through my interviews veteran John Santorelli suggested I use the VFW hall on Peaceable Hill Road for the Brewster interviews.

I arrived for my first interview of the day on September 11, 2001 when John met me. He had not had his television on, so as I started to say something about what I had heard on my car radio around 9 a.m., I could see an expression of disbelief come over his face. And then we went into the VFW lounge and watched the early reports of the terrorist attack on the World Trade Center. Somehow I felt that for a WWII veteran who had gone through what John had, this attack must have had a deeper meaning than I could imagine. Although I enjoyed being welcomed into many homes, the use of the Veteran's hall helped a great deal.

Then other people, relatives and friends responded with addresses. My original plan was to include all the Southeast veterans in this book, living or deceased. The Honor Roll list has 572 names. My original list had 131 names. Some of those veterans were deceased, and I could not obtain stories from relatives, or there were no relatives to my knowledge to contact. There were those whose whereabouts we did not know. There were only a few stories promised which never materialized. Numerous veterans were not well but were eager to talk with me or sent their stories. Several sent me short, concise histories with the bare essentials including dates, training and rank. I am certain some found it too emotionally taxing to call up the memories of their combat duties. Many widows and children were eager to have their family veteran's story told and either sat with me in an interview or wrote the story. In several cases where a veteran could not for one reason or another be interviewed or write his own story, I mailed a form with pertinent questions from which I wrote the story. In these cases, the story may be short, but I felt they were at least included. There were those I interviewed who were too young to enlist during the war years but entered the military after hostilities ceased and served. They are included in the home front section.

One thing I sometimes fault myself for is not being aggressive enough to get more combat stories, the death, the horror, the loneliness of our soldiers, sailors, coastguardsmen, marines, and airmen. But as I would reflect on this, I felt I simply could not further invade their memories. Perhaps if I had been a total stranger to them, and I had prodded more, they would have given me more details They told me what they wanted to tell me, and I respect them for what they said and for what they did not say; for behind the blank spaces I know were their own horrors of war.

At the stage where I had done multiple interviews and written up seventy plus stories, I received a list containing the balance of the honor roll veterans. There were no addresses, and I was not familiar with most of the names. I did not know how many on the list were still living. At that point I realized that to start pursuing addresses on this list would mean at least another two years. I had started in 2000 and it was now 2002.

As I received stories in the mail and did interviews, I realized that I had to decide just how these stories were to be written. There were some which were so complete and readable that I took them verbatim. Others had to have some repetitions removed and some juxtaposing of paragraphs. Whatever changes were made from the original were minimal, as I did not want to spoil the integrity of the tellers' words. And most of all I wanted it to sound like the veteran speaking, not the compiler of the memoirs.

Throughout the process of writing, there was editing, and my husband, Mallory, joined me in the later stages of editing and proof reading. He also plowed through information on the publishing process, the part I least enjoyed. There were decisions to make. I wanted to get on with the book and see these veterans' stories in print. I wanted to tell them they could now read about themselves and their fellow veterans. Time was also taking its toll. I was encouraged to go with the original list and not prolong the process. My final act of search was to put a notice in the local Putnam and Dutchess County newspapers asking veterans and families to contact me if they had a story to contribute.

My last thought is about the veterans themselves. They were very supportive, appreciative and simply a great group. I regret being unable to obtain stories about the women who served during that time except for my sister. Some are not well, and others have passed away. They were a great service to their country.

In several stories there are Brewster friends who met far from home. Some were in the same battles but didn't know it at the time. I encouraged the veterans to tell me what medals they received. Many did so. But the fact that the awarding of medals to any particular veteran does not appear in a story does not mean they were not earned – only that they were not reported. I also encouraged the veterans to talk about their beginnings in Brewster – what life was like, their friendships and their activities. They were all products of the Great Depression.

I finish the book with the greatest respect for them all, and it is a privilege that, having grown up in Brewster, I happen to have known most of them. One thing they all have in common besides having honorably served their country is their love for their hometown, Brewster, New York.

Dolores Beal Stephens

The Village of Brewster, Photo Courtesy of Denis Castelli.

Army

Malcolm T. Beal

Two times I tried to enlist in the Army but was turned down. I couldn't pass the physical because of my flat feet. After I graduated from Brewster High School in 1943, I again tried to enlist and that time, because I volunteered, they had to accept me but in the category of Limited Enlistment.

I went for basic training at Ft. Dix, New Jersey. From there I was sent for engineer training at Fort Belvoir, Virginia, then to Camp Reynolds, Pennsylvania for more training. While I was at Fort Belvoir in 1944, my Uncle Ross Beal, who had returned from drilling wells for the troops in North Africa and Sicily, was until his release assigned to Fort Belvoir as Ass't Post Engineer. One day in August I was out on maneuvers when my sergeant told me someone had come to see me and told me where to meet him. It was pouring rain. Soon I saw my uncle who was in uniform and my cousin Dodie walking toward me. My Aunt Florence was in the car. We visited only a few minutes in the rain.

My service after that was in the Engineer Corps on Amchitka, one of the Aleutian Islands. Our work was mostly related to repairing and maintaining airfields on Adak and Attu; however, because I was a replacement, I could be asked to do anything that had to be done. The airfields were used as stopping points for the Air Force airplanes on their way to the Pacific Theatre. There was great concern over whether the U.S. would be attacked by the Japanese; they had already made a landing on two of the islands and had been driven back by our troops. The weather on the Aleutian Islands was harsh. In order to get from one building to the next, it was necessary to use a rope strung between buildings; otherwise it was easy to become lost in the blowing snow only a short distance from the buildings. I found out that there was a battalion of troops on the island who had been sent there as a punishment for acts they had engaged in. The isolation and weather were certainly punishment.

My father, Philip F. Beal, Jr. had carried on the business at P. F. Beal & Sons after my uncle had joined the Army. When he got back to the business, I was still in the Army. I learned while still in the Aleutians that my father was terminally ill. He and my uncle were very close; my uncle was then carrying on with the business alone.

At that point I wanted to get home to be with my dad, and my uncle needed help running the business. So he enlisted the help of a friend who was a retired army colonel to expedite my release. The atomic bomb had been dropped, and after two years in the Army I was released in January of 1946, and returned to my father before he died. I rejoined the business, being partner with my Uncle Ross until his retirement. Then I ran the business, bringing in my two sons, and eventually their sons. I retired and left the business in good hands.

Having been engaged before entering the Army, I married my childhood sweetheart, Marjorie Lane of Brewster in March of 1946. We have four children.[1]

William Ross Beal

Some of Ross's fondest recollections were being a Boy Scout and love for the woods and streams. As a young scout he won an award for collecting and naming the most wild flowers. His award was a copy of the book, *Black Beauty*. He knew all the lakes and streams around Brewster and became a good fisherman and hunter, and he knew the names of all the trees. He attended Brewster school until his junior year, and then graduated from Pawling Preparatory School.

During WW I at age seventeen Ross joined the Navy and served on the ship, *USS Amphitrite* which patrolled the eastern coast of the United States.

When Ross returned to civilian life he joined his father's well drilling firm, which later would become P. F. Beal & Sons. He and his brother Phil worked with their father, and later when their father retired they were partners. They were a good team, talking over various jobs and working on company situations – and joking with each other.

Ross had met Florence Simms at a beach in Connecticut and fell instantly in love with this lovely girl who was a part time artist's model in Westport, Connecticut. They married in April of 1919 when Florence was 19 years old and Ross was 22. In time Ross and Florence had three daughters. When they were children he would take them out into the countryside on an autumn Sunday, where he had spotted a hickory tree. They would all scramble to pick up hickory nuts, and in the weeks following he would make penuche in their kitchen. When the local lakes were solidly frozen, he took Florence and the girls to Vreeland's Pond on Turk Hill and captured the family outing on his movie camera. On the 4th of July he purchased small firecrackers for the girls, showing them how to light them with a punk and do it safely.

In 1938 Ross Jr. was born and became the center of attention for all and made his father especially proud. There seemed to be enough love to go around for all, however, and the girls felt sure that each one was his favorite.

When the Japanese attacked Pearl Harbor on December 7, 1941, the dynamics of most families in the U. S. changed. And so it was with this family. Soon after that, Ross wanted to join the armed services. At 44 years old he was beyond draft age and had a family.

Sometime in early 1942 he went to the Pentagon in Washington, D.C. to offer his services to the Navy, hoping to get a commission. The Navy turned him down, but when the Army learned of his business experience he was immediately accepted. He was needed for the scheduled North African campaign. Capt. Beal was told he could choose two of his former employees who were experienced well drillers and were now in the Army. He selected Le Roy (Louis) Barrett and Arthur Ashby.

9-21-42 - From the Mayflower Hotel in Washington, D.C., he wrote to Florence: "Things are beginning to move very swiftly. I don't think that I will be in the country more than a month or six weeks. I know about where I am to be sent, and it is very far away...I realize fully the awful burden I am giving you, but I know how well you will hold up under it. I realize too well how hard it is going to be for me to leave you all. Well, let's be brave. Think of thousands who have already gone into service who feel just as we do"...

On his last leave before departing New York harbor, it was difficult for all the family. When the final hour came he dressed in his uniform, and in the early morning hours he went to the bedrooms of his children and kissed them goodbye. Then he hugged and kissed Florence and went out the door to his waiting car and driver. The convoy was to leave on 2 November 1942.

Ross was taken into the Engineer Corps. commissioned as a captain for the specific duty of overseeing the drilling of wells to provide fresh water for our troops as they moved forward. " The 401st Engineer Battalion was activated at Plattsburg Barracks, N.Y. on 18 April 1942... by the War Department, assigned to First Army. Only two officers had prior experience in civil life with water supply activities. On 3 May the unit was attached to VI Corps...Gathering and training personnel was a hasty process...Time was short... The Battalion was able to secure trained drillers who were hurriedly transferred to the unit from organizations in the east and middle west. Trained drillers ordered to the unit by the War Dept. arrived singly and in small groups during the month of October. As a result, the 401st was able, with a minimum of equipment, orientation and training, to place operating drilling teams in the field overseas...The last two drilling rigs arrived at the N. Y. Port of Embarkation just 8 days before embarkation...the battalion embarked at New York Port of Embarkation, at 0300 hours, 2 November 1942." The convoy was headed for North Africa.

The following are excerpts from letters to Ross's family at home as well as excerpts from his diary as stated:

Nov. 2, 1942 - ..."Well, we got started... We have been ordered to sleep with our clothes on"...

Nov. 11, 1948 - ..."We expect to land any day now (Casablanca). Today we were given maps of the country and dry field rations for four days. I received a report of the water supply of each city. They are very crude. Some of the water flows through concrete pipes that were put in by the Moors several centuries ago. In some cases the pipes are broken and open to sunlight...We have been ordered not to drink any water – only what is provided by the Water Supply Battalion"...

Nov. 18, 1942 – ..."Well, we thought we would land long before this... It seems the docking facilities have been shattered, and we must navigate until repairs are made"...

Nov. 19, 1942 – ..."Things must be very bad where we are headed. I am assuming this because of the delay. We are still cruising around. It seems the trip will never end. We are so anxious to get ashore and get busy"...

Nov. 25, 1942 – ..."I have been here six days since leaving the ship. I am going to try to get the letter on the same ship today before it leaves for the States. When we pulled in the harbor, there was much evidence of the terrific battle"...

Dec. 9, 1942 – ..."I am writing this out at the field of operations. (wells). We have a crew of sixteen men here that I am in charge of. They are camping at the site. I go back and forth to the main camp the other side of the city"...

Dec. 28, 1942 – ..."After coming to the new job quite a few miles north of where I originally landed, I made a reconnaissance many miles inland. At the head of the valley, I encountered a camp of soldiers that have been in a concentration camp since the French Armistice. In this camp, there are Germans, French, Czechs, Russians, Italians, Spaniards, Swiss and Dutch, including French Foreign Legionnaires. There are about 80 in all. They are anti-Nazi. They were very glad to see me. I gave them all the rations, cigarettes and candy that we had. They are a very nice bunch of men. Among them are doctors, lawyers, manufacturers, chemists, etc. that were made to leave Germany because of, I think, Jewish blood, or on account of their unfriendliness to Nazism. Among them was a German who speaks fairly good English. He invited me to bring two of my men with me for a party with his men on Christmas Eve. I took Louis Barrett (Brewster) and a boy from Texas. They had killed a pig a few days before, and we really had a banquet, soldier style. The German cooks (and Dad will be interested in this) made several different kinds of sausage. We had about an eight-course dinner. They had a Christmas tree in one corner of their hovel with cotton and tangerines tied on it for ornaments. These men are a wonder. They were happy and contented outwardly – most of them are separated from their families, but they try to make the best of it. They are very friendly to Americans and only want to fight under our command. I stayed out on the job and didn't go back to the main camp. I only get back there every few days for a couple of hours"...

Jan 12, 1943 - ..." I am not sorry I joined the Army, realizing the importance of my work. Our battalion has done a good job so far, and it is a big one...civilians are not allowed to use a car...everyone rides a bicycle. I have never seen so many in my life. They also use mules, ponies, and velo-taxis (for one person). What cars and trucks that operate are using charcoal and alcohol. It seems funny to see a car with the back end covered with two big boilers, pipes, etc. You can see the fire in them as you go by"...

Jan 13, 1943 - ..."I didn't tell you I had a trailer hook put on the back of my little car. Now when I have to go a long way off, I'll pull my bed and room along with me...I obtained the hook from a wrecked Jeep"...

Jan 26, 1943 – ..."Sunday I had a most interesting day at my friend's house. His name is Mohammed Bouelal...At this dinner was a Sahib representing the Sultan of Morocco, and six other Arabs dressed, of course, in their native way... After the meal, my friend put his arm around me in good old American style and offered me the graciousness of his house at any time I wanted to come. He is planning to send his boy to study in the U.S. to be a doctor"...

Feb. 10, 1943 – ..."I had a nice Valentine today – General Patton and General Harmon stopped in to inspect my installation, and they both commended me on the way I handled the job and stuck to it"...

Feb. 14, 1943 – ..."Tell Phil the ground water temperature here is 68 degrees which is the annual mean temperature. In New York it is 50 – 51 degrees"...

Feb. 17, 1943 – ..."I had a very interesting assignment today. I was asked to make a reconnaissance for work in my line for the Sultan of

Morocco"...

Feb. 27, 1943 - ..."I believe the work mentioned for one of the Sultan's palaces will be a success. I am putting in the pump tomorrow..."

March 7, 1943 – ..."I had a very nice dinner with the French Consul General on Thursday...Afterwards, I took him to show him the final installation of the well and pump. He was very pleased with it. The Sultan had been there already, unknown to me and passed approval...There are rumors that we will be moving up in a month or so... The fact that we will be in action may not be so bad...I do not look toward it with any sense of fear. All officers here are anxious to get started, realizing that the sooner it starts, the nearer the end of the war"...

March 10, 1943 – ..."Monday I received a letter from the French Consul General. It said in French, and I am writing the translation, 'Dear Friend, I have been asked to invite you to dinner next Thursday, March 11th at 12:30 with one of the important ministers. This should be very interesting and you will see a beautiful palace. Come... at 12:25. Bring your camera. Very Cordially,'...I have a job coming up now that will take me many hundreds of miles away from my base...Don't worry though. I have a crew of men that will go through anything for me including Art Ashby and Louis Barrett"... (former employees)

March 14, 1943 – ..."Well, this week I have had an experience that few American soldiers, or in fact, few people have had. The privilege was accorded me on account of work satisfactorily completed for His Majesty, the Sultan of Morocco...On Thursday a dinner was given in my honor... On Friday I was invited to visit the gardens at the Palace, and part of the Palace... An interesting thing happened when we arrived at the end of one of the balconies, and I knew the next place we would visit would be the zoo. I turned toward the door that I thought would take us to the garden below. The Arabic First Minister said, 'No! No!' He turned to the French Consul and said in French, 'That is the door of the Harem, and no one is allowed to go in there.'"

March 18, 1943 – "...I have left my battalion behind again... I am on an extremely important job from the standpoint of success or failure. Another unit did not make out so well; in fact they did not make out at all....

March 18, 1943 – "... a telephone call from the Adjutant General's Office... He said, 'I have a letter from the French Consul General that

I would like to read to you... (Quote) His Majesty, the Sultan of Morocco would like to have Captain Beal of the United States Army come to the Palace and present himself as soon as possible to Si Mammeri, Chief Protocol of the Cherffien (native) Government'...I had already sent my clothes on in a truck. I borrowed a blouse, shined my fatigue shoes and went to see the Consul General. I didn't look very good but it was the best I could do under the conditions...I was taken to the second floor of the Palace where His Majesty sat in a huge chair, his feet on a cushion and an electric heater under his feet. On entering, we all bowed from the hips. Halfway to his chair we bowed again, and the same when we were a few feet from him. I was presented to him, and shook hands. I sat in a chair with M. Lemaire next to me. M. Lemaire was the interpreter for me. He asked me where I am from in the U.S. and if I was married and had a family. I showed him all the pictures of you all which I carry in my wallet. He was very cordial, but brief. He then told me that he appreciated very much the work I was accomplishing here as water was very important to his people... he appreciated also the prompt and efficient manner in which it was done... and said, 'In view of all this I would like to honor you by bestowing upon you this decoration'. He stood up and I walked over to him. He then pinned a medal on my blouse. The AGO Office had sent an Army photographer down. He took a flash photo of the ceremony and another examining an Arab knife and silver sheath that was given to me immediately after he pinned the medal on me...After a few more minutes of conversation, we said goodbye. I shook hands with him again and thanked him very much. We then bowed our way out as we had entered. As we passed all the native guards, they all bowed from their hips to me. I'll tell you I couldn't help but wish you could have seen it all. It was certainly a thrill"...

March 23, 1943 - ... "I have learned that there is much more work for me ahead than I thought. I am glad as it keeps my mind occupied. I am a long way up toward the front from my Battalion... The knife I told you of in my last letter is supposed to be a symbol of rank...this one is comparable to a Shiek. The order is Pasha 1st, Caid 2nd, and Shiek 3rd. It is held in very high esteem by the Moors and Arabs... sacred to them...the one given to General Patton was comparable to a Pasha. The length and amount of engraving denotes its owner's rank"...

March 26, 1943 – "Tell Dodie not to worry about the Arabs. I get along very well with them. They are around wherever one goes. If it's way back toward the mountains, and you stop your car, they will come up to it seemingly from nowhere. They live very close to the soil."

March 28, 1943 - ... "General Clark inspected a job I did here the other day. I shook hands with him"...

March 30, 1943 - ... "I am doing some work at an airport near here, and I saw some bombers come in yesterday. I hung around the plane and helped the pilot load his gear... When he climbed back on board, he opened a sliding window, put his thumb and forefinger together in a circle and took off. I watched him until he went out of sight up toward the front"...

April 2, 1943 - ..."I also forgot to tell you that each man that worked on the job for the Sultan was given a pair of silver bracelets. They are a matched pair"...

April 14, 1943 - ... "I saw some very interesting water wells today... One was drilled to a depth of 200 feet and had a flow of 300 gallons per minute. The other one was at a depth of 800 feet with a flow of 1500 GPM...Near this site was an area approximately 100 feet across that was filled with boiling springs (cold water). Where the water came up out of the ground, it would carry a certain amount of sand making little conical mounds. This area was filled with these mounds, and it was a strange sight. From this area and the overflow from the wells, a river starts that is ten feet across and with a variation in depth. Small edible fish live in this stream... More work is coming in all the time. I think I will have to have an additional machine to handle it. That pleases me; the more work I have, the better I like it".

April 27, 1943 - ... "I stopped in to see M. Robert Lemaire, the French Consul General. While there, he informed me that I was to receive the affidavit...accompanying the medal...given to me by the Sultan...I have since heard that in the paper it states, that 'all wild beasts will quake at my approach, lions will slink away, and foxes will crawl in their holes'...Won't that be interesting to get?"...

May 4, 1943 – ..."Where I am now is about two miles out on a level plain in a huge valley... I am set up right in the center of a hundred acre field of wheat"...

May 6 – ..." I washed all my clothes, took a bath in a bucket, and cleaned all my guns. I hung my blankets and bedding roll on top of the wheat, so I should sleep very comfortably tonight, what with clean pajamas and a fresh bed"...

May 26, 1943 - ...." This A.M. I left before breakfast in a jeep with a captain in the Air Force for a hunt in the desert... When we arrived at the mountain, we began to see gazelle ...I shot two, and the captain with me shot three. We brought enough back for our whole camp to have some... On our way to the hunting ground, we stopped to chat with a nomad Arab. He informed us that his Sheik wished to have us have dinner with him on our return. We stopped on our way back and found a delicious meal prepared for us"...

June 3, 1943 -... "I found out today that because of the record and success we have had, that the whole well drilling section of our battalion has been selected for a special mission. It is probably no more than we did before, but it makes me feel good. We have been given a deadline of a little more than a week to get cleaned up here, and I have just started an important job. I am working this machine twenty-four hours a day, so I may finish...Whenever I hear of our movement, I immediately think of home – I would like so to talk things over with you. I know more now of what is ahead for me than I can say... You will probably know by the news"...

Somewhere in Sicily:

July 11, 1943 – (diary) ..." birthday, 46 years old. Had a bottle of Coca-Cola, first in almost 9 months. K-rations for 1 day received for use after landing"...

July 13, 1943 – (diary)..."Pulled in and anchored about one mile off shore from Gela at 6 A.M. Left ship and good food on an invasion barge at 3 P.M. Evidence of a tough time on D-day – two large ships sunk. One bomb landed in the funnel of the ship and 134 soldiers and sailors lost their lives. Marched 4 miles, full pack – air mattress and blanket. Bivouacked in an almond and olive grove...Our co. captured a machine gun, 500 rounds of ammunition and some Italian rifles"...

July 14, 1943 – (diary)..." marched back to the beach to find trucks. Gela, population 20,000 had its water main broken and the city is without water. Truck and machine has not been delivered on shore yet."...

July 15, 1943 – (diary)..." Lt. Mitchell and Colonel Hurley were killed by a mine. They were in a Jeep with another officer and driver. Gunfire is almost over, but there is much aerial patrol by Spitfires"...

July 16, 1943 – (diary)..." left the company to put in a well at Gela, Sicily airport. About ¼ mile north of airport found a frame building used formerly for two 20 mm. Italian gun positions...cleared out the building and are using it for my crew... placed the two guns in position and have 2000 rounds of ammunition"...

July 17, 1943 – (diary)..."8 Italian prisoners came into our camp and gave themselves up. I turned them over to the M.P for P.O.W. camp... bad bugs and fleas in the shack... slept two hours and was all bitten up. All hands moved out in the open...Enemy planes bombed runways of the airport with delayed action bombs which killed 8 men and a lieutenant in the 809th Aviation Engineers...I took a bath in a bucket today, and received all of my gear. There is a full moon tonight and that is bad"...

July 18, 1943 – (diary) ..." expect a big raid at the airport tonight... am running the drilling machine and 4 ton Piamont and ½ ton Dodge on Italian gas – the dump is close by... enemy left their barracks in such a hurry, that spaghetti was still on their plates."...

July 19, 1943...." Things are pretty rough, but I am all right... I have just completed my first job here. It only took me two and a half days, flow of well 250 GPM – pump 50 GPM. Things are progressing way ahead of schedule here so I will be pushing on soon, I hope...I have lots to tell you when I can write in peace"...

July 24, 1943 –..." German mine went off near machine while I was away. Killed three boys (shepherds) who came to building for clothes...While in Salwisetta found that 2 engines (RR) were not running due to lack of water. Called HQ and advised them. They gave me OK to call Col. Carter, Second Corps. who has C Co. attached to them. They gave me approval for No. 4 tank trucks to haul water to the engines. Waiting for Capt. Talcott for final approval. When arriving back at North Station, our bivouac area, I found that explosion had occurred in my absence. Priest made one small box and two large ones for bodies. Condition of ground is bad. Low on water. No food - Just getting by – everybody asked for something to eat – all buildings in town shattered and a good many completely demolished"...

July 25, 1943 – (diary)..." Lice very bad since arriving in Sicily – two or three hours of sleep lost every night. Flea powder no good"...

July 25, 1943 – ..."I just lost my four ton Brockway truck and trailer, both fully loaded, which were left on a grade last night. At eleven o'clock today, it went down over the bank, and the truck turned over. The machine wasn't hurt, but the truck was a complete wreck... Truck and machine have already been pulled out, and the truck turned in for salvage. It is quite a loss to me, and I feel as badly as though it were mine – I need it badly"...

July 26, 1943 (diary) ..."found two bodies near RR station. Notified priest"...

July 28, 1943 (diary) ..."Thrilled to hear that Mussolini has been put out. Perhaps I am a little nearer home now"...

July 30, 1943 (diary) ..."Left Caltinissetta Station (R.R.) at 6 A.M. Went to Palermo and reported at Engineer office. On my way back took a short cut and almost went through a bombed bridge – 30 ft. drop. Oil line on brakes broke on way home. Muffler fell off. Very bad road. Returned home at 7 P.M...Prices have started to skyrocket just like Morocco and Algiers. Had a dinner in an Italian Inn with wine, vinegar and oil on tomatoes – delicious"...

July 31, 1943 – ..."I made a water reconnaissance today to two very old cities. It was very interesting but heartrending to see the pitiful condition of the people. We receive fruit drops in lifesaver form with our rations, and I gave away about a dozen rolls today. It is pitiful to see people digging around in the wreckage of their homes trying to find some of the things they know are there...I saw a boy waiting for diggers to uncover the body of his father. It was awful to see. He crossed himself and knelt down by the remains and cried pitifully. I walked away after that"...

August 1, 1943 – (diary)..."Florence's birthday. Wish I could be home with her"...

August 8, 1943 – ..."It has been such a nice day here. The wind is blowing in right off the sea...it made me think of home; then of course, I decided to write a letter to you...I go along all day with a longing in my heart to see you and the children. Then when mail comes along, momentarily I drift back home in my thoughts, and you are all nearer to me"...

August 15, 1943 (diary) ..."Moved machine to hospital. Set up. Drilled 10 feet. Water at 60 feet. Coquina rock (Florida) (Shells) - Very poor"...

August 17, 1943 (diary)..."Fleas very bad. Sand flies"...

August 18, 1943 – (diary) ..."Tested well. Got a letter from Florence and Dodie"...

August 19, 1943 (diary) ..."Sent package to Florence. Had bad day. Moved machine to 59th Evac. Hospital. Gave instructions to proceed with building stone pump house"...

14

August 23, 1943 – (diary) …"Very bad air raid. Flack dropped all around hospital and bivouac…British ship on fire and lit up harbor; then they bombed ship and sank it. Number of dead and missing 16. Wounded 46. German fliers brought in to 56th evac. Hospital and 91st evac. Hospital"…

August 25, 1943 – (diary) …"Went to 91st hosp. to check pipe line and 56th to check pump…Turned on pump…Turbine pump – big flow. Handles satisfactorily"…

August 26, 1943 – (diary) "…Moved machine from 56 evac hospital to Mondela staging area. Started drilling at 3 P.M. Drilled 20 ft. All sand and shell rock"…

August 28, 1943 – (diary)…"Went to Mondella. Returned to area after having written letter home. Truck hit a shell hole and threw me out while out on job. Hurt my back. Did not do anything about it"…

August 29, 1943 – (diary) … "Couldn't get out of my bunk. Taken to 91st hospital. Doctors all good to me. X-ray shows no bone broken. Very bad pain in my back. Upset stomach. In misery, trying to lie flat on my back"…

August 30, 1943 – (diary) …" Lt. Sheffield, Capt. Soltroff in to see me. Another X-ray picture – nothing shows broken." Diary stopped at this point.

Capt. Beal was put in a plaster cast in hospital for two weeks, and then flown to Africa. He was on two hospital ships, and when he returned home was in three hospitals, one at Atlantic City and the last at Fort Dix, N. J. He had a 21 - day leave before being assigned to the EORP Field Maintenance Office in Columbus, Ohio. He went to Marion, Ohio and after only one month on TDY was assigned to Fort Belvoir, VA. as Assistant Post Engineer. He had charge of the post dump, which he sanitized by having all trash bulldozed to the periphery, continually leveling the mound. His other duty was maintenance of the chlorinating and filtration equipment at the Fort Belvoir swimming pools. He and his family lived in a house on the post. By chance Ross met Tom Lottreciano from Brewster who was in the Navy. Tom was invited with a friend for dinner, and everyone had a good visit. When Ross got to Fort Belvoir he learned that his nephew Malcolm Beal was in training there and received permission to visit him while he was out on maneuvers. This assignment lasted until the following May of 1945 at which time he was released from the Army.

Ross went back to P.F. Beal & Sons where he was partner with his brother Philip F. Beal. Phil became terminally ill and in time Malcolm who had served in the Aleutian Islands was able to get home before his father's death. Malcolm then joined the firm. Ross retired to his Tonetta Lake home. He died in 1963.[2][3]

Emmett Brennan

Emmett Brennan enlisted in the Army in September 1940 and was in the Infantry, stationed at Fort Dix, N.J. for a year. He became a civilian again in September 1941. On April 23, 1942 he was drafted into the Army, and since he had already served for a year and didn't need more basic training, he was sent immediately to Hawaii. He was stationed on Oahu, 762nd M.P. Battalion. While on the island of Oahu he met with Cpl. Phil Ryan, Sgt. Bill Murtha and Sgt. Len Butler, all Brewster men.

From there he was sent to join "Operation Iceberg", the 1945 invasion of Okinawa. Amongst the more than 180,000 men who participated in this invasion were other Brewster men some of whom were Howard Dingee (Marines) and Philip F. Beal (Navy).

On December 29, 1945 Emmett married Gertrude Benziger, and they lived in Lake Purdy. He worked for American Export Lines and went to photography school at night under the G.I. Bill. He used the knowledge he gained to enjoy many hours of picture taking. In 1951 he changed positions going to work for IGE (international division of General Electric). After thirty-one years of service he retired from the Aerospace Division of IGE and moved to Venice, Florida. Emmett died in October of 2000. [4]

Joseph G. Brennan

Joe Brennan, like his brothers, graduated from Brewster High School. He enlisted in the Army, and after graduating from Officers' Candidate School married Mary Dick.

Joseph Brennan met with his brother Leo in England. He took part in the invasion of Normandy, and it was at that time that he was promoted to Captain. He met up with his brother Leo again in Valognes about twenty miles from Cherbourg, just before the fighting ended in that city. He was wounded July 15, 1944 six days after Leo was wounded at Tribehon, France. Joe had been shot in the right arm between the shoulder and the elbow by a German sniper. The bone was badly shattered, and it would take six months for him to recover. He was hospitalized in England before being sent back to the states.

After the war he went back to work for the New York Central Railroad where he worked as a conductor until he retired. They moved to Sun City, Arizona, and several years later his wife, Mary, died. Joseph later married Madonna Beck.

Joseph and his first wife, Mary had six children: two boys and four girls.[5]

Leo A. Brennan

In the class of 1941, Leo was on the Brewster High School track team and acted in the senior play, *Meet The Folks* which according to the 1941 issue of *Resumé* was "known as the best senior play in years." Also from that issue of his yearbook he used a favorite expression of the time, "What's the matter – tired of living?" He was also known by most of the people in Brewster because he faithfully delivered their newspapers. His story follows:

"In February 1943 I entered military service and shipped overseas to England in January 1944. I was assigned to Company C, 297th Engineer (combat) Battalion, VII Corps. First Army. We landed on Omaha Beach on D+3 (June 9). On our way crossing the English Channel our Navy friends operating the LCI assured us they would bring us up on the beach when we landed. It didn't happen that way. They dropped us in hip-deep water, and as we waded ashore we had to dodge the shell holes or go under water. I'll never know how the Rangers scaled those cliffs on D-day with the Germans firing at them from pillboxes on the top.

Our first assignment on the continent was to keep the MSR (Main Supply Route) to Cherbourg open. We cleared roadblocks, mines and built culverts and a POW enclosure; VII Corps captured 33,000 German troops before the fighting ended in Cherbourg on June 27th.

Across France, Belgium and Germany we constructed 45 bridges. These included: single, double and triple Bailey bridges, steel tread-way, floating Bailey, floating tread-way, timber trestle and pontoon bridges. Most of these bridges ranged between 100 and 300 feet long, and most were built under fire and many under cover of darkness. The longest bridge was over the Rhine River at Rolandseck, Germany just south of Cologne. It was a floating tread-way 1,128 feet long completed in 23 1/2 hours and ready for use March 1945. In addition to our engineer work we were engaged in infantry operations while assigned to the 4th Cavalry Group from September 19 to November 10, 1944. During this period, our operations included holding segments of the front line at the Siegfried Line at Lamersdorf and in the Hurtgen Forest. Just before Christmas we were forced to retreat back into Belgium during the Battle of the Bulge, which started on December 16, and we spent Christmas in a small town, Houffalize, Belgium. The winter was bitter cold, and we were required to keep the roads open 24 hours a day for both troops, tanks and heavy equipment moving in both directions (to the front and from the front).

We reentered Germany a second time in the middle of February, and on February 23 we completed a bridge across the Ruhr River at Durem, Germany. We continued to travel east and constructed 19 more bridges in Germany. Our final bridge was completed on April 19, 1945 at Halle, Germany over the Elbe River.

Just before we reached Halle, on April 1 we moved into Nordhausen. In this town was a concentration camp where Russian, Polish, and other political prisoners were sent by the Germans to work and then die. Just outside of town above a huge underground V2 plant where the slave labor was forced to work was a crematory. When they were too weak to work, they were left to starve to death and then wait their turn for the furnace. Over 6,000 bodies were found here and several thousand more in various stages of starvation. We required the German civilians from the town to bury the dead bodies.

We were involved in the five major campaigns of World War II in the European Theatre of Operations (ETO), namely:

June 6 – July 25	Normandy
July 26 – Sept. 14	Northern France
Sept. 15 – Dec. 14	Rhineland I
Dec. 15 – Jan. 25	Ardennes
Jan 26 – Mar. 2	Rhineland II
Mar. 22 – May 12	Central Europe

Rhineland is in two parts because of the Battle of the Bulge.

I saw my brother Joe (U. S. Army) in England and again in Valognes, France, which is about 20 miles from Cherbourg just before fighting ended in that city. I also saw Donald Smith once. I believe it was somewhere in Germany that I ran into Bob Palmer. He was assigned to another engineer outfit.

My brother Joe was wounded July 15, 1944. I was wounded July 21 in Tribihon, France and was sent back to an Army Field Hospital. I spent a week there and was lucky to catch up with my outfit, since they had not moved forward. This was just before the Allied breakthrough at St. Lo, and the march across France, which began July 26, 1944.

My decorations include: Bronze Star*, Purple Heart, ETO with five battle stars and two Letters of Commendation with several endorsements on each. I was discharged from the service in October 1945."

*Leo's citation reads, "The Bronze Star Medal for meritorious service in connection with military operations against an enemy of the United States during the period 9 June 1944 to 20 March 1945, in France, Belgium and Germany. He has at all times performed his duties under combat conditions in an outstanding manner. His courage, devotion to duty and leadership under fire was an inspiration to all. His work has aided materially in the success of his unit in combat." [6]

Bernard H. Brewer

When I was a child my father and mother ran B. H. Brewer, a dry goods store in Brewster, and after school my Aunt Gertrude Brewer, Grace Hine and Mallory Stephens would wait there for the train going north, as Aunt Gert lived in Towners and Mallory lived in Patterson; there were no schools there. Grace lived in the old saltbox near the entrance to Tonetta Lake Park. Aunt Gert, Grace, her brother George Hine and Mallory were close friends from childhood. Grace married Mallory, and they eventually moved to Brewster. Aunt Gert married George, and they lived in Brewster.

Before the war I worked at Eaton Kelly Co. in Carmel. In 1940 there was conscription, taking men into the military for a year. Henry Wells, a Spanish American War veteran, was on the Draft Board, and he used to walk from Brewster over to Carmel daily. I said to him, "I work in Carmel and have to go there every day. There's no point in your walking over there every day, when I have to drive there; so why don't you let me pick you up at your house?" He said, "You want to do that?" So that is what I did. People began to talk in both communities when they saw me driving Henry (Harry) to Carmel. They were saying look at Brewer; he's going to get out of the draft, taking Harry over there to Carmel every day. Finally Henry said we're going to have to do something about this.

So my turn came, and I was sent down to the camp on Long Island where we got inducted and got all our uniforms. They began calling out draft numbers coming to mine, "32338802. Brewer, Brewer, from Brewster". I was told I was wanted in the office and that I must know somebody, because they wanted me to go to Camp Croft, S.C.; but that camp was full, and it was going to be about 10 – 15 days before they started the new session. So I was given a furlough. When my parents saw me in uniform they were beside themselves. When I went back, I was sent to Spartanburg, S.C. for thirteen weeks basic training. That was 1940. While I was there Bob Hope and his crew came, and that was quite exciting. At the end of thirteen weeks the commanding officer told us we were going on a 25-mile hike the next day and that during the breaks each soldier would be interviewed and told where each one would be going. He was sitting on a big oak tree, and the First Sergeant was nearby. "Private Brewer?" he said. Yes, sir. "You are going to Fort Bragg, N. C. You were so good on every piece of

firearm, we're going to send you up there" So I asked him if that was
armored, and when you graduate you are an officer. And he said yes. I
told him I'd prefer not to go there, because I don't want to be an
officer. He took off his cap and said, "You don't talk to an officer in
the Army like that. Sergeant, didn't I see where the Military Police
needed a couple of bastards?" He said yes, they do. The officer said,
"We have a bastard right here. You are going to the Military Police."

So I went into the MP's, and I was sent down to Gadsden,
Alabama. I was pulling city duty. An M.P had to accompany every
military patrol car that went into the city where there was a camp. I
pulled that for about four days and had to have a bagged lunch and
have an early breakfast. So I went into the mess hall to get my
breakfast and bagged lunch. Not a soul was there, and I heard cussing
and carrying on. I went into the back. It was an officer. He said to me,
"You're a private, right?" I told him yes, and that I was there for my
breakfast and my lunch. He said, "Can you imagine in the MP's the
Mess Sergeant is drunk and two of the cooks are drunk. It's going to
be a while. You're going to have to help me get breakfast." So I
helped him get breakfast, and after breakfast he told me to go to my
tent and stay there until I was called. I was in my tent writing a letter
home, when I got a call telling me to report to the Provost Marshal's
office. The Provost Marshal said, "We looked up your records, and in
them you said that your hobby is cooking." Back when I was going to
school, they started a home economic department with a very
attractive teacher. I told my Uncle George who was then on the
School Board that I had three study periods and that I would like to
take the cooking course. He spoke to the principal, Herman Donley,
who said it would be all right. Three of us boys took the course – and
that's why I put that down.

He said, "You know what is going to happen? You're going into
the mess hall, okay, Corporal?" I said, "Corporal?" He said, "yes,
you're a T5 now". So I went into the mess hall, and I probably cooked
there four weeks; I did a lot of baking. I got a call from the Provost
Marshal. In his office he said that I was doing a wonderful job. I was
told General Patton was not happy with the Infantry they've given
him to run alongside the tanks. So he was going to start an Armored
Infantry Battalion in Fort Smith, Arkansas – Camp Chaffee. I was
going to be the Mess Sergeant at the new place.

While in Gadsden, Alabama I married Dorothy Minerley. She
called me and said she was finished school, and it was time we got

married. So, she came down. We planned on having a big camp wedding, but the camp became quarantined. We went to the public building in the city and got our license. The man standing next to us asked us where we were going to be married. I told him about the quarantine, and he said it's my lucky day because he was a Presbyterian minister, and if we wanted he could marry us right there. So we went into the file room with the cabinets all around, he grabbed a woman to be witness and we got married.

When we got to Fort Smith – Camp Chaffee, my wife wanted to get a job. I was now involved with the Officers' Mess. At Fort Smith they trained all the officers and non-coms and others in armored infantry. I was still a corporal, but was acting sergeant in charge of the mess hall. I wasn't attached to any unit. Because it was an Officers' Mess, they paid for their meals. I had to go to the commissary once a week to buy the food, and whatever money was left over from that week was mine. I took half the money and divided it up with the cooks. So, I made a good amount. My wife went to work for the PX, and we were there for probably a good six months. A group of officers were transferred to Little Rock, Arkansas.

One day we got a big surprise. General George Patton secretly flew out and came to Little Rock before we left. It was after the North African Campaign and before the invasions of Italy. The officers told me he liked apple pie so I made an apple cobbler, and General Patton thought that was the greatest. I got all kinds of comments on it. He gave a speech to the officers. He said he wanted a show of hands of those that liked him, and everyone put up their hands. He said, " I never want to see that again. I don't want any son of a bitch out there to like me."

We were there probably five weeks and then transferred to Ozark where I was mess sergeant. This was a Chemical Warfare center, but while there it was decided to cut out chemical warfare training, as the Germans were not using chemicals. They sent us about seventy-five officers. I had two cooks and one fellow who didn't have the capacity to do anything else in the Army, so they sent him to me to see if I could use him. He was excellent with pots and pans, cleaning them and putting them away. The officers used to come around to do a white-glove inspection. He also did a good job on the stoves and grills. So I said I would keep this fellow.

I was being transferred to Orangeburg, N.Y. We were headed overseas. My grandfather Brewer was dying and wanted to see me. I couldn't get a furlough and Mrs. Hall who worked for the American Red Cross in Brewster went to work. She worked hard for the servicemen's families and the servicemen. My officer told me I could have a furlough and drive my wife home if I would drop his wife off at Myrtle Beach where she lived.

In December 1943 we left by boat from New York harbor and arrived at Lime Regis, south of London, England. We were in a large hotel on the fourth floor. There was a problem. There were no facilities for baking, so we couldn't have any bread or cake, and the officers lived on it. I told the officer that when I looked out my hotel window I saw a sign that said, *Bakery – Tea and Crumpets*. There might be an oven there. He said, "You have a big mouth, why don't you go over there and see what you can do." So, I went to the bakery and the hostess greeted me. I asked her if they had a bakery there, and she said yes. I told her my difficulties. "Well", she said, "I'll tell you right off the bat that Mr. Alpin, the owner, does not like Americans, because you are ruining our little town with this heavy equipment going up and down these narrow streets. One of those tanks is going to hit the corner of one of our buildings. Let me bring out Mrs. Alpin."

I was holding her kitten when she came out and she said, "Do you like kittens?" When I said yes, she told me, "You can't be too bad then." She told me that Mr. Alpin doesn't like Americans, but said she would see what she could do. She returned and said he would see me. I went in and asked him what time he used his bakery and equipment. He said he used it from three to ten in the morning. So I told him we could come in at ten. We would not only pay him, but since I could see his shelves were quite empty I could provide him with flour, sugar and everything under the sun that would help him.

He said to me, "My wife says that you're a nice fellow. So I'll do it." So I left, went back and loaded up all my equipment. My officer said to send two cooks over who were bakers. MP's were also assigned there. An hour after they went to the bakery, they were back. The men said that the owner did not make the agreement with the guys I sent there; he made the agreement with me, and if I wanted to go there the agreement stands. If not, it's off.

My officer said, "What choice do we have? We have to have baked goods. We have to have bread." So back I go and unload everything and left to go back to my hotel room.

In those days whenever there was any Army material whatsoever, there had to be a guard. So out in front of the bakery are two guards with rifles walking back and forth. Mr. Alpin said he wouldn't have that. Mrs. Alpin came up with the idea that I use their spare room. She pointed out that I would have a rifle and wouldn't that suffice? Back I go to my officer with this arrangement, and he said, "Move right over."

At some point in 1944 we were ready to leave England. There hadn't been a German U-boat in the channel in a long while. One struck the ship ahead of us and sank it. Seeing those bodies floating by was something. We had to anchor down right away, because we were four miles off the coast of England. The ship was an English ship from 1928, made of wood but iron clad. We sat there for five days while they cleaned up the harbor, and we could get in. On the boat there was very little to eat, only tea and corned beef. That's all we had. There were no facilities on board for men's rooms so it was over the side of the boat. An airplane got the submarine, and we got started for France. We went into Cherbourg.

We were sent to a huge brick building on the coast. The officers would be there maybe one and a half months waiting to be assigned. They had hired three French people to show us around and show us how to operate everything in the building. The mess hall was going to be down on the lower floor like hotels. I smelled this peculiar odor. When I went outside I asked what the smell was. The man said come, come, and he took me down below and showed me three large heating units for heating the building. He told me that when the Germans came here, the building housed 6,000 mental patients. They took all the women and cut their hair off, so they walked around with small caps. When the Germans left they threw the 6,000 patients into the furnaces. I was told that what I smelled was the smell of the burned flesh. The odor was awful. No one knows about that. We were there until the war was over.

They sent us down to Marseilles, attached to the 66th Division. The officers had to run the camp for the soldiers who had enough points to be sent home. Those who didn't have enough points were sent to Japan. The war in Europe was over.

When I was in Fort Smith, Arkansas and Little Rock, every Friday night they put on a dance for the officers. I didn't have to do this, but I baked up pastries and made tea and coffee. They really appreciated that. My wife came, and I loved to dance. In Marseilles one of the officers told me I had done things way beyond duty, and I had been good to them. They were sorry I had never been attached to any unit. Even though I was getting sergeant's pay, I was still a corporal. Because of all these things, they wanted to take me to Paris for three days. So we went there by train and had a very nice dinner. Then I was told that the officers had a big surprise for me. I was going to dance with a French professional dancer. I was told my name would be announced both in English and French. When the lights came on, I was to go out on the dance floor. The announcer said, "The mess sergeant is coming out even though he doesn't have sergeant stripes." Then, out comes a girl who had nothing on but body makeup, similar to the leg make-up American girls were wearing.

When I left to go overseas my wife was pregnant, and she said I wasn't to touch another girl. I danced with that French girl and never touched her. My daughter was nine months old while I was overseas. That was some experience. My face was red.

While still in Marseilles one of the officers asked me how many pies I had, and I told him twenty-five. He said, "I always wanted to throw a pie in somebody's face." He did, and then everyone was throwing pies. What a mess! I said, "Who is going to clean up this mess? " All the officers went and took showers and dressed and then came back and cleaned it all up.

It was 1945, and it was my turn to leave Marseilles for Norfolk, Virginia. We got through the Straits of Gibraltar, but then it was discovered that one of two propellers wasn't functioning. Everyone was sick, and since I hadn't told anyone I was a cook I was put in charge of the latrines. We had a choice of going back to Marseilles for repairs or to limp home. Everyone said, "straight ahead". We took off and got to Norfolk a little late, the day before Christmas, and we all wanted to get home. When disembarked, we were told they had a big surprise for us – doughnuts and as many glasses of milk as we wanted. We got on the train heading north. The grade going up was steep, and the drive shaft let loose and fell down. It took four hours to get that repaired. We arrived in New Jersey Christmas Eve. We disbursed according to states, and the New York group went to the New York sector. As the five of us got there, the sergeant gets up and announces he's leaving, and he left. We all needed passes, and there was no one to give them to us. Our officer said he saw what was coming and had called a taxi, which would cost us fifty dollars or ten dollars each. He told us we would be AWOL, but he knew we wanted to get home for Christmas. I got on the train at Grand Central Station and ran into Joan Beal (a WAVE) from Brewster. So we sat and talked all the way home and had a lovely visit.

When I reached home, I met my nine-month old daughter. She wouldn't have anything to do with me. She was actually three years old before she would let me touch her. All she did was cry. Two days after Christmas I went down to Fort Dix for my discharge papers and was told, "We can't issue any because you're AWOL." One of the officers in my unit came over and said, "This whole damn place can go plum to hell. I don't care whether I am AWOL or not; I am going home – are you going home?" I said yes, and I came home. When I was home I talked with Mallory Stephens, and he suggested I see Harry Barrett, the county clerk. He provided me with a card stating, "Bernard Brewer, Draft No. 32338801 is Honorably Discharged." I carried it in my wallet, but didn't care about it until three years ago, when a friend suggested we go over to Castle Point Veterans Hospital. When it came time to fill out the Medicare form I was told I wasn't listed. I had to go to Peekskill and fill out a form. It took six months, but I finally received my discharge papers.

One day I received word from England that Mr. Alpin was getting out of the bakery business. They had no children, and so he wanted to offer the business to me. I was very pleased, but my wife and I decided we didn't want to leave the United States. I went back to work for Eaton-Kelly and continued later in that business elsewhere.

Whenever I went to a veterans meeting, I always felt guilty because I didn't see any action.

We had three children.[7]

Ernest R. Buckstine, Jr.

Ernest R. Buckstine, Jr. grew up on Center Street in Brewster living with his widowed mother Daisy and sister, Naomi. He attended Brewster High School with childhood friends Johnny Truran, Bill Cox, Elizabeth and Beatrice Denton, Alice Stephens, and graduated in 1935. After two years of training at Gaines Business School, Ernie worked as an executive secretary at Quigley & Co. in New York City. In anticipation of his draft into the Army, Ernie and Elizabeth Denton married in October 1942. They were living in Mt. Kisco, N.Y. when he was drafted and inducted into the army on March 25, 1943.

After only three weeks at Camp Dix, Ernie was assigned to the newly created 66th Black Panther Division and transferred to Camp Blanding in Florida. Based on his administrative skills, he was assigned as secretary to the 66th's Commanding General. Elizabeth took the *Silver Meteor* to Florida to visit Ernie, and they decided she would move to Florida becoming a camp follower. After having returned to Brewster and then driven back to Florida in a used '38 Buick convertible, she found a job as a registered nurse at St. Vincent's hospital in Jacksonville. This entailed a daily commute of fifty-two miles, and as one might expect a lot of negotiation with the Office of Price Administration for gasoline rationing appeals.

Clearly there were some advantages to being secretary to the General – including foreknowledge of impending troop movements. So, as Ernie was ordered to Little Rock, Arkansas as part of a small contingent to arrange movement of the 66th to Camp Joseph T. Robinson, Elizabeth and a friend drove straight through to Little Rock to get a head start on house hunting. They found a place soon after their arrival.

Only a week later the car was again the center of attention when it was stolen. Ernie and Liz had taken it into Little Rock, and it seems they were "conned" by a local. The man posing as a manager of a parking lot took their keys and was of course, along with the car, nowhere to be found when they returned from dinner and a movie. Fortunately it was found late the next day when a police officer noticed it with its top down in the pouring rain. There was no damage and only a spare tire, wheel and tube were missing. They were replaced, and the Buckstines were forever convinced of the value of insurance, as John Ralph Truran Sr's insurance agency paid them the $43.29 replacement cost.

Little Rock continued to be exciting when Ernie and Liz moved to another apartment shortly thereafter. After a long day of moving, they fell into bed and slept soundly – only to awaken the next morning, look out the back door and find that a tornado had passed through. The row of houses immediately behind their home had disappeared!

At the end of October Ernie went on furlough, and they drove home to Brewster. They visited with family and friends and had the opportunity to see Sergeant Johnny Truran before he shipped out to England with the Headquarters of the 1st Army. Upon his return to Little Rock, Ernie was promoted to T5 Sergeant in the Adjutant General section.

On April 10, 1944 Ernie was ordered to Camp Rucker in Alabama, again as part of the headquarters contingent preparing for the transfer of the 66th into the IX Corps. of the Second Army. A nursing job at Station Hospital's Out Patient Clinic was found for Liz, and the Buckstines settled into life at Camp Rucker. Ernie was even able to spend most nights off base at their apartment. In July there was a furlough back home and another promotion to T3.

By the end of September rumors of overseas orders were a "penny a piece"; overseas furloughs started and Ernie's furlough was supposed to be from October 16th to the 28th. They drove to Savannah, Georgia, stored the car and took the *Champion* to Penn Station in New York City. After only thirty-six hours in Brewster they received a telegram ordering Ernie back to Camp Rucker immediately. In the end, it was nearly a month and a half before he shipped out to Europe, and they had a lot of time together before he left. Liz and her friend Ruth Bercaw quickly drove back to the northeast in order to see their husbands off when they embarked for Europe from New York.

The 66th shipped out of New York on November 15th, went to England for preparations to land on the continent, and in December 1944 disembarked in Cherbourg, France. It was assigned to the 12th Army Group Coastal Sector to relieve the 94th Infantry Division, which had been containing the German garrisons in Lorient and St. Nazaire. At the time Ernie was still in the Adjutant General's section of the 66th Headquarters. Until their surrender in May 1945, over 53,000 German troops were contained in the two pockets. During that action, 78 Black Panther officers and 2,170 men were killed or injured.

In mid-May, the 66th moved to Koblenz in the Fifteenth U.S Army Rhine Province, and under the control of XXIII Corps. assumed responsibility for the occupation and the military government of Regierrungs Bezirke Koblenz. Early in 1946 the division moved through Marseilles and returned to New York.

Ernie was honorably discharged from the Army on April 9, 1946 as a Tech. Sergeant. He carried his discharge papers in his wallet until he retired, and when asked why, he said, "My final orders were to 'keep your discharge papers with you'"... So, he did.

Ernie returned to Elizabeth, and two and a half years later they had their first child, Ernest R. Buckstine III. A second son, William Townsend Buckstine, was born in June of 1952.

Ernie worked his entire career for D. Mallory Stephens and his son Willis H. Stephens. He held various State of New York positions on the staffs of Messrs. Stephens, as they were State Assemblymen. This included Chief of Staff for the Assembly Ways & Means Committee when the Republicans were in the majority and the Assemblymen were Chairmen of the committee. Liz continued her nursing at Northern Westchester Hospital for several years and then as the office nurse in several physicians' practices in Pleasantville and Mt. Kisco, N.Y.

The Buckstines lived in Pleasantville, N.Y. for over twenty-five years. Their lives were full of teaching Sunday School, managing the acolytes and helping with antique and rummage sales at St. Johns Episcopal Church, summers at Barnegat Light, N.J. and hardly ever missing a New York Giants' football game. They retired to Barnegat Light N.J. and Port Orange, FL when Ernie became sixty-five in 1983.

Ernest R. Buckstine, Jr. died in July 1987.[8]

George J. Carlone

In 1942 before my graduation I left school, enlisted in the Army and was given a war diploma (given to those who enlisted before graduation). I went into the 8th Air Force and planned to be a tail gunner, spending six weeks in Miami Beach, then to Mobile, Alabama and Chinook, Illinois. I took six weeks basic training in Oxford, England. I left the Air Force and went into the 2nd Division 23rd Infantry. On June 6, 1944 I was amongst the invasion troops that landed on Omaha Beach, D-day, 1944. I went through Paris, France, Belgium and on into Germany. The 23rd made a 365-mile drive in 23 days to Merseburg, west of Leipzig. We went on to Prague, Czechoslovakia until V-E Day, May 8th 1945. By then I had enough points to go home. I had been overseas for thirty two months. I was discharged at Camp Fanin, Texas on August 27, 1945.

Back home I worked on the New York Central Railroad for thirty-eight years, retiring as a locomotive engineer.

In 1947 I married Doris Kilburn. We have a son and a daughter.[9]

Patrick M. Carlone

After graduating from Brewster High School in 1938, I traveled by rail daily to the Gaines Business School in New York City and received my degree in Business Administration.

On September 4, 1942 I was inducted into the Army at Ft. Jay, New York. The first thing they checked was my schooling in business, and I was immediately placed in Battalion Headquarters of the 444th Antiaircraft Division as an administrative officer with the rank of Technical Sergeant. I supervised the work done by six clerks in Battalion Headquarters, in charge of payrolls, morning reports, duty rosters, ration reports and battalion strength. It was also my duty to write up courts-martial and special orders.

During 1945 I served overseas for five months in the Asiatic Pacific Theatre Operations. While waiting to be discharged I took the opportunity to take courses at the University of Hawaii.

Medals received were the Asiatic Pacific Service Medal, Good Conduct Medal and the American Service Medal, Sharp Shooter Medal and World War II Victory Medal.

I worked with the Spain Insurance Agency in Mahopac, N.Y. for thirty-five years. It was there I met my wife Rose Ann Veschi. We were married in May of 1946 and have four children.[10]

Anthony Carollo

Anthony Carollo was born in New York City December 14, 1908. He attended school in the Bronx. Anthony's family moved to Brewster in 1919 when he was eleven years old. He then transferred to the Brewster Schools.

He was from a family of eight, one girl and seven boys, Fred, Vinnie and five who served in World War II, Anthony, Charles, Archimedes, Victor and Joseph.

Previous to his induction in the Army, Anthony worked as a plumber for S.D. Avery Plumbing Co. in Brewster.

Anthony joined the U.S. Army March 31, 1941. He was included in a group of fourteen in the "Eighth Contingent of Putnam Draftees from Brewster". They were one of the first groups to be inducted in the Army from this area. He joined the infantry. His tour of duty took him to Mitchell Field, Long Island, N.Y., Fort Eustis, Virginia, Salt Lake City and Ogden, Utah, Fort McDowell near San Francisco, California and to Hawaii.

He was in Hawaii, when he received a notice of "Demobilization by the Government" which in his case meant he could be discharged (age 28 and older). On November 21, 1941 at Fort McDowell, California he was discharged and his records transferred to "Enlisted Reserve". From March 31, 1941 to November 21, 1941 Anthony served as a Private, Coast Artillery, unassigned.

He was home just a short time when the Japanese bombed Pearl Harbor, December 7, 1941 (16 days since he left Hawaii). What a blessing he escaped the bombing!

He was called back to service January 19, 1942 at Fort Dix, N.J. At that time he took a three week Military Education Course at Bell Laboratories in New York City. The course was given in maintenance work in the Information Center. On July 17, 1942 at Fort Dix, Anthony was promoted from Private to Technician 5th Grade, Company "D" 583rd Signal A. W. Battalion.

"Summary of Military Occupational Specialty":
Anthony was an Aircraft Warning Plotter # 510. He placed small markers on plotting and filter boards to indicate the presence, type, direction and altitude of aircraft approaching, receiving information by telephone from radar stations.

He went on to Manila, the Philippines and Australia and was on active duty in Luzon and New Guinea.

Anthony was discharged from the service December 5, 1945 at Fort Dix, New Jersey.

Foreign Service:
Asiatic Pacific area, 2 years, 1 month, 26 days
Continental Service: 2 years, 4 months, 11 days
Total time served: 4 years, 6 months, 7 days

He received several medals and documents of appreciation from the U.S. Army as well as from the U.S. Air Force.

After his discharge from the Army, he again went to work as a plumber for S.O. Avery Plumbing Co. in Brewster. Subsequently he established his own plumbing and heating business in Brewster where he worked until his retirement in 1980.

On May 19, 1951 Anthony married Dorothy Cummings from Benedicta, Maine. At that time she was working as an R.N. at the White Plains Hospital in White Plains, N.Y. They had two daughters. He died at his home in Brewster in October of 1983.

Anthony never wanted to talk about his war experiences undoubtedly because there were too many sad memories.[11]

Joseph Carollo

On June 1, 1944 I entered the military, receiving sixteen weeks of infantry training at Camp Wheeler, Georgia. I was then shipped overseas as a replacement on December first and assigned to Co. B, 409th Regiment, 103rd Infantry Division. We fought in the Rhineland, Germany. On December twentieth I was hit in the left arm by artillery shrapnel and spent time in hospitals in France and England before being shipped to Camp Edwards, Massachusetts. I received the Purple Heart and was discharged October 25, 1945.

The Carollo family had seven boys and one girl, and five boys served in the Army during World War II. The oldest, Anthony was the first to be drafted, followed by Charles, Arky, Victor and then the baby of the family Joe. Anthony served in the South Pacific; Charles was shuttled across country in the United States; Arky was in England, France and Germany. Victor was in North Africa where he had a passing hello with Rooster (Donald) Smith. He then went to Sicily and Italy. Out of five brothers who served in the Army, I was the only one injured. God was good to the Carollo family. [12]

Joseph J. Cioccolanti

On Sunday, December 7, 1941 I was at the movies with Malcolm Beal, Ted Turnrose and a bunch of kids. They stopped the movie, and they announced that Pearl Harbor had been bombed by Japan and that war was being declared. Everybody said, Wow! We were unprepared. I can remember they were training with stovepipes instead of guns. To show you what a great country we are, we were able to gear up our manufacturing processes and everyone got behind the effort.

In 1944 I was seventeen years old when the Defense Dept. was offering an exam, which if I passed, I could choose the branch of service. I was too young for the regular service. To go in the usual way I would have had to be eighteen years old. In a month or so I was notified that I had passed the exam, and in September I was assigned to Harvard University where I was to start the course in Civil Engineering. My father took me to the station; we shook hands and said good-bye. We didn't show much emotion in those days. At the end of the semester they did away with the ASTP, and we were all sent to the infantry. They had so many casualties, the highest being amongst the lieutenants. Ferd Vetare was in the Navy program and was at Middlebury College. He was there quite a while.

I took a bus from Brewster to Fort Devens, Mass. and from there to Camp Blanding, Florida. In the three or four months training program I was learning the basics of being an infantryman, learning to take orders, marching, learning how to shoot a rifle. We were training in the swamp, pinewoods and wetlands, so we thought we would be sent to the Pacific. I ended up in the 106th Infantry Division at Camp Atterbury, Indiana, near Bloomington. One day I was walking down the street, and who do I bump into but Ulindo Tranquilli. He was in the Headquarters Company. After three or four months we were sent to Fort Meade, Maryland to be sent overseas. On a Saturday night we were all on the train headed for the ship, and they came through with a big list; some names had been red-lined, meaning that those men would not be getting on the ship. I found out that a congressman had a son who had enlisted or was drafted and was sent overseas immediately after basic training. There was a hue and cry that these young men were being sent overseas into battle fresh out of basic training. Changes were made and the soldiers from then on had to spend more months in training. After basic, I was assigned to Camp Butner, N.C., near Durham and spent three or four months there.

In January of 1945 I took a train to Massachusetts and sailed with the 89th Division from Boston. We landed in England and were immediately put on landing crafts headed for Le Havre where we went to Camp Lucky Strike, a mobilization camp. It was a bunch of tents in a field of mud. I remember slogging around in mud up to my knees every day; it was like chocolate pudding. It was terrible - you couldn't dry your feet. Our leather shoes and our socks would get wet, and we couldn't dry them. They really didn't prepare us for those conditions. It was cold sleeping on a cot in unheated tents with no sleeping bag, nothing. We slept with our clothes on; it was really cold. We used to burn some kind of grease to waterproof the boots, and the soot just hung on the tent. We were given two meals a day – breakfast and dinner, because they didn't have enough food. Jazz music was played, only two pieces, and they were played a hundred times a day and very loud. C rations were good; we didn't mind them. We could heat up the scrambled eggs and beef stew; sometimes we had to eat it cold. The A rations were not very good, a tough biscuit and Spam, always the same.

When orders came to move, we were going so fast, walking didn't do it. We'd ride in trucks until such time as we would run into resistance, then get out of the trucks and walk through fields and villages. We were in the countryside, never in cities, and if we were going to be there overnight, we would knock on the door in a German country village. We'd ask in German if they had any eggs. The woman might say yes and give us eggs. Sometimes she would say, "nein". We could look through and see a cupboard with hams, and smoked meat. We would say in German "you have". If she was very difficult, we would walk in and not only take eggs, but also a ham. We would never abuse anybody, and we wouldn't take a lot. We might cut salami in half. We couldn't carry much. The fresh eggs were wonderful. We could always find a frying pan and cook them.

We were bathing ourselves in big hot pots, and just as we were bathing they called us to leave on an antitank outpost. We had to hurry and dress. It was very tense. They hadn't given us the password to get through the American lines. An American soldier was going to shoot us because of not having the password, but we finally got through. Three of us were staying near a little train station that night, and about fifty feet away we could hear German tanks and armored cars all night. I'll tell you I was never so scared in my life. We only had a bazooka and a carbine. At night we couldn't do anything. We weren't sure what they were. They may have been retreating. I don't know. We just stood there. It was scary. We had a concrete floor to sleep on, but I didn't sleep all night not knowing whether they were going to blow us up. Fear wasn't too bad. Some guys would really get rattled. They'd become blubbering idiots. I saw that happen only once. There was a G.I. from Pittsburgh, Pa, a loudmouth, always bragging about this and that. When things got tough, he turned into... just fell apart.

We were mobilizing and went to Luxembourg. We got into the fighting outside Luxembourg; we came to the Trier River Valley where Moselle wines come from. As we got near the Rhine we really got into fighting; we were either being shelled by the Americans or the Germans. In the afternoon we would get some air support. Hundreds of bombers came overhead; you could hear them for twenty minutes before they got to us. Then way off in the distance there would be flashes of light. A half hour later they would over on their way back to England.

I did see American and German fighter planes in battle, and it was spectacular. In one particular fight I saw the American shoot down the German plane. German fighter planes strafed us, and we would shoot at them with our rifles, but it didn't do any good. I should have led the plane; I hadn't done enough duck hunting.

We went through Gothe, Germany. I left the 106th Infantry that Tranquilli was in. He was captured and put in prison. I was in an antitank company with 57 mm. cannons. They found out that these guns weren't suitable, so they gave us a bazooka. The bazooka packed a big wallop but was inaccurate. The way they selected a bazooka man was to take us out to a field where there was a pile of wood. We each shot the bazooka at the pile, and whoever came closest became a bazooka man....that's the scientific method. I had learned something about shooting because I used to go hunting as a kid. So, since I was one of the guys who came the closest, I became a bazooka man. The nice thing about being a bazooka man was that we only had to carry the bazooka, plus either a 45 or a carbine. Then you had three ammo bearers following with sacks of three shells apiece.

It was 1945. We crossed the Trier and captured Ohrdruf, a death camp. We had trouble keeping up with the retreating Germans. We were going through Bavaria and being shot at by snipers on mountainous roads in the woods. There was a brook about seventy feet wide and deep with a lot of water coming off the mountain. Some of the guys jumped into the water along the edge of the road to get out of sight. There was a replacement from Erie, Pennsylvania being shot at by snipers. We were ordered to get out of there, but he stayed out there looking for the snipers. He was gung-ho. I went to get this kid. I told him we've gotta' get out of here. Just as I got to him he reached up to his chest; I thought he was reaching for a hand grenade, but he had been shot through the heart by a sniper. I called for a medic, but there wasn't much we could do. There was a large hole in his back. I tried to put some sulfa powder on the wound, but it was too late. We were really angry, because the sniper took a life for no reason. We captured the snipers and put them on the back of a truck. There were a couple of guys from Texas, and they wanted to kill them. I said we couldn't do it; it's against the Geneva Convention rules of war. I was such a proper guy. They would have killed them. That buddy shot by a sniper - that wasn't smart fighting. When snipers are shooting at you, you want to hide, because you are a target. The snipers were really after him. I was lucky. Unfortunately this wasn't the only accident on the last day of a long tour.

We lived in a town where we took over a house. It was near Czechoslovakia. The German soldiers were coming from the eastern front by the tens of thousands marching in formation toward the west. The day President Roosevelt died we all got orders to stop fighting, but outside the billet there was a German jeep with two soldiers. The jeep was burned up. They were killed, and because they were so full of fat the bodies burned almost all day long. We dug out their wallets and looked at the pictures. It was sad. There were pictures of kids. These guys were probably in their thirties and were probably officers in their Volkswagen jeep.

We were sent on peacekeeping duty to Wells, then Salzburg and up the mountain where we were stationed near Badgenstein, not far from Bertesgarten. What a beautiful place with thermal baths! We stayed in one of those hotels on the side of a beautiful valley for close to a month – guarding piles of coal and other supplies, and then I was detached for a few days to guard another pile of coal in a town nearby. It was great. I stayed in another hotel. I wish I had taken up skiing then; they had big wooden skis there, and they would have given us lessons. I ate in this hotel very formally at night, with soup and nice crusted rolls, the dinner cooked by a German chef.

I was sent back to Camp Lucky Strike, a big tent camp, and spent two to three weeks there waiting for a boat to come home.

Being in the service during this time was a good thing in some ways, because when you go through something like that you grow up awfully fast.

I married Mary Palmer of Brewster in 1952. We have four children.

Business: Builder/developer and Supervisor for The Town of Southeast.[13]

Robert Folchetti

Robert Folchetti was inducted into the Army on June 5, 1941 at Fort Jay, N.Y. From 1941 to 1943 he was operating a winch and balloons protecting the Panama Canal from enemy airplanes. From 1943 to 1944 he was at Camp Cook, California where he trained young men in Engineer Basics and then was put in charge of their work. With the rank of T4 he was section leader of 30 men. The following year he was sent to Leyte in the Pacific where he operated cranes and loaded war supplies which were being sent to the Americans on the surrounding Philippine Islands.

His military occupational specialties are listed as: Bas Tng CA (521), Crewman Balloon (526), Winch Operator (473), Section Leader (583) and Crane Operator (063).

His medals included the American Defense Service Medal, American Service Medal, Asiatic-Pacific Service Medal, Good Conduct Medal, World War II Victory Medal and the Philippines Liberation Ribbon.

Date of separation was December 10, 1945. Deb's army years were not the happiest years of his life; consolation was he did his duty for his country. He married Anna Lotrecchiano of Brewster.

After discharge, he became an Assistant Conductor on the Penn Central Railroad, retired after 42 years and moved to Florida.[14]

Behrend Goossen

"Ben was born August 4, 1915 in New Rochelle, New York and moved to Brewster in 1927 with his grandparents, parents, brother Fred and sister Dorothy. He graduated from Brewster High School in 1932. He married Margery (Midge) Hopkins on May 10, 1941 at a ceremony at Midge's family home on Prospect Street in Brewster.

Ben was working at Vapyre Gas Corporation (subsequently purchased by Suburban Propane Gas) on Sunday, December 7, 1941 when he heard the news about Pearl Harbor. Two days later he, Midge and Elsebeth Heinen were on their way to South Carolina to meet Eddie Tuttle who was stationed there. Eddie and Elsebeth were married on December 11th with Ben and Midge in attendance.

Ben enlisted in the Army November 6, 1942 and went to Camp Lee in Petersburg, Virginia for basic training and graduated from Quartermaster Officer's Candidate School on April 29, 1943. Midge joined him and lived in a boarding house in town. From May to July he attended Ordinance Automotive School in Atlanta, Georgia and then transferred to Fort Knox in Louisville, Kentucky. They attended John Kelly's graduation from OCS at Fort Knox and Midge pinned his Lieutenant's bars on him. While there they also met with Faye Pinckney.

In October 1943 it was back to Camp Lee where they ran into Barney Waters who was also in the Quartermasters. He went on to Cooks and Bakers School and Ben to Automotive/Transportation.

Ben transferred from Quartermaster to the Corps of Engineers and graduated from Engineer Training Course No. 5 at Fort Belvoir, Virginia. Upon assignment to the 86th Blackhawk Division he served as battalion motor officer of the 311 Engineer Combat Battalion. He trained in Louisiana at Camp Livingston and in California at Camp San Luis Obispo and Cooke before shipping off to Europe in February 1945. The Blackhawks were originally trained for land and amphibious fighting and were destined for war duty in the Pacific. The Battle of the Bulge in Europe changed the assignment.

Midge returned home to Brewster when the division moved to California. In October 1944 their first child, Chloe, was born. Ben did not see his daughter until he was on leave before departing for Europe. In fact, he was in the hospital in San Luis Obispo recuperating from a hernia repair operation at the time Chloe was born.

The Blackhawk Division was the last to leave the U.S. for Europe. Under Major General Harris Melasky, commanding general, the 86th fought for forty-two days in Europe, pushing far into Bavaria before the war ended. Ben served as Motor Transportation Officer responsible for maintenance and operation of vehicles and construction equipment. The European war over, the 86th eventually returned to the U.S. After a month leave the division regrouped at Camp Gruber in Oklahoma and were assigned to the Philippines.

The 86th Division spent eight months in the Philippines. Ben served as Headquarters Company Commander of the 311th Engineer (C) Brigade responsible for all administration, housing, feeding, and general welfare of the unit. Since the war was essentially over during this time, the company was involved in clean up. Except for being away from home and his family, Ben enjoyed his time in Asia living among the Philippine people and developing lasting relationships.

The company returned to the United States in June 1946. Ben was discharged from the regular Army in July but remained in the Reserve. He retired in 1964 with the rank of Lt. Colonel.

Ben returned to civilian life in Brewster. He was District Manager of Suburban Propane until his retirement in 1976 and served as Councilman, Town of Southeast from 1950 to 1955 and as Town Justice from 1955 to 1981. He was active in the Brewster Lions Club (past President), the Landmarks Preservation Society and the Southeast Museum. He also served for a time as Town Historian and as a member of the Milltown Cemetery Board.

Midge and Ben had two more children, sons Dean and Reed. On May 10, 2001 they celebrated their 60th wedding anniversary." Ben's brother Fred also served in the Army. [15]

Frederick L. Goossen

My family moved to Brewster in 1927 from New Rochelle where I was born. When Hitler's troops invaded Poland in 1939, the war seemed a long way off, and although I think most people believed we would eventually become involved, it did not seem imminent.

I had graduated from B.H.S. in 1934 and was married and had two children at the time of the bombing of Pearl Harbor and the subsequent declaration of war against Japan and then Germany. I did various menial jobs: laborer, truck driver and manager, Brewster station for Leahy Oil Co.

Growing up in Brewster in those years was a wonderful experience. There was great pride in our town and school. Most everyone had the opportunity to participate in sports and other activities. I lettered in football, basketball, baseball and was elected Captain of the 1934 baseball team. Another of my favorite interests was drama, and I participated in high school productions and later in Brewster's Little Theatre Group as well as appearing several times in plays at Starlight Theatre in Pawling, a summer stock company.

In 1943 I was drafted into the Army, being sworn in November 26. We traveled to New York from Carmel on the old Putnam Division. The exact details are hazy, but my next stop was Camp Upton on Long Island. We were there a couple of weeks in the coldest weather ever seen on Long Island – about 4 degrees below zero.

The next stop was Fort McClellan, Alabama, an Infantry Replacement Training Center (I.R.T.C.). This huge camp was devoted to basic training of individual infantry soldiers. Every man was trained to be a rifleman (plain old foot soldier) first and then possibly some other specialty as a secondary classification.

My basic training ended about April 2, 1944, and after a ten-day delay en route I reported to Fort Meade, Maryland, a staging area for shipment overseas. I was in Ft. Meade on D-day, June 6, 1944. The highlight of my stay at Fort Meade was when I was offered the opportunity of evading a night march if I would box three rounds instead. I boxed a young kid from New York City and won the first round handily, drew the second, and got shellacked in the third. That constituted my entire lifetime boxing career.

From Ft. Meade we went to Camp Kilmer, New Jersey and then after two days embarked from New York City docks about June 15 on the *U.S.S. Hermitage* for England. The Hermitage was the former Italian luxury liner *Count di Biancomana*, which the U.S. had seized in the Panama Canal when the war started. The *Hermitage* carried 7000 troops and was part of a huge convoy shepherded across the Atlantic by some destroyers. One night we were attacked by a sub or subs, which were dispersed by the destroyers.

After landing in Liverpool July 1, we went by train somewhere in the north of England to a base called Warminster Barracks. About two weeks later we went by train to Southampton and shipped out to France two days later. While at Southampton, we experienced a "Buzz Bomb" attack. As I recall those were called V-2 bombs which were launched from Europe with enough fuel to reach a target and then fall. They were quite inaccurate, but effective on concentrated targets. We suffered no casualties, but a civilian house was hit.

We crossed the English Channel on L.C.I.'s (landing craft infantry) and landed on Utah Beach, which had been secured several weeks earlier. After a seven-mile walk inland with 125 pounds of equipment, we arrived at a replacement depot and were eventually split up and assigned to various units. I was sent to "C" Company, 1st Battalion, 329th Infantry, 83rd Division with whom I spent the rest of my combat career in Europe.

The 83rd (Thunderbolt Division) was in constant combat with the enemy for eleven months. For me it meant fighting on the beaches, fighting in the hedgerows of Normandy, the break-out at St. Lo, pursuit of Germans to the south, Loire Valley, Luxembourg, the bloody battle of the Hurtgen Forest, releasing prisoners in two death camps, the first crossing of the Elbe River where we met the Russians, and the last battle on the other side. Having said that, it does not mean that all units were engaged at all times, but we were pretty busy.

My own record contains five campaign stars for campaigns in the Ardennes, Central Europe, Normandy, Northern France, and the Rhineland. My medals include European African Middle Eastern Service Medal, Purple Heart, Good Conduct Medal, German Occupation Medal, World War II Victory Medal and Bronze Star Citation and Medal. My proudest possession, I think, is the Combat Infantry Badge. No war is ever won until the infantry soldier puts his big flat feet on the enemy's home turf.

My Purple Heart was earned when I was hit by machine gun fire while crossing a logging road in the Hurtgen Forest. At the time I was hit, I was operating as a scout for the 1st Platoon of "C" Company, as we were attacking the Siegfried Line. Ironically, after I was retrieved from the woods, I was placed on a litter-bearing jeep next to a German soldier who told me he was a machine gunner. From what I was told he was routed out of the area we were trying to take, and I believe he was the one who shot me. We proceeded to a field hospital at peace with each other at that time. He was badly wounded, and I don't believe he survived.

I was transported from Germany by ambulance to a field hospital; then after a stabilizing operation on my leg, I was taken by train to a general hospital in Paris and later flown to England to a hospital in Cheltenham.

After recuperation from a patching up operation in Cheltenham, I was routed back to my outfit at Neuess, Germany on the Rhine River. We crossed the Rhine River on a British pontoon bridge and started our dash across Germany, culminating with our crossing of the Elbe. We picked up all kinds of transportation on the way: motorcycles, German scout cars, Mercedes sedans and anything else that we could make run. When V-E Day was announced, we had pulled back and were located outside of Brunschweig, Germany.

We were then sent to a German training area called Graffenwohr to train for an invasion of Japan. While there V-J Day was announced and our fighting was over. After V-J Day we went down into Bavaria for occupation duty. That was good living with good beer, horseback riding and trips to a rest center in a castle on the Danube once owned by crazy King Ludwig. I was eventually rotated home via Marseilles. My European adventure took me to England, France, Luxembourg, Belgium, Germany, the Netherlands, Austria and Czechoslovakia.

I received my Honorable Discharge on November 2, 1945 at Fort Dix, New Jersey. Returning to civilian life was not difficult, although we had to start over. We lost a couple of prime years, but our country honored us, and we were about to enter the greatest age America had ever experienced.

My business experience is as follows: Prudential Insurance Co., Sales Agent;Goossen Furniture Co., President and General Manager; Frederick L. Goossen – Real Estate, Broker/Owner; South Seas Realty Co., Sales Director/Partner; Tripp Day & Mahan – Marine Construction, V.P. Sales. Retired 1988.

I have belonged or do belong to the following organizations:
Brewster Chamber of Commerce – Charter Member, 2nd President

Brewster Lions Club – Member – President
Brewster School Board – Member
V.F.W. (Veterans of Foreign Wars – Marco Island –Charter
    Member – Vice Commander
D.A.V. (Disabled American Veterans) – Member – Naples,
    Florida
Trinity Lutheran Church – Council Member
In 1939 I married Ruth Stiles – divorced in 1946. In 1951 I
married Nina Menichelli (deceased). In 1962 I married Bettina B.
Butler. I have a blended family of seven children.[16]

Nicolas Lovallo

I was born in Port Chester, N. Y. and stayed there to finish high school in 1933. Then, I went to join my father who worked on the farm in historic Milltown, Brewster owned by W. R. Kirkland, Jr. His beautiful house on Gage Road was built by one of the best Brewster contractors, Kenneth Newcomb. There was also a dog kennel, and my father built the greenhouse.

On April 14, 1941 I enlisted in the Army, and on July 9, 1941 I married Elvy I. Anderson from Georgetown, Connecticut. When I was inducted, I wasn't given any military training, only medical training for the medical corps. I studied anatomy, psychology, physiology and celestial navigation. First I went to Camp Jackson, later called Fort Jackson in South Carolina. We called it Stump City, because there were stumps all over, and we slept in tents. There were no barracks.

I was a cadre man and wore a red cross on my arm. It was my duty to train recruits to be medics. I wasn't sent overseas, but was sent to numerous camps to train medics and run dispensaries at Ft. Leonard Wood in Missouri, Fort Taylor, Key West, Florida and others. It was also my responsibility to weed out those who were sick from those who were faking it. If someone was very ill, he was sent to a field hospital.

There were many cases of "gold-bricking". One guy came in one morning and said he didn't feel too well. Then he said, "Come on, Herbie, come on, Herbie. I'm all messed up, and my dog is having problems" I told him to go back and take it easy. I gave him some placebo pills and told him to return in a couple of days. When he came back, it was the same story: "Come on, Herbie." He came several times, so I went to see the colonel. I told him that this guy was bucking for a Section 8. When I saw this soldier again, I told him we were going to see the colonel, and he said, "Good, come on Herbie, we're going to see the colonel". This guy wanted to get out.

Leaving the colonel's office, he gave the colonel a big hi five! And said, "Come on, Herbie, we've got to go now." I talked with the colonel, and he thought we had to let this fellow out. One more time I took this guy to see the colonel, and again he was talking to his "dog, Herbie". The colonel told him he could go. As the soldier left, he gave a good about-face and said to the colonel, "Colonel, some one of these days, you're going to need that dog". He got his discharge. He was as sane as anyone. He had worked on getting out. But the Army couldn't keep someone in like that.

There was another case: A soldier came in and said, "Hey, doc, I am in some pain. I can't lift my arm." I told him to try to move it, and he complained that he couldn't move it. So, I put his arm in a sling and told him to come back to see me in a few days. When he returned, it was the same problem. "I can't lift my arm or bend it." I took the sling off, and talked with him. After a while, I told him I wanted him to do one more thing for me. I said, "Now, take your right hand and touch it to your left earlobe. Without thinking, he touched his left ear with his right hand. I said, "You dirty rat. Out." There was nothing wrong with that guy. We had all kinds. It's been sixty years. I can't remember all the stories.

I was offered a field commission. It would have been strictly an administrative title. I even took a test and got 156 correct out of 160. The top man got a perfect score. There were three officers on the panel. I wasn't interested. A captain's pay was $225 per month and he had to buy his clothes, food and shelter. I was getting $156 a month, and I didn't have to buy anything. I was twenty-three years old.

After discharge, I went to work for P.F. Beal & Sons, Inc. in Brewster and worked for them about five years. Then I started a gas station, but the rent was too high. After that I became a bus driver. My wife and I had four children, two boys and two girls.[17]

Louis G. Manes

Louis Manes was born in Italy on January 22, 1922. He was inducted into the U. S. Army on August 21, 1941 and after training was assigned to the 34th Division. He took part in the North African Campaign in 1942 going into Tunisia then through Sicily and on to Italy, where he took part in the occupation of Naples-Foggia, North Apennines, Po Valley, and Rome-Arno. He was given the following decorations and citations: European African Middle Eastern Service Medal. He was discharged October 5, 1945.

After the war he was trained in electronics at the Delehanty Institute, School of Radio, Electronics and Television. He worked from April 1953 to February 1984 as an Electronics Technician at Perkin-Elmer in Norwalk, Connecticut. He married Teresa D'Matteo of Italy and they had four children.[18]

David C. Maroney

I was born in Brewster, N.Y. on January 10, 1913. While working on the railroad, I was called to serve during the peacetime draft. The period of time was from January 21, 1941 to November 14, 1941. I re-entered service Pearl Harbor Day, Dec. 7, 1941 and was assigned to the Coast Artillery Mine Planter Battery as a Technician #5. I had sea duty aboard the U. S. Mine Planter *"Mayback"* - Fort Hancock.

I did have a wonderful relationship with my shipmates, and a great friendship existed with one in particular, until he passed away several years ago. He was a commercial fisherman from Eastport, Maine, and for years we went on fishing trips there – and renewed our friendship.

I served four years, ten months, and 25 days. Date of discharge was December 14, 1945. When I was released, I went back to my work with the New York Central Railroad on passenger service, retiring Feb. 11, 1976 from Penn Central after 38 years of service.

I married in Jan. 1952 – a high school friend from Katonah, N.Y. – Camille V. Virtuoso, a dental technician who was employed by her brother (a dentist) and his associate in Katonah, N.Y. We have no children. We built a home on Drewville Road and have lived here for approximately 50 years.

Citations: American Service Medal
World War II Victory Medal[19]

Robert E. Palmer

After working for one year on the New York Central Railroad, on August 19, 1941 at the age of 21 I was drafted into the U.S. Army, inducted in New York City and sent to Camp Dix, New Jersey. The men were mostly from Putnam and Westchester Counties. In order to make up the full complement of men needed, men from the Bronx and New Jersey were added. It became evident that those from Westchester and Putnam County had been used to more hardships in country life and therefore adapted more readily to Army life than those from cities. Some complained about the accommodations, the 30 - mile hikes out and back, and some lined up for sick call in order to get out of hiking and other work. But there were some from the city who persevered and were good guys. We were given a box for our "civies", which we mailed home. There we received our army clothing, and after three or four days we boarded a train and eventually arrived at Camp Davis, North Carolina, which was thirty miles north of Wilmington, N.C.

We became acquainted with army life, including physical training, gradually receiving our rifles and our commissioned officers. Our guns were 40 mm. antiaircraft and four 50 caliber guns mounted in a turret and on a six-wheel trailer - later mounted on a half-track.

We remained in this area for about one year while training with our guns and equipment and learning how to maintain them. We took 30-mile over-night hikes twice a month and took part in simulated battle maneuvers. After being located near the Atlantic coast, we moved to the coastal camp, Fort Fisher, for target practice. At this area we practiced using targets towed by small aircraft, our guns – 40 mm. and 50 caliber - only being good for targets a mile or less away.

We were moving northward toward our eventual destination, New York City. Our next move was to Camp Pickett, Virginia for more specialized training and then to Norfolk, Virginia for amphibious training with the U.S. Navy. The one thing we all remembered about this training was how well we ate while there, as the Navy food was wonderful compared to what we had received in the Army. From here we moved to Pennsylvania near Harrisburg, to train at Fort Indiantown Gap and then to Fort Dix, New Jersey, where we received many new replacements. We had a number of men, some as old as 45 years old. There was a father and son named Jackson Rose, Sr. and Jr. from Cold Spring, N.Y. who had been inducted with our group from Putnam County. While at Fort Dix all of the men over 35 were replaced with new, fresh, young soldiers from Mississippi. From Fort Dix, N.J. we went to a camp in Brooklyn, N.Y., where soon after we boarded ship in New York harbor along with 5,000 other troops. Our ship was a large and fast French luxury liner that the British captured, and it was used to convoy troops from New York to Liverpool, England. It was very hot on the boat, and so crowded many of us slept on the steps between decks. I believe it was a nine or ten day voyage. It was winter and we traveled alone unescorted on a southern route, eventually entering the North Sea on the northeast side of Ireland, landing in Liverpool, England in February 1944. We changed course every nine minutes so that enemy submarines could not attack us due to our constant maneuvering. Our food was tea and fish three times a day; needless to say not very many ate the meals, so we lived on Hershey chocolate bars, which we were able to purchase by the box of twelve in the ship's store.

Our group was called on to remain on the boat until all the other troops disembarked, and then we had to clean the ship. At this time we watched the English crew leaving with all of the fruit and good food, which was probably destined for our troops. After leaving the ship we were taken to the country of Wales where we gradually received our guns, two trucks and necessary supplies. From there we went to the southeast coast of England near the seaport of Dartmouth. We set up our guns on a farm overlooking the Dart River, north of Dartmouth, England. The Dart River was filled with landing craft, which were to be used in the landing on D-day, June 6th 1944. Our duty here was to protect the landing craft and equipment from strafing German aircraft. We remained here from March 1944 until the ships departed to cross the English Channel.

While stationed at this area, two British officers came to me one day and requested permission to check our gunnery emplacements. I courteously followed them while they measured the number of square feet used by our guns, ammunition storage area, and our living area under two large oak trees where sixteen of us slept in eight pup tents. When they finished, one of them said, "Sergeant, you must have a latrine." I replied, "yes", whereupon we had to measure for a ditch in the ground about eight feet long and eight inches wide. After completing this, I inquired what the purpose of this was. They informed me that the U.S.A. was to pay England for the use of this measured area. It was quite depressing for us to think we were in their country protecting them, and our citizens were paying them for the use of their land.

We were sleeping in a very deep area with our raincoats under us to shield us from the dampness. It was insufficient, so I asked the farmer, owner of the farm we were camping on, if he would consider giving us some hay from his barn full of hay to put under us while we slept. He said he couldn't do such a thing. Soon after, my crew of sixteen took it upon themselves to help themselves to some hay. He turned us in to the British government, and as a result our army had to please the British Army by notifying them that I was immediately reduced to private as punishment for my behavior. My superior officer informed me of all this. He told me the British were sent a letter telling them of my punishment, satisfying them; but on the q.t. I was told to carry on my duties as usual.

Soon the landing vessels all left the Dart River for the Normandy Invasion. We were then assigned to the Eighth Infantry Division, 445th AAA battalion and departed from Dartmouth Harbor for Normandy, landing there some time the first week of July. It was our duty to protect the Eighth Infantry troops and engineers from strafing German aircraft. We came across dead children, animals and great mounds of bricks. We figured we could not survive the war, so we didn't worry about anything.

There were several men from Brewster in the 445th AAA Battalion. Michael Green who delivered beef was in Headquarters Company. Tony Vanaria was in A Co., Frank Killarne was in B. Co., Joe Foster was a medic in C Co., and I was in D Co. I would bump into these fellows no more than every two months.

We struggled through Normandy, from Omaha Beach to St. Lo, France, when finally we broke the German resistance with plenty of help from the U. S. Army Air Corps. They bombed this area twenty-four hours a day for several days. Our main force was pushing the German Army into a wholesale retreat to the German border where they had a magnificent defense area set up at the Siegfried Line with steel and concrete barricades and underground quarters, 3 or 4 stories for troops and supplies. When we left St. Lo we traveled at night. We had our front and rear lights covered so that there were only small holes of light. It was hard to see the truck ahead, and very often one truck would run into another. We saw trucks that had lost their way and had fallen into a bomb crater, down 15 feet and were almost buried. Just before daybreak, they ordered us into an orchard to take cover and wait for further orders. We dug out our frying pans and had our breakfast. Upon seeing daylight, we discovered the Germans in their retreat had left behind a horse-drawn headquarters group of several teams of horses still hooked onto them. There were some snipers around that we had to clean out. Some of them surrendered. The fellows opened up some of the trunks on these wagons, and they were full of money, brown and purple, large bills with numbers. It was to pay the German troops at the end of the month. The payroll list had all the German names on it. Some of the fellows stuffed their pockets with this paper money, and later some of them cashed in the money for American money and were able to send thousands of dollars home. It was a government rule that you could only send twice what the monthly pay was.

A good number of German troops surrendered to us except for a few remaining snipers. Over the hedgerows we could see a big farm with barns; the farmers discovered we were American troops, and they could see our trucks. We could see their heads looking at us from over the hedgerows. They immediately started coming over the hedgerows like ants over an anthill. It was early morning, and I was the first one at the latrine doing my business; I saw these people looking at me. Then they came over and hugged and kissed me. They didn't care what I was doing. They were so happy to be free. The guys were laughing at me trying to get my pants on. They kept on hugging and kissing us. I get broken up talking of this. They were so delighted to be free of German rule. It was their freedom. When they saw us, they evidently realized that all that bombing was for a good end. They hugged and squeezed us. There were maybe two families.

The next day around noontime, a courier was sent around with a march order to back our trucks around and get ready to go. Then someone else came through and told us when to go. We were given a map and told to get underway and were taken through some small towns. Word must have gotten around, because the people lined the streets four and five deep, waving the American flags. I don't know where they got the flags. They knew they were free again.

We had little burners plus C rations and canned rations. Every once in a while they would come around and replenish our supplies. We had cans of bacon; we would use the grease, and make bacon sandwiches. When we were done, the grease was saved in the frying pan, and the frying pan was thrown up onto the truck with all kinds of stuff on top of it. They threw duffle bags and every other thing on top of the pan. When it came time to eat again, the guy designated as cook would dig out that frying pan, stir the stuff up, heat it a little bit… It was a marvel that none of us ever got sick. We also ate stew, stew, stew. But we were young. We were the cream of the crop. Nobody got in with any stomach problems or other sickness, because they didn't want problems. You'd be more trouble than you'd be worth. That's why they say wars are terrible; they take the cream, the healthiest.

From there we went south cleaning out small groups of German resistance that we encountered. We (the 8th Infantry Div.) were then assigned along with the 2nd and 29th Infantry Divisions to overtake the Brest Peninsula, which had been shut off from the rest of the German forces. After a period of time we conquered the Brest Peninsula and then made our way across France and into a rather dormant area of Luxembourg to regroup, that is to get us up to full strength in regards to injured, dead troops and damaged equipment.

After being here for a short period of time, we were sent to Aachen, Germany to replace the 28th Infantry Div., which was nearly destroyed. It was a slaughter. It was around Thanksgiving, and we were living in the mud up to our knees. Our colonel saw that we were sloshing around in the mud, so he did something about it. He and his driver arrived one day in a jeep, and he had the back filled with arctics. They weren't the right size, but he told us to take a pair, as they were rubber and would keep the water out. We had some trench foot in our outfit and some men had to be hospitalized. This old colonel was a fine gentleman. He was great. It was very cold there and very muddy with a lot of snow. One day the colonel came around with two raincoats. They were long and were lined and also had warm hoods, which we hadn't seen before. They kept the wind away from the neck. These two coats were to be used by our two men on guard duty. They would pass the coats to their two replacements. When we got into Germany our attitudes changed to one of optimism. We felt then that we were going to make it. However, we never discussed our feelings - and we never felt down.

We survived the Battle of Aachen and went into the Hurtgen Forest, which was a disaster area. The radio on our truck wasn't that good, but one of our guys heard a woman (Axis Sally) talking to the American GI's. She said, "All of you GI's out there – if any of you fellows have any friends in the 28th Division, they're all dead. If you think you're going to replace them, you're going to be in the same boat." I don't think our guys were affected by her. We were 16 men, and we stayed pretty much to ourselves. We ate together and stayed together all the time. We had two AA guns protecting the 13th Combat Infantry Regiment with 1,500 men in A, B, C, and D companies. One time we had two trucks stuck in the mud, exposed to enemy airplane fire. I asked for volunteers to go out and pull the trucks out of the mud. No one volunteered. So, I went out and pulled them out myself. I wouldn't ask anyone to do what I wouldn't do myself. I pulled guard duty along with all the other men, even though as their sergeant I wasn't required to do so.

We got so low on fuel that we were stalled on the highway. That's when I saw Frank Piazza (from Brewster) going by on a tank. Traveling in the opposite direction was General Patton standing in his jeep hollering as he passed that everybody should get out with their bazooka. Shells were going off around us, but he didn't care about anybody, not even himself. Nobody paid attention to his order that I could see.

Our forces never had to retreat but kept pushing the German forces further each day, across the Elbe River and back to the Rhine River. We arrived at the Rhine River just as the Remagen Bridge was blown up. Our 8th Div. Engineers (the 12th Engineer Battalion) built the pontoon bridge alongside the blown-up bridge so that our troops could cross the river and continue to push the German troops back. Tony Vanaria and Frank Killarny were injured and sent home. Joe Flannagan whom I saw occasionally was in the 12th Combat Engineers Bn. with us, but we were separated by several hedgerows. One night I was with Joe Flanagan and his outfit. He got talking about playing football in Brewster and told about the signals he and Vic Carollo had worked out. If he hit Joe in the stomach, he knew they were to block a guy in one direction; if Joe hit him in the stomach, they were to block a player in another direction. Joe found some cognac and some jelly glasses. I had never had anything stronger than beer, but I drank it and crawled in my foxhole and went to sleep. When I woke up in early morning, I was covered with dirt from the shelling. I had dirt in my mouth. That cognac was powerful stuff. It was so wonderful seeing Joe, but I had to get back to my outfit. As I walked back I would come across an MP at each hedgerow who would challenge me. The password changed every day, and I had to come up with the password and come forward and be recognized. When I got back to my outfit I caught the devil for leaving my troops. The captain had come around the night before and found I wasn't there.

We were with Joe Flanagan at the Roer River crossing. During the time of the construction of the pontoon bridge he was badly mangled, hospitalized and sent home. The sad thing - it was our own artillery fire that killed many of us. They were shelling the Germans, but their fire was directed incorrectly and fell on our own troops. Joe never fully recovered and died a few years later. We moved on through Germany until we were stopped sixty miles west of Berlin. The German troops and civilians were surrendering to us by the thousands, as they feared surrendering to the Russian troops. At one point there was an airfield nearby, and we ordered all the German troops and people to make some form of shelter for themselves, and they were told the U.S. Government would feed them.

Shortly after that we went to take shelter in a German schoolhouse where we slept on the floor but in nice dry and warm quarters. Sometime later we moved to Belgium, where we were put to work removing a gasoline pipeline that was used as a supply line from the big boat tankers in Amsterdam, Holland. We moved to Holland and then finally to a seaport, which was our last stop. We boarded a troop ship and had a wild, wintry ride across the North Atlantic Ocean arriving at Boston Harbor two days before Thanksgiving, November, 1945. On Thanksgiving Day we traveled by train from a camp near Boston to Camp Dix, N. J., where we were discharged on the following Sunday evening.

My three brothers Henry, Ed and John were in service. Henry and Ed were both in the Army Air Force. John was delayed in getting in, because when he went to enlist, they found he had a hernia that needed an operation. So they sent him into defense work. After six months and the operation taken care of, the Army took him in 1946, and he was sent to the Philippines. My sister Mary was in college at New Paltz.

On my return home I went to work for the New York Central Railroad starting as a fireman on a steam engine. Eventually I moved up to diesel engineer and spent 41 years, the latter years working for Metro-North. I retired in 1982.

One of the soldiers I knew, Anthony Aderno, who was in Tony Vanaria's company was doing amphibious training on Myrtle Beach,

N.C. before going overseas and lost his dog tags with his blood type, religion, etc. He was from Akron, Ohio and was stationed at Fort Fisher. Forty-eight years later a retired Marine was walking in the grasses near the beach using a Geiger counter and picked up those dog tags. It was a couple of hundred miles south from where they had been lost. From surf and winds in heavy storms, the tags had been washed up into the grasses. The address on the tags was a restaurant owned by Aderno's family. The man who found the tags took a chance and wrote to that address. The family still owned the restaurant, and the dog tags were finally returned to the owner.

This is a humorous story: I was having a conversation with a seven-year old girl. She said her grandfather had told her he had saved all the sailors on his ship. I asked her how he had done that, and she said, "He threw the cook overboard."

On January 22, 1944 I married Marjorie Jean Edmondson. We have three children.[20]

Frank Piazza

My father built a three-story house on Allview Avenue, and that is where I grew up. We had a garden as large as a farm, and my mom used to can the tomatoes, which we used the whole year. What a job that was. She worked like a dog. We lost the house during the depression. Mr. Henry Wells who was the Mayor of Brewster at the time was an angel. He offered to rent us a house on Center Street.

In 1937 I graduated from Brewster High School. I had odd jobs for a while, and then my mother financed me to go to business school for shorthand and typing. Where she scraped up the money to send me to business school, I don't know. It was probably the best thing that ever happened to me. When I graduated I got a job in New York City at a food company as a typist and did that job for close to two years.

On June 16, 1941 I was conscripted into the Army, and I was to get out after six months. Several of us recruits were saying that in two more weeks we would be out, going home. Then Pearl Harbor was struck, so that was it.

In the beginning when the Army needed typists very badly, I was put on special duty at Ft. Dix. The policy at the time was that a new recruit could be kept there for only 30 days, and after that he had to be re-assigned for his basic training. I hadn't gone through basic training at that point, so I was sent to Aberdeen, Maryland. I got to know the captain, and I asked him if there was any chance of getting my brother Salvatore down there, since he was being inducted. The colonel arranged to have him sent to Aberdeen where he got his basic training and spent a year and a half. Then he was sent to Indiana. Four of us brothers were in the service at the same time. August was in Europe, Frank in Asia, John was in the states and Salvatore was sent to India. George went in after I was home. My other brother was Angelo, and I had a sister Antoinette. After being in Aberdeen for probably a year and a half, I was in a position that called for a Master Sergeant's rating, but I was a Private First Class. The colonel in charge of the department liked my work, so about every month, I got a promotion and reached Master Sergeant. I was probably the youngest Master Sergeant in Aberdeen as I wasn't yet 24 years old. One day I walked into his office, and he handed me a paper and told me to fill it out. He was sending me to Officers' Candidate School. When someone is accepted into O.C.S. an investigator is always sent out to question neighbors about the candidate. One went to our neighbors, the Durkin's, and they thought surely I was in trouble.

It was near the end of 1943 when I went to Texarkana, Texas for a year. We had a good time there. We weren't fighting people; we were partying people. Then I was transferred to Pearl Harbor. That was an ideal place, and I ask myself why I left.

I was a lieutenant, and we operated the 346th Power Training Rebuilt Company. We rebuilt power transmissions and rear ends of vehicles. I knew nothing about automobiles, but I read and learned. Any vehicle that needed rebuilding on any Pacific island would be sent to us. We had a production line doing this heavy-duty stuff. It was specialized work. After close to a year, the early part of 1945, we were shipped to Okinawa and operated a base there also. We worked under a tent and continued the same work. I was promoted to Captain, and I felt good about that. When the war was over, they wanted officers to stay in service, so that they could help with demobilization - getting the kids home. Anyone who volunteered to stay in another six months would get an automatic promotion. I could have become a major. With the prestige involved, why didn't I do it? I was away from home for over two years; that was the reason.

In February 1946 I got home and was discharged at Ft. Dix. I went back to the food company in New York City. They gave me a chance to sell and after about a year and a half one of my accounts was looking to sell his store. So I bought the store in Yonkers in 1951. I married Barbara Brundage on July 2, 1951. After fifteen years I was looking to semi-retire and bought another store in Patterson, N.Y. My son has that store now; I retired in 1985.[21]

Earl E. Pinckney

On December 7, 1941 I was in Yonkers, New York working in the Signal Construction Department of the New York Central Railroad. Having graduated from Brewster High School the previous June, I was taking correspondence classes preparing to learn about diesel engines. Without consulting my parents, I enlisted in the US Army June 26, 1942 and was sent to Fort Knox for basic training in tanks because of my interest in diesel engines. During basic training I took special classes and was considered a potential officer candidate. I also helped train soldiers in tanks, teaching everything from driving to firing the guns of a tank. When it was decided that I qualified for officer training, it was determined that I could not remain in a combat unit because of poor eyesight and thus selected to serve in the Ordinance Corps. I went to Officer Training School at Aberdeen Proving Grounds, Aberdeen, Maryland and graduated March 25, 1943 and was commissioned a second lieutenant. I returned to Fort Knox and was assigned to the 486th Tank Recovery Unit.

My brother LaVern had as his bunkmate on a sub chaser the movie actor Victor Mature. His mother lived in Louisville, Kentucky, and so he suggested that I contact her. I did and she adopted me as her son all the while I was at Fort Knox. After training we were shipped out in March 1944 to England sailing on the Queen Mary from New York City. We traveled unescorted across the Atlantic making a zigzag course arriving in the Firth of Clyde in Scotland. We proceeded to Stroud near Cheltenham and Gloucester just north of Bristol. Just before the invasion I met my brother LaFayette (Fay) in Cambridge. He served with the 8th Air Force near Norwich, Norfolk, England.

Our job was to transport tanks to units preparing for the invasion. We also had to prepare our vehicles including the large M25 armored tank transports to operate under water up to a certain level. We were scheduled to arrive on Omaha Beach in Normandy D-day plus 6. However, because of the special call for a Canadian Tank unit, we were not able to leave until D-day plus 10. We were transported on LCTs (Landing Craft Tanks). The fighting by this time had advanced inland, so that there was no enemy fire near the beach.

Our first task was to pull out of the water the tanks that did not make shore. I transferred into the 532nd Heavy Maintenance Company, which was assigned to provide back up maintenance for the 2nd Armored Division. One of the men in our company designed blades to be welded onto the front of tanks enabling them to cut through the hedgerows, which were very dangerous obstacles for the tanks. This proved to be most effective and undoubtedly saved many lives.

We followed the 2nd Armored Division from the breakthrough at St. Lo up to Maastricht in Holland. We were transferred to the town of Marche in Belgium to help re-equip units which were sent there for a rest. This was before the German breakthrough, so we were there for some time. We would get our food rations at the very areas in which the Germans made their initial breakthrough in the Battle of the Bulge. We would frequently pass through Bastogne, and the day of the German breakthrough I was in Malmedy getting parts for tanks. On the way back we were stopped by roadblocks checking identifications, since Germans in American uniforms had infiltrated our lines.

One of the units, which passed through our town, was the 106th Infantry Division, fresh from the States. Among the troops was Ulindo Tranquilli, a classmate of mine from Brewster, New York. They did not even have a chance to get ready when the Germans attacked; the division suffered severe casualties, and Ulindo was taken prisoner and remained so until the end of the war. You cannot imagine the confusion of these days with troops moving to the rear and with a heavy fog setting in. Our unit sent ten tanks to Bastogne, which were turned over to the parachute units. They had been rushed in to hold that strategic city. Because we had about 50 replacement tanks, we were eventually ordered to move back across the Meuse River into the city of Liege. Here we received many German rockets. They were psychologically unnerving, since you would hear them coming, and then the motor would stop and come down. Because you did not know where, you were concerned until you heard an explosion. As you can imagine these were days of deep concern for us all. During that time I met John Truran in Reims, France where he served in First Army Headquarters. John and I lived on the same street in Brewster. I also met Mario Caruso from Brewster. Mario served in the 7th Armored Division which our company was assigned to help re-equip. They had suffered many casualties having faced the brunt of the German army at the first onslaught of the breakthrough.

Our unit went through the cities of Aachen and Frankfort, when they were reduced to rubble as a result of the fighting. On one occasion when we were delivering a tank to a unit, we crossed the Rhine River just up stream from the Remagen Bridge. We then drove under it, and before we could return later that day, the bridge had collapsed. We gave a ride to members of the engineering group that was working on the bridge. Many of their friends had died when the bridge collapsed.

We followed the fighting troops until we arrived at Gera near Leipzig and the Czechoslovakian border. We then moved back into St. Dizir near Nancy, France preparing to be transferred to the South Pacific Theatre. We were so thankful that the war with Japan ended when it did. I was separated from active duty on January 28, 1946.

Most of the time in the service I drank in moderation. However, when we were in France waiting to return to the States I found myself drinking too much. I was the battalion special service officer, and among other duties was that of a nightclub for the enlisted men. When I would go and check on its operations, I would often have some drinks. When we went for noon dinner, we would often have a few drinks before the meal. I had a friend who ran the brewery in town for the army. After hours some of us would also drink, and I found myself in a vicious cycle of drinking which was getting out of hand. I prayed for help in getting the drinking under control. I talked with the chaplain and developed an interest in the Bible. It was then that I decided to prepare for the ministry rather than to become an engineer as I had previously considered. Through the GI Bill I was able to go to Bible College and seminary preparing for the ministry. When I joined the army, I would read the bible and pray before going to bed. I attended chapel and church regularly. I did not understand just how my worshiping God related to death and even life.

I want to express my deep felt thanks for all of the service men who faced combat and kept those of us in service units safe. I also have fond memories of Bunky O'Brien and Harding O'Hara who were killed in the line-of-duty. May we not fail them by letting our freedoms be taken away from us.

On June 25, 1949 I married Marion Ruth Drigers from New York City and Lake Secor. We have two sons.[22]

Frederick Rapp

Before the war I was working as an office boy for a pharmaceutical company and attending Pace Institute (now Pace University) studying to be an accountant, following in my father's footsteps. I realized after two semesters that this was not my calling. At that time Connecticut celebrated Thanksgiving a week later than New York, and this gave me an opportunity to look for another job without losing a day's pay. In December of 1940 I got a job as an apprentice toolmaker and thought, now I don't have to work a half-day on Saturdays. I was now working for Bard Parker Co. in Danbury, Connecticut who manufactured surgical blades. Evidently the company had just received a big contract from England, and we were making gun parts for the 10 mm. Orlikon antiaircraft gun. Soon we were working twelve hours a day, six and one half days a week, deeply involved in the war effort.

After two and one half years of working in an essential war effort program, all those under twenty-six years of age were no longer deferred and were eligible for being drafted into the military. Upon learning this, I immediately went down to join the Navy and was classified as a selective volunteer. After boot camp at Sampson, New York, I was advised that I could pick any service school except Fire Control. Rather than get stuck on a freighter as a gunner's mate I chose to be a torpedo-man, so I would be on a war ship.

After sixteen weeks of Torpedo School, I went to the west coast and sailed to New Caledonia in the south Pacific. We zigzagged for fifteen days before arriving at our destination. In order to aim a torpedo accurately there are three factors involved: 1. the ship's speed, 2. the distance from ship and 3. the target ship's angle. If the ship keeps changing course, it changes the aim of the torpedo making our ship less of a target.

I was stationed at a Navy dispensing station waiting for assignment and was assigned to temporary duty on a garbage truck. There was a call for volunteer lifeguards at a navy recreational area for incoming ships. (I was a certified Lifeguard before going in service). This job lasted about three months, and I was shipped to Hawaii for assignment. The day finally came; with my sea bag packed and lashed to my hammock, I marched down the beach where there were five destroyers at anchor waiting for a change in crewmembers. I thought, now I am going to sea. I was assigned a bunk in a quonset hut awaiting assignment the next day.

About 1 a.m. there was a lot of noise outside. The rockets on the ships were going off. The navy band was parading around, all in celebration of the Japanese surrender. Thank God, the war was over! What was left was to separate all personnel back into civilian life. Having had a background in accounting and being able to type, I was assigned to Con Des Pac. Flag allowance is the number of personnel permitted for each task, such as 10 cooks, 20 gunner's mates, 10 torpedo men, postmasters, yeomen, etc. I had to account for the personnel on about thirty destroyers so that they wouldn't get a surplus of help in any area. There was a constant change in personnel, especially after combat with the wounded or killed in action.

I was in New Caledonia when I received word from my mother that my brother Robert was missing. Her words were, "Needless to say, I am heartbroken". My mother was living alone and despondent; I was therefore given an early discharge to go home. [23]

Note: As explained at the end of Richard Rapp's story, Fred Rapp does not technically belong in this collection. After reading the contribution all brothers made to the defense of the U.S. I decided not to separate them.

Richard Rapp

I went to school in North Salem. When Pearl Harbor was attacked I was in New York City at the Savage School for Physical Education. The dean called us all out and told us what had happened. In December of 1943 I was drafted into the Army before my brother Fred went into the Navy and took my basic training at Jefferson Barracks in St. Louis, Missouri. I went to several schools for training and became a part of the Air Transport Command. I was in the United States for eighteen months, then in Casablanca for eighteen months. It was our duty to transport everything into the European Theatre. By the time I got over there, we were supplying India, Italy and the European Theater. Casablanca was a big airfield, and we loaded the planes and sent them on their way. I didn't fly.

I ended up a Staff Sergeant in the Education Department, keeping the pilots healthy. Our job was to make sure the pilots had good recreation programs. These men were mostly officers of C-46's and C-47's. The crews were small, and they were in their twenties. That was part of the Air Transport Command, and that is what I did for eighteen months. A gymnasium was set up, and there were weight lifting and exercise programs. The men were supplied with all the equipment needed for tennis, softball and golf.

Whenever the pilots would go to their planes or get off, they would always run because of the poor Arabs who would kill them to take their clothes. If the officers were in the casbah or got drunk, they would be accosted and stripped. They would do a job on them and steal their clothes, because the Arabs had very few. I never walked; I always ran. The Arabs who worked for the Army were poor. Our food came in large containers, and when they were empty the Arabs would scoop out what was left, and that is how they fed their families. The French treated them terribly. When we went hunting and would shoot coyotes and birds, we gave the Arabs all the game.

My mother wrote me about my brother Robert who was missing in action. She wanted me to go to Italy to look for him, but there was nothing I could do. I think my mother realized my brother was killed in action long before the government notified her of that.

On my return to civilian life, I became a student at Springfield College earning a Bachelors degree in 1948 and subsequently a

Masters Degree at Teachers College, Columbia University followed by a professional diploma in Administration. I married Rita O'Hara of Brewster on September 1, 1947. We have two sons.[24]

Note: After much thought, I made a decision about including the three Rapp brothers in this book. Robert is on the Honor Roll of The Town of Southeast. The Rapps lived on Daisy Lane in The Town of Carmel; the houses across the road were in The Town of Southeast. Technically Richard and Fred do not belong in a book about Southeast veterans. The extenuating circumstances are, as follows:
Three brothers served our country. One brother, Robert who is on the Southeast Honor Roll, lost his life trying to save the life of one of his men. Another brother Fred served his country in a defense factory and also served in the Pacific theatre. A third brother Richard served in North Africa. On his return he married a young Brewster woman who had lost her brother, Harding O'Hara when his B-24 Liberator was shot down somewhere over the North Sea in 1943. These great losses were a common bond.

Robert C. Rapp (KIA)

Robert Rapp, the youngest of three brothers, enlisted in the 10th Mountain Division at the age of nineteen, the same division in which Crosby Wells of Brewster served and lost a leg. Sen. Robert Dole also served with this division and was seriously injured. In the spring of 1945 the 10th Mountain Division led the Allies' final offensive over the Italian Alps.

As a ski trooper, Sergeant Rapp had specialized training in survival, but nothing prepared him for what happened. His outfit was crossing the Po River at night, when his boat hit a log and overturned. He started to swim for shore when one of his men hollered for help. He went to help this trooper, but they both went down. In a letter written by Robert's closest buddy, PFC H.W. McMahon to Mr. Knobloch*, "at 7 o'clock I saw Bob leave me to join another boat group... He last said 'take it easy Mac I'll see you on the other side'. When we reached the other side of the Po I looked around for Bob and his boat crew, but couldn't find him. I waited there for a half hour thinking they may have gotten stuck. Then one of the boats came in giving us the news that one of the boats had hit a sunken log and turned over. After getting more news we found out that Bob was on that boat. Several of the boys made it to shore and from them I got the following information. They say most of the boys had belts full of ammo and they went straight to the bottom without coming up and some of them said they saw Bob go down and come up with all of his weight clear of his body, and they say he went to save another boy who couldn't swim and neither were ever seen again. They dragged the river over and over again, but with no sign of them. They also made a check of all hospitals and aid stations without any luck...there is very little hope of him being alive, but I still hope and pray that he might have drifted down stream and got picked up some place, but all hopes of that are going now, as no reports have come in from any place. I would like you to write Mrs. Rapp this news as I couldn't word it right and also tell her we feel deeply sorry for her loss, as he was as good a boy as they come, and I miss him as I would my brother... This letter is the toughest thing I have had to do in this war; you can't imagine how it is to write some one that their friend and yours is gone." It is his brother Fred's opinion that the two men "suffered from hypothermia due to the spring time thaws and the very cold water." He also expressed his sadness in light of the fact that the war was nearing an end, and had Hitler's officers succeeded in their assassination attempt his brother's life would likely have been spared.

A letter written to Mrs. Lillian B. Rapp states, "Your son was the leader of a rifle squad in a front line rifle company, whose mission was to cross a river under cover of darkness and assault the positions of the enemy. Their boat overturned in the swift current of the river, and although some survivors were rescued by other craft, Robert was not among them."

At the time of Robert's death, his older brother Fred was in New Caledonia in the Navy, and his brother Richard was in North Africa in the Army. At that time only one son had to be in service, which meant that one of the Rapp brothers could be released to go home. Fred wrote to Richard telling him that he could be released to go home, but Dick's decision was to stay and do his job in North Africa. So Fred received an early discharge and went home to be with his mother. He said, "It was near Christmas, but there was no happiness in our house for some time" [25]

*Mr. Knobloch was a father figure for the Rapp brothers. He had a vacation home on Daisy Lane not far from the Rapp home. The boys' father had died when Robert was 12 years old, Richard was 14 and Fred 17; Mr. Knobloch took the boys hunting and fishing. He did what a father would have done, contacting people who knew Robert in the 10th Mountain Division, and who had written to Mrs. Rapp.

Benjamin Rosenberg

In 1938 at the age of 23 and unmarried I came to Brewster and started my stationery store business on the corner across from the New York Central Railroad station. I wasn't too aware of what was going on in Europe or Asia until Pearl Harbor was attacked on December 7, 1941.

I was drafted, took a physical exam and was declared 4F – not fit for service. A second time I was called and rejected. A third time I was called and rejected because of my eyesight. When I was called a fourth time and was examined by an optometrist, I told him I thought I should go into service, because I said I'm Jewish and I think I have an obligation to serve. The war had been going on for about a year. The optometrist looked at me with a little amazement and asked if I really wanted to go. I said I don't want to go, but I feel I have an obligation to serve. I told him about limited service, and that I could serve in some capacity. He said all right, you're in.

I remember that Leo Susnitzky went in the same time as I under limited service, but in about six months he was released. When I heard that, I expected to be released also, but I wasn't. They did away with limited service. I guess they thought I was fighting material, so I stayed in. I was then in the regular service.

A couple of months later I wasn't so happy about it. I'll never forget my drill sergeant. He was very tough. I thought I was going to kill him, but when we graduated after 13 weeks I found he was one of the nicest guys you could find. We even went out drinking beer. So I wasn't going to kill him anymore. They had to tear you down and then build you up, so you automatically responded to orders. If he said jump, you had to automatically jump. If you were in combat and he said go, you weren't supposed to think or hesitate about going.

I was sent to Signal Corps School in Camp Crowder, Missouri and also Ft. Monmouth, N.Y. I had been accepted in OCS in Chemical Warfare, but one day someone came to me with a proposition. There were such a limited number of men being taken into Chemical Warfare; there probably wouldn't be any call for me. But they were having a special program called the Army Special Training Program in which they wanted to turn out engineers for the Army. I had had two years of college, so I went to the University of Santa Clara in California and spent the year studying electrical engineering. After the year they closed that program down, and I was released from that. For a short while I was in the MP's. Can you imagine me being in the MP's? I was stationed at Chula Vista, between San Diego and the Mexican border. There I was patrolling outside a manufacturing plant that made airplane motors.

I ended up in Alaska in the Signal Corps. in a place called Northway, 90 miles north of the Yukon border. In the winter we only had two or three hours of daylight. An Indian set out a trap line for me. I carried a rifle, and figured I was going to shoot something. I didn't care whether it was two-legged or four-legged; I was going to shoot that rifle. In my trap line all I caught were three ravens and two rabbits – no ermine, no mink, no wolf, no bear – nothing like that, and I never saw a live animal in all the time I was in Alaska. The winters are brutal, 30 to 40 degrees below zero. I used to go ice fishing on the Yukon border and had to keep chopping just to keep the line free, but I never caught a fish.

As part of the Signal Corps, we worked the Repeater and Carrier System that boosted the volume of the telephone, Teletype and even radio, because radios didn't work in those mountains. They had to work by wire by plugging them in. We were between Fairbanks and Dawson Creek.

When I got out of the Army I had a hernia, so I was on disability. My wife Edith thought I had a mental problem at the time because I told her I had difficulty sleeping, and she connected that with the disability. I never talked about my time in service to my wife or children, and they didn't know I had a hernia. I did go to Dr. Eliot about my sleeplessness after getting home. He said I was fine; that I had the same problem millions of other veterans had and advised me to find a way to relax or go to a psychiatrist. So, I took a fishing pole and went down to the reservoir below the railroad station. I'd throw a line in, and I'd fall asleep, but never caught a fish. That straightened me out pretty well. One day I had to call my wife, because the hernia had popped out. I wanted her to come to the store so I could tell her, but she insisted I tell her on the telephone. That was the first time she learned about what the disability was.

My life in service was bouncing from one school or assignment to another. I never stayed with a group of men that I could establish a friendship with. I kept losing that. Of course I wasn't really happy in service, because I wasn't really a soldier. I was a civilian who carried a gun.

It hit me very hard last Memorial Day. I was in the parade in the front line and discovered I was the oldest veteran in the parade. I assumed there were older veterans who didn't go to the parades anymore. So, the next day I went to Rotary, and I wanted to tell them about my feelings in the parade. I just couldn't talk. It was too emotional for me. It was the young men who lost their lives. It never hit me all those years. I never fired a gun at anybody; I never saw anyone killed. I was never a part of any combat. I went where they told me to go. It just hit me that I'm here, and I have feelings of guilt; why am I here, and these young men, vigorous, strong, good guys didn't make it.

I had a cousin who was in the Army six months. He was sent over to the battle in France, and he got hit. He was on the battlefield all night long before the medics reached him. They thought he was dead; then one of them noticed he was breathing. He got 100% disability and has been suffering all these years; his pain is part of his life. He paid a terrible price. Here I am vigorous, healthy, living well and enjoying my life. I know I had no control of my life in the Army. At this time of my life I realize you didn't have to shoot a gun. I keep telling myself I didn't have a choice in the matter.

I was in the Army 3 years, 3 months and 3 weeks. I didn't think I would ever get out. It was no kind of life for a guy used to his independence.

Besides having a business in Brewster, I was elected to the Village Board for about six years and enjoyed that. I enjoyed my business but never made a lot of money at it.

I married Edith Tobias from the Bronx, and we have three children.[26]

Edward G. Roth

Eddie Roth was born in New York City. His mother was a city girl, and when she came to Brewster she was very unhappy. She deserted her family and went back to the city. This had a lasting effect on him, so that he did not like saying "good bye" to anyone. He was very sentimental and loving to those close to him. So, his father, Leo Roth and the grandmother he loved like a mother raised Ed. When he came home after the war, he took care of her until she died.

Edward left Brewster High School early to join the Navy, but the Navy turned him down, because he had a heart murmur. He believed then that the Army would also turn him down, which later proved to be unfounded. So he found a job surveying in Vermont and Massachusetts.

Ed was inducted into the Army on January 15, 1943 and became engaged to his Brewster sweetheart, Ruth Godfrey before going overseas. He was in the 2nd Battalion, 320th Infantry. When he got home he told Ruth, "You really don't want to know what I did or where I've been". He drove officers in jeeps and trucks up to the front lines. They needed everyone at that time.

Eddie and I married on September 30, 1945, soon after he came home. He was very thin. We went to Vermont on our honeymoon. One day an airplane flew overhead, and Eddie dropped to the ground. He had nightmares for quite a while and had to adjust to being home and being with family. He had bad experiences and never wanted to talk about them. He was discharged on November 6, 1945.

Edward Roth received a Citation for Bronze Star Medal which reads as follows: "To First Class Edward G. Roth, Headquarters Company Second Battalion, 320th Infantry, for meritorious service in connection with military operations against an enemy of the U.S., near Chambrey, France on 7 October 1944. Private Roth, a truck driver and another man volunteered to go forward and repair a quarter-ton truck that was badly damaged. Despite the fact that the area was under enemy observation and subjected to heavy shellfire, Private Roth worked coolly and efficiently for a period of two hours, succeeded in placing the vehicle in operating condition, and removed it to the rear...1 Nov. 44 "

The following story relates to the experiences Ed had in the war and is told by his widow Ruth Godfrey Roth: "When I worked at Guidepost Magazine, I had a boss who expected a lot from everyone. One day someone asked him why he pushed so hard. He told us that when he was a pilot during WWII he was shot down and was held prisoner in Germany for three or four years. He said that he vowed that when he was freed he would not miss a minute of life – that he would keep very busy and not waste any time, because there had been so much time as a prisoner. He talked about being taken prisoner, and then he mentioned the group Eddie was in. I told him that was my husband's unit. Later, his wife called me and invited Eddie and me for dinner at their home. They were very social people; we had a lovely dinner. Then the two men went out to talk about their experiences. Eddie had been in the group that released the prisoners from the POW camp and had released my boss".

Eddie was a plumber and worked on many jobs where asbestos was involved. He died at age 65. We have one child.

His medals were for service in the European-African-Middle Eastern Theatre, the Good Conduct Medal, Bronze Star and the American Service Medal.[27]

Army of the United States

Honorable Discharge

This is to certify that

EDWARD G ROTH 32 719 384 PRIVATE FIRST CLASS

SERVICE COMPANY 320TH INFANTRY

Army of the United States

is hereby Honorably Discharged from the military service of the United States of America.

This certificate is awarded as a testimonial of Honest and Faithful Service to this country.

Given at SEPARATION CENTER FOR T DIX NEW JERSEY

Date 6 NOVEMBER 1945

J H Gunter

J. H. GUNTER
MAJOR, INFANTRY

Aldo Sagrati

In 1936 I was eighteen years old. When I graduated from Brewster High, I went to work for my uncle, Harry Tranquilli, who was in the building business. (It was his son, Lindy Tranquilli who was taken prisoner in Germany.)

President Roosevelt called for the conscription of troops for one year, and in January 1941 I was called. I was in Anderson, Alabama the entire time and was supposed to get out the first or second week of January 1942. I was really looking forward to it. I had even gone to a haberdashery shop and bought a new suit; it was a zoot suit with pin stripes and long double-breasted jacket, the big broad brimmed hat and the whole shmear. I couldn't even pay for it and had to charge it. I was only making twenty-one dollars a month and part of that went to laundry and other necessities. You could wear civilians at that time, and I was buying the suit to go home after I was released. I didn't care too much for the army because I was in the infantry, and that was the worst part of the army. On Sunday, December 7, 1941 I was at a movie and all of a sudden all the lights came on, and the MPs came in; they told us all to get back to the post, that Pearl Harbor had been attacked. I looked at my friend and he looked at me, and we said where is Pearl Harbor? We didn't know where Pearl Harbor was. The Navy took an awful shellacking there. So we went back to camp. From then on I was moving. It was only one week until we were in California. (When Aldo was in California waiting to be shipped out to the Pacific, he and a buddy were hitchhiking towards L.A. one evening. A car stopped and in conversation they were asked where they were from. When Aldo said Brewster, N.Y. the man said that he used to go through Brewster on his way to Towners, N.Y where he would visit Robert Montgomery, the movie actor. The man who picked up the servicemen was Ronald Reagan, the future California governor and the future president of the United States.)*

We didn't get much training, and the equipment was very poor. What we had was WWI materiel: old crummy helmets, leggings. They didn't have weapons; some of us had to use simulated weapons like broomsticks. It was terrible. I was there three months when we went to Hawaii for further training. It was a mess when I got there. I trained on Hawaii for about eight months, transferring from the New

York State National Guard outfit to the regular Army, the 25th Division and the 27th Infantry. So at least I was going to be with experienced people. The equipment we trained with there was no better. I was in a demolition section.

We left there and went to Guadalcanal. It was after the Marines had landed. That was the beginning of the island series. It was the first island that was bombed. There were Bougainville, The Mariana Islands, Arundel, and the Philippines on forward. They were trying to establish air bases closer and closer to Japan. The Japanese were on all these islands, and they had to be taken for the air force to have air bases. I did get back to the Philippines.

While I was on duty on one of the Pacific islands, I became sick with malaria and had a fever of around 105 degrees. From then on I was a sucker for malaria, getting it like you get colds. It really hits you very hard. My outfit was coming off the front lines for relief. I was rushed to a base hospital. While I was there, my division, 12,000 to 15,000 men got shipped to New Zealand. They needed relief and went there to re-coup, have some beer and some ice-cream. We'd been on the front lines a long time. When I got out of the hospital I was hoping I'd get sent back to the states, but it didn't happen. I had to hitchhike to New Zealand to join my outfit.

I did get back to the Philippines just before coming home. We were taking them back, and had things pretty much under control. That's when Mac Arthur returned. That was the happiest moment I had. Here I had made half a dozen landings, and it was just a question of time when I was going to get hit. You don't know when it's going to come. Fortunately, I was never wounded. Just a little "shrap" in my shoulder, that's the only thing.

I was in the Philippines, and the greatest thing happened to me. I was on the front lines and my First Sergeant came to me and said come on back here. He told me I was getting out on points. I couldn't believe it. Tears started coming from my eyes. I was in almost five years. I went in a year before the war, not on my own conditions. It was... don't say I didn't hate it. I wasted the best years of my life in the service - from age twenty-two to twenty seven. They're your productive years, but it all fell apart. I don't think I benefited personally. It took a lot out of me. I got malaria once when I got home and went to Dr. Cleaver.

When I was getting out I went to the distribution center in the Philippines; they gave us a "ruptured duck". That meant you didn't have to salute anyone. I was supposed to ship out from there, but I couldn't get a plane or anything. There were thousands and thousands of people there – replacements for the wounded. The war wasn't over then. Twelve of us waited about a month, and finally we got on a freighter, one of these Norwegian freighters. It was an Army escort - they'd go about six to eight knots. We'd go this way and that way, and it took us about thirty days to Hawaii. Once I got to Hawaii, I got a flight out to the states. When I got to San Francisco, they rolled out the red carpet. They treated me like...who the hell was I? They couldn't do enough for me. [28]

Aldo Sagrati was an inspector with the New York Racing Assoc. for 16 years, retiring September 28, 1975. He was a member of the Italian-American club.

*Aldo Sagrati told this story to his friend, Doris Vichi, and she passed it along to me.

Salvatore Salvia

I was in the Pacific from 1944 to 1946 with Earl Tuttle. We both went through the Philippine Campaign. We both landed in Manila; I went south; he went north. We liberated the island and got ready to go to Japan, having gotten a new issue of everything: guns, trucks, clothes. Thank God the bomb was dropped, and the war was over. Then I went to Japan as part of the occupation forces for about seven months.

When I came home, I saw Earl Tuttle and married his sister Mary. She was in the Navy (WAVES) and was stationed in Washington, D.C.[29]

80

Donald Smith

My brother Eddie was the first born, and I was the second. We were born on 183rd Street in the Bronx, and when I was a year old, my parents came to Brewster. Robert ("Snuffy") was the third boy, and then there was Paul and Margaret. It was a handful for my mom, especially during the depression years, but as kids we didn't suffer. My folks took care of us, and we got by. My dad was first a farmer in Amenia, N.Y; then he went to Brewster and he went to work on the New York Central Railroad and became a conductor. This was a railroad town. Right in this area around Putnam Terrace there was Charlie Drum, Crowley, O'Connor, engineer, Ernest Hopkins, Fred Burdge, Walt Benson, Robert Collins, Engineer, Joe Durkin, and a half mile away Pinckney and others, all working on the railroad.

By 1937 I had graduated from BHS and worked as a soda jerk for Sam Seifert in Hope's Drug Store. Then I worked doing the same thing at the Brewster Bakery run by Tom O'Loughlin. I also helped bring pies down. Soon I became a brakeman on the railroad out of Chatham. It was when they were building the aqueduct, and we brought cement cars down. It was a heavy freight line as well as a passenger line. We also brought Rutland milk down out of Chatham. We would go through the towns to North White Plains, change to electric power, then go right to the west side of New York City with milk cars. Local milk came down later.

The news about Europe was in the paper, and I read that. I was conscripted into the Army before the war started. Just before I was released Pearl Harbor was bombed, and I was drafted. I went from Fort Dix to Fort Hustis, Virginia for basic training. We wore spats at that time; some wore wraparounds from WWI on their legs, because there weren't enough spats. Other equipment was pretty good.

In 1941 after Pearl Harbor, we were guarding the power plants in Chicago. Some soldiers from Ft. Sheridan, Ill. were sent to Chicago to round up Japanese and bring them to internment camps. We left Ft. Sheridan for Indiantown Gap and loaded up to go overseas. I was with the 103rd Automatic Weapons Antiaircraft. We got to know the guys on our guns better than we knew our own brothers. We were in the First Army for a while.

We left Indiantown Gap, shipped out and met a convoy around Nova Scotia. It was one of the biggest convoys going across the north

Atlantic and we had U.S. Navy protection with destroyers. They were worried about submarines. You could see the Navy guys throwing the ash cans off the stern of the ships to get the submarines following us. We were taken to Northern Ireland where we continued training with the British. We didn't know where we were going.

I went into North Africa after the initial landings. If anyone needed an antiaircraft unit, they grabbed us. We guarded Oran and Algiers along the coastline and continued training for the Sicilian invasion. During the invasion, the Italian Army didn't resist. We went to Syracuse and Mt. Etna, which was active at the time. When I went to Port Petigo, the people there couldn't get any fish. So we took a battery from the truck. We had dynamite, fuses and wire. So, we threw the dynamite into the water, set off an explosion, and the fish came up by the hundreds. The people came out in rowboats grabbing the fish. That night they brought us vino and melons; they came with an accordion and a violin, and we had a party. We had a Captain Poe; he lined us up before going into Sicily, and he said if any of you guys are caught raping or doing anything you'll be shot at sundown. You go in there, do the fighting and leave the civilians alone. The soldiers would save their chocolates and then give them to children.

After Sicily we went back to England. We thought we were on our way home. We were training, but we didn't know what for. My brother "Snuffy" was in England training with the 341st Engineers, and I got permission to go see him. I walked into the headquarters, and a captain was at the desk. We saluted – I had some decorations from Africa and Sicily. I asked him if I could see my brother Robert Smith. He asked me if that's the guy they call "Snuffy". He said it's too bad about what happened to your brother, Eddie. I asked what he meant. He said, "Don't you know what happened to your brother, Eddie? I said no. He said, "nobody told you? Your brother got killed on the Alaskan Highway. He said your brother "Snuffy" can have off as much time as you have off. I didn't have much time, because we were training for something. So I walked down where "Snuffy" was training. It was raining and muddy. We walked for a while and talked about Eddie. He had to go and identify the body, and fly it home for the funeral. He lay right here in this house where we grew up. My mother wrote to me as though he was alive. She never told me. Somebody told me she would walk from our house, up to the Catholic Church every day while we were away, never missing a day. The funny part about it, she was all right until we all got home. She died soon after.

We were on our way to Normandy, but we got out into the channel, and it was stormy. We stayed out there in the choppy waves, and about the 4th or 5th day we went in. We saw that a lot of the soldiers were killed - Jeeps with dead soldiers covered up. Once we got into Normandy, they started shelling there. There were A, B, and C Companies. I was in C Company. I think it was B Company that got a direct hit, and five or six guys were killed. Ray Corsetto lived, and every Christmas since, he has sent us a newsletter with news of all the fellows.

We were behind the First Division. Aachen was the first German city to fall. Then we pulled back and were going to make a push in the Cologne Plains, but that fell through when the Germans broke through, and we had to go up to the Battle of the Bulge. As soon as the weather broke, we left there and moved fast across Holland and Germany with General Patton's Third Army. There was one general I thought was great, and that was General Omar Bradley. He thought things out in order to save as many infantrymen as he could. They all liked Bradley.

We wound up in Czechoslovakia. When the Russians got there, we withdrew. We moved back to a small town in Germany. One night, I think it was in the Harz Mountains when German soldiers surrendered to us. There were only a handful of us, and thousands of them. We got them all into a lot and set machine guns guarding them. The next day they loaded the prisoners in trucks. They pushed them right in. We had to drive so many miles to take them back to a prison camp; we were told to keep going regardless of any needs to stop along the way. As we went through the German towns, the people were throwing rocks at the German soldiers. The captured German officer said if he knew there were only a handful of us they would never have surrendered.

In that small German town they made beer, but their equipment wasn't operating. They needed coal. We found a big dump with stored tanks of poisoned gas. There was also some soft coal there. We backed a two and a half ton truck up and loaded it with soft coal. An officer came by at that time and asked what we were going to do with the coal. We said we were going to use it. He said, "no you aren't – you're going to unload it, because we're going to need this coal." So when he got out of sight we took off anyway, back to the town, backed into the alleyway and unloaded the coal. They started up their beer making, and all the people in the town were happy that they got the equipment going. The American soldiers were awfully good to the civilians in Germany or anywhere else they went.

We left that town riding in the 40 & 8 freight cars. We went through the middle of a huge supply depot. Food was stacked up as high as you could see. When the train stopped, we jumped out and ate better than we had in a long time. We helped ourselves to boxes of canned chicken. The guard came out and told us to put it back, or he would shoot us. We told him he would have to shoot us all. Then somebody came out and said we could have some, but not to take too much. So we took what we wanted. They had some great supply of food.

My brother Paul was in army communications in Europe. Mr. O'Brien, the Brewster freight agent had taught Paul the Morse code when he worked at the freight office in high school, as they had to use the code. Because of his knowledge and experience they put him in communications.

We were on our way to Marseilles, a staging area. Those who had many points from all the campaigns were slated to go home. Those without enough points would be going to the Pacific. I flew from Marseilles to Casablanca in a B-17. We hit an air pocket, and the propellers shut down, and the wing was flapping. We got out of the pockets, and things went back to normal. It was a scary thing. From Casablanca we went to Dakar on the equator in a C-46 or C-47, then across to Brazil and British Guiana. From there we went to Puerto Rico and then Miami. I kissed the earth. Soon I was on a train to Fort Dix where I was discharged, and in July 1945 I was home.

It has always bothered me when I'd see pictures of our American flag being burned.

Once home I was employed by the railroad as an assistant conductor and worked for forty years.

I married Barbara Sheridan, a Brewster girl. We have two boys and a girl.[30] [31]

Thomas B. Smith

Our family lived in a large, rented house on Rt. 124 in Brewster, which is where I was born. The house was on the old Bailey Farm. I had nine brothers and five sisters. When war came, John the oldest went into the Army as did Frank, Kaleb, Donald and I. Howard went into the Navy.

My father John worked on the New York Central Railroad as a crane inspector. We all went to the Brewster school. In seventh grade, after moving to Mahopac, I went to school there. After three years we moved to Goldens Bridge. I went to the second year of high school, but because I lost my father in 1941 I had to go out and support the family. I went to work in 1943 for the railroad as machinist helper for 23 cents an hour.

On September 22, 1944 I was drafted into the Army. My choice was to go into the Navy, but I was told, sorry the Army needs you. The guy ahead of me wanted the Army, and he was told, sorry the Navy needs you. I went to Ft. Dix, N.J. and Ft. McClellan, Alabama for infantry training including maneuvers using the M1 rifle and machine gun. I was shipped back to Ft. Dix and departed for the European Theater of Operations on March 7, 1945, landing at Le Havre, France on March 18, 1945. We anchored way out and had to be transported to shore on PT Boats, because of so many sunken ships in the harbor. I first went into combat on March 20, joining the 70th Division, Co. F, 275th Infantry. We crossed the Saar River in small boats and rafts where it was narrow but swift water. It was just before getting to Saarbrucken, Germany. We were lucky that the Germans didn't fire on us, because they were retreating. I was scared to death every minute I was over there, and anyone who says he wasn't is lying. We were just following orders.

We stopped at the line at Wiesbaden, but some outfits continued on and had to dig their foxholes. We stopped to clean out snipers, stragglers left behind. They were told to stay there, and they did. When you were eighteen years old, that's what you did. We went to Frankfurt, Germany, cleaning out snipers and patrolling the city. We went back on the line at Bauhomberg, fighting and digging foxholes. The 70th Division stopped, patrolling the city. I was young, and they placed me with another outfit, but I didn't know it. I thought I was still in the 70th. I learned more recently that the 70th had stopped at Frankfurt.

In about three days I was hurt. Shelling was going on, and I was in my foxhole. We figure that a shell exploded next to me giving me a concussion. I was unconscious for two days. I had no wounds, and I didn't bleed, so I didn't get the Purple Heart – not like some people who received a Purple Heart after cutting their hands on C-Rations. I didn't know what had happened to me.

It was a long road back. They sent me back to Frankfurt, which was the closest field evacuation hospital – just tents. Then I was flown to the 198th General Hospital in Paris, France. They diagnosed me with a concussion. It fouled up my back, shoulders and neck. I had been in a foxhole so I wasn't thrown very far, and they didn't call that a battle injury.

On June 1, 1945 I left Paris and was put on a hospital ship called the *Wakefield*. It landed June 16, 1945 at Pier 5, Boston, Massachusetts. From there I went to the William Beaumont General Hospital, El Paso, Texas. Coming back on the ship they told us to pick a hospital closest to home, and they would ship us there so our parents could come and visit. I got the orders to William Beaumont. I was on the train almost a week, as we delivered people on the way. There were two litter patients; I was one, and there was another kid. I could walk better than 95% of the veterans on the train. They wouldn't let me get up. After five days on the train I was told to roll over, and I asked why. I was told I hadn't called for a bedpan, and they gave me an enema. I had been getting up, going nights. I never did get to feel better, especially my neck. After a month and a half at Beaumont, I was discharged there on August 21, 1945. I was getting 16 aspirin a day in the Army. I'm down to 2 a day now and am on 20% disability.

My medals included the European African Middle Eastern Medals with one cluster (the Battle of the Bulge), Bronze Service Star (for bravery beyond the line of duty), Combat Infantry Badge, WWII Victory Medal, Lapel Button (Ruptured Duck), Good Conduct Medal (engraved with name on back so that only recipient could wear it), New York State Medal for serving from N.Y.S.

I went back to the railroad the week after discharge as a machinist helper, not applying for the 52-20 unemployment. In 1946 I made machinist. In 1974 I became a supervisor of the entire system.

In 1946 I married Madelyn Hunter from Woodlawn in the Bronx. We had one boy and two girls. I moved back to Brewster in 1952, joined the VFW 1961-62, was post commander VFW 1965-66 and commander Putnam County VFW 1966. I retired from Metro-North in 1986.[32]

Peter J. Tavino

In June 1944 I graduated from Brewster High School. I didn't enlist; my father wouldn't hear of it, so I waited to be drafted which happened in November 1944. I was sent to Camp Blanding, Florida for fifteen weeks of infantry training. Because the war was accelerating so fast, the training period was cut from twenty - one weeks to fifteen weeks to get the troops overseas quickly. At the end of training I was given a thirty day furlough, then put on a ship in New York and sent overseas.

I landed in Glasgow, Scotland, took a train to Liverpool, England and then shipped across the channel to Le Havre, France. Once there, they put us on a train called "forty and eight". It was a troop ship, but it was a freight train with boxcars. The boxcars held either forty men or eight horses. As a replacement I wasn't assigned to any outfit, but would be sent where needed. We then went through France, Belgium and down into Germany. In Bonn, Germany I was put in a building that had been bombed out; all the windows were open. We threw blankets down and slept on the floor. This was in April of 1945, just after the Battle of the Bulge was over, and the United Stated Army was advancing pretty close to Berlin. I developed pneumonia and ended up in an army general hospital.

I was discharged from the hospital on May 4th, and the next day the war was over. There were a whole bunch of replacements and no outfits that needed troops; so they shifted us from one Replacement Depot to another. This went on for about three months. They had all these men over there but didn't want to ship them back home, as they were getting ready to send the old troops back and would need replacements.

The war in the Pacific was still going on, so they decided to take the extra replacements in Germany and send them over to the Pacific. I thought, O boy! Here I go; I'm going to wind up in the Pacific. I did all right here, but now I'm going to the Pacific. Now I'm going to be in trouble. As fate would have it, they needed a typist at the Replacement Depot Headquarters. So I spent the rest of my service time there.

In that office, I typed up orders for replacements, shipping men to different places, many going to the States. I was there about sixteen months. I typed fifteen to twenty thousand names a day - never came across a name from Brewster and none named Tavino. The war was over; there was no danger. We didn't need furloughs, as we could go anywhere in Germany. That's when the black market started. Some men made out like bandits – until the Army caught up with them. They saw what was happening. The men were sending money back to the states. They could buy cigarettes for fifty cents at the PX and sell a carton for one hundred dollars. A cheap watch would sell for one hundred to one hundred fifty dollars, and men would hitchhike into Berlin to sell watches and cigarettes. In Germany a cigarette took the place of money. A German would rather take a cigarette than ten dollars or ten marks. My barber would take a cigarette to cut my hair. He could trade it for whatever he wanted.

The buildings were all rubble. I complained every day I was there. I wanted to get home. But when I got home I said what am I doing here - what am I going to do now? I had a good life over there. I should have stayed.

While in Europe, I was able to go to Italy and visit relatives. I got to my uncle's house in Benevento on Christmas Eve. They were all happy the war was over - just very unhappy that their city and church had been bombed. They complained like hell. Many people had left the city to go into the mountains. Otherwise, they were happy.

Until my retirement I was a building contractor in Brewster for many years.

I married Nellie Lato in 1951, and we have five children.[33]

Anthony Vanaria

I grew up in Brewster. In September 1942 after being drafted into the Army I was sent to Ft. Dix and then to Fort Bragg, a new camp at the time. I was there for three months, going back and forth into Virginia on maneuvers and then was assigned to the 445th Antiaircraft Battalion. We headed for England on the former French passenger liner, *Louis Pasteur*. There were 5,000 men aboard, three or four people stacked up on bunks. It was cramped. We didn't know what we were in for. We landed in Liverpool and stayed there for eighteen months doing more training. We left England for Normandy landing there in July. We went to Brest, France. There was action in the area, but I didn't see any at that time. We were there two or three days. The infantry was pushing the German army back. We went up to Hurtgen Forest, and then crossed the Elbe River. Bombs were dropping, and our AA unit was doing its job protecting the infantry. In that area I went to a church where I ran into Frank Killarney, B Company and Auggie Piazza. Bob Palmer was in the same AA outfit; he was in D Battery and I was in A Battery.

In February 1945 I was on the Cologne Plains when shrapnel from a German 88 tank hit me. One of my buddies got hit in the stomach. They got eight of us that day. We didn't have anything to match that tank. I was laid up for two months in the Versailles Army Hospital. I went back to my outfit, and we were guarding German prisoners in Antwerp. V-E Day was May 8th. By then I was a T 5 Corporal and expected to be shipped to Japan, but in August the war with Japan was over.

I was put on a Victory Ship headed for Boston, a small ship holding 2,000 men. Many were sick during the trip. When I got to Boston I called my family, and I arrived in Brewster on Thanksgiving Day, 1945. A lot of men never got back. I was lucky.

While I was in Europe, I got a lot of V-mail. Marge Addis, the publisher of The Brewster Standard, used to send us all the weekly papers. It had articles and pictures of the Brewster people in service. Our buddies would be sitting around and see me coming, and they would say, "here comes the hub of the Harlem Valley". That was on the top of our newspaper and they knew it. I got ribbed about that.

When I got home I was working on Ford tractors; then I got my own agency. It was a tough business. I started on a shoestring and had three or four people working for me. Then I went into servicing lawns. Finally, I got into real estate and still do some of that.

We have had reunions of the 445th, but there aren't too many of us left.

In 1949 I married Denise Gilhooly from the Bronx. I had met her in Lake Carmel. We have two sons.[34]

Alexander Vanderburgh, M.D.

My grandfather had gone to China in 1896 as a medical missionary starting a hospital near Shanghai and spent many years there. My father had married in 1925, and I was born in 1926 in Kuling in central China. Of course the Communists were in power and were trying to overthrow Chiang Kai-shek. And they wanted the Americans out of China. My own mother died when I was very young and my father came to Brewster to set up his medical practice.

Even though my dad was 45 years old and had five children, he was conscripted into the U.S. Army in 1941 before the attack on Pearl Harbor and was given the rank of Captain. Having spent two years as a medical missionary in China from 1925 to 1927, he spoke, read and understood the Mandarin dialect and could understand Cantonese. When he left home, he promised my stepmother that he would not let on that he could speak or understand Chinese. In 1941 he was assigned to a camp in Kentucky, mostly taking care of scrapes and men who got into brawls, and he didn't feel very useful. He asked my mother to release him from his promise and informed those above him that he could speak and understand Chinese. He was instantly shipped to Oregon, where he was stationed for a couple of months and then sent right over to China.

My dad was born in China and lived on the mainland as a boy in the area of Shanghai. For a time the officers' quarters he lived in during WWII was the same house he had lived in when he was a boy. He was assigned to a field hospital. The Japanese were bombing the mainland, and there were casualties at the camps, including American pilots and Chinese civilians. He had to operate on a young man who had been wounded in his eye. The eyeball had to be removed, even though he had never done that before. There was a book that showed step by step how to do the operation, and he did it while reading the book. The fellow lost the sight of one eye, but he apparently healed well. My father didn't like the Chinese doctors, but he did think the nurses were good and compassionate.

There were many times when he had to make the trip by plane over the Himalayan Mountains to Karachi, India taking the wounded. He was apparently in southern China in part of the China/Burma Theatre and went over the Lido Road and the Burma Road several times in a truck convoy. He said it was scarier than flying in an airplane, as there were precipitous drops without railings. He could see trucks that had gone off the road – and he didn't like heights.

He probably got over there in 1942. I believe he met Chiang Kai-shek once. He did meet General Clare Chenault, head of the Flying Tigers. Some of them had to be treated. They were a wild bunch.

There were quite a few Army medics, Captains and higher in rank. I don't really know why that unit was there. There was one time when the big brass was meeting with the high Chinese officials, and Dad went as an interpreter. At the banquet before every course, each person was given a glass of some sort of wine and was expected as a courtesy to drink it. He didn't drink at all, and he knew there were many toasts ahead for each course. So he just tipped his glass at the toasts. Everyone who came to the banquet left the banquet intoxicated, and he was the only one sober and could drive the whole group back. He didn't expect that he would have to do this, of course. The Chinese people all said that my father had a very good command of the Chinese dialect which is unusual for a foreigner, but he had lived there for years as a boy.

My grandfather and grandmother said the Chinese peasants were gentle, lovely people. He liked Pearl Buck's writings, and he might have met her.

My father returned to the U.S. in 1945 and got busy re-opening his medical practice at our home on Main Street in Brewster.[35]

Isaac Van Vlack

Isaac Van Vlack was born in 1919 and grew up in Brewster on his family's farm on Peaceable Hill. There were five children in the family. If his mother found him playing sports, she would tell him he had to get home to feed the animals. He didn't have the luxury of completing high school, as he had to work on the farm. At the age of fifteen or sixteen he was also working at P. F. Beal & Sons as a well driller.

"Ike and I (Jeanne Jenkins) were married in June of 1941. 'Ike' was working for Ross and Phil (P. F. Beal & Sons) as a well driller before war began.

Our first child, a son, was born February 4, 1943 and 'Ike' received his draft notice February 10, 1943. He entered the service February 25, 1943. Mayor Wells saw him off at Brewster Station carrying the American flag, as he did for all who left for war. He went to Ft. Dix, N.J. for his early training, and because of his previous employment he was placed in the Army Engineer Corps.

I was pregnant with our second child when 'Ike' was going overseas. His destination was the Azores Islands where he was assigned to an Army Air Force Squadron. They built airstrips for our planes to land and refuel, and he was there for the duration of the war. He learned through the Red Cross that he had a daughter born August 15, 1944.

While 'Ike' was away, I worked at the Barden Corp. defense plant in Danbury, Connecticut. I worked evenings so I could take care of my children during the day. My parents watched over them in the evening.

'Ike' was separated from service at Camp Grant, Illinois on October 22, 1945.

He established his own well drilling company after the war and continued in that business for many years. We moved to Florida in 1977 and 'Ike' passed away January 7, 1998." [36]

Bernard J. Waters

In 1934 I graduated from Brewster High School, having received three scholarships for college basketball. They were Holy Cross, Villanova and Fordham. My father had been injured in a fall and died soon afterward, so I had to take care of my mother and went to work at the First National Store on Main Street.

On July 19, 1942 I married Kathryn Hubbard from Coxsackie, N.Y. who had graduated from Russell Sage College. She taught typing, shorthand and business English at Brewster High School. The class of 1939 wanted Kay to go to Washington on their class trip. Bobby Collins (a Marine who was killed in action in the Pacific) was president of the class. One night in Washington, Bobby went to Kay and told her they were going to sneak a bottle of wine into their room. She told him she didn't hear him and let them do it. She figured one bottle of wine for eight kids, and each one wouldn't get much.

On December 7, 1942 I enlisted in the Army Quartermaster Corps. We went to Camp Upton for assignment and then to Camp Lee, Virginia for basic training. I went to Officer Candidate School and the men in charge of us were 2nd Lieutenants who had been separated from their units. While their units went overseas they had this assignment at OCS, and they didn't like it. So they sent us out on 40-mile marches as fast as we could go. It was hot as hell. They were 6 ft 2 in. and we were smaller guys. I went from 180 lbs. to 157 lbs. I graduated a 2nd Lieutenant, and my mother, sisters Mary and Betty and Kay drove down to attend graduation. Kay would teach all year and then join me for the summer.

After more training I was sent for basic training in fundamentals at Fort George Meade, Maryland as instructor. Ft. Meade was a permanent, old Army post with a golf course and swimming pool. One day a lieutenant came out all dressed up and asked Kay, "Don't I look nice?" Kay looked at him and said "yes, but you have two different shoes on". One shoe had a buckle, and one shoe had laces. The lieutenant said, "I do? Nobody will ever notice it". He was going on a date.

My next assignment was to Camp Reynolds, 90 miles north of Pittsburgh, Pa. I brought men with me. This was a Cooks and Bakers School, and I was the officer in charge of twenty-five enlisted men who were already cooks. The men wanted their own building and mess hall, so I made the request of the commanding general. He granted my wish and gave the men their own building. They were teaching guys to cook. Everything was timing when cooking, when to start a dish that had to be eaten at a given time. I told my men they were to discipline themselves and hand out punishments. One soldier broke curfew and showed up drunk. They made him take 25 laps around the baseball field and made him go to bed at nine o'clock every night for a week plus doing KP work. They knew this worked, because they understood they would have to come back to me if it didn't. The men fixed up their mess hall, taking grass sections from the golf course where it wouldn't be missed and planted it. They also made a walkway of crushed stone.

Now that the war was over, the general wanted my men to give a dinner for the Red Cross volunteers who had been so helpful to the soldiers who were returning from overseas. Sixty people came.

A buddy from Pittsburgh was with me in the mess hall one day, and he stood up and said, "I'm a Catholic, and I want to go to church – anybody want to join me?" So I went with him. We became best friends, and when he got married, I was his best man. He had gone with a beautiful girl who could have been an actress, she was so stunning. Her mother kept pushing him on her daughter to the point where he gave her up and married someone else. He went to Ohio State, and then had his own bakery distributing business. He wanted me to go out there and be his sales manager, but Kay said no because her mother was still alive and she wanted to be near her.

I was sent to Indian Town Gap, Pa. and was promoted to Captain from 1st Lieutenant. I was placed on orders to go over to Europe, so I went home and said good-bye to everyone. Back at Indian Town Gap the orders were cancelled. Later I was on orders to go to Japan. President Truman ordered the dropping of the atomic bomb and shortly thereafter all orders were cancelled.

The army suggested I stay in the army six months and be promoted from Captain to Major. My wife Kay said, "stay in the army six months and I will divorce you". I got out of the Army. I was in three years and seven months, discharged in 1946.

I worked at the First National Store on Main Street, Brewster and became manager. We moved to Route 6 opposite Love's Restaurant when the store became a super market. We have one son.[37]

Richard Weizenecker

We lived in my grandfather's house in North Brewster off Peaceable Hill Road. As kids we wore knickers. In winter we would have great sleigh riding down Peaceable Hill; there weren't many cars – maybe one in a half-hour would come by.

"Bunky" O'Brien lived up the street from me, and although I was younger, we were good friends. He was a great guy, and I went down and saw him off when he went in service. He and his sister used to write back and forth. He was on a B-17 and was killed in action over Europe.

I was inducted into the Army April 11, 1945 in New York City. Mayor Wells saw our group off in Brewster. We were put on a Liberty ship in Seattle, Washington headed for the invasion of Japan. I was a Tech, Fifth Grade, Battery B, 89th Field Artillery Battalion, and I was scared to death. Those ships would go up and flop down making a loud racket, and often cracks would occur. You couldn't get any sleep. Everyone was sick. If you could get up on deck and tie yourself to a lifeboat you would feel better – you could handle it. But if you weren't tied to a lifeboat you could go overboard. We had guys welding the cracks in the bulkhead, and they had to be tied down. We were too sick to do anything; we had a clean-up crew cleaning up the mess. If we had landed on Japan, we would have scared them to death, we were in such bad shape.

Our ship was way off the coast of Japan waiting for the surrender. We didn't know the A-bomb was going to be used, but we knew something was about to happen. The first, then the second bomb was dropped, and we were then told about them. If the Japanese had not surrendered we would have invaded. I was in the Occupation Force and was in Osaka and Nagasaki.

I was honorably discharged at Fort Dix, N.J. on December 14, 1946. My medals included the WWII Victory Medal, Army of Occupation Medal and Asiatic Medal.

On August 28, 1965 I married Jacqueline Sniffen who lived in Brewster her entire life. We had two children, a boy and a girl who both live in Brewster. I have owned my own business, Weizenecker's Plumbing and Heating, for over forty years.[38]

H. Crosby Wells

I left Yale to join the ski troops, the 10th Mountain Division, which trained at Camp Hale, Colorado (alt. 9,500 feet) and was later deployed in the Apennines in Italy. I was Squad leader of an infantry rifle platoon. During an early advance all but two of my infantry squad of twelve became casualties, and I was elevated to the lofty rank of Staff Sergeant. I had called back the two scouts for rotation and the replacements had not yet moved forward. So I ended up being the first one through a small hillside orchard that turned out to be a minefield. I became a casualty soon thereafter, losing part of my left leg several inches below the knee and ended up spending sixteen months in military hospitals (not nearly as long as Senator Bob Dole, also of the 10th Mountain Division). I received excellent medical treatment. While so ensconced, I worked on and received my B.A. from Yale. Upon discharge I enrolled at the University of Virginia Law School in Charlottesville, Virginia and began really enjoying life for the first time.

For forty years I practiced law in New York City including a four-year assignment in Athens, Greece as General Counsel of the Greek State Power Company, the public power corporation.

I am now retired and living with my wonderful wife Chany in the lovely village of Salisbury in the northwest corner of Connecticut. I have two sons.

I was awarded the Bronze star.

Brothers, Tomlinson Wells served in the Military Police as a 2nd Lieutenant and Henry H. Wells Jr. served as a 1st Lieutenant in the Chemical Corps. They did not go overseas.[3940]

Left:
Wm. Ross Beal
meeting the Sultan
of Morocco.

Below:
Wm. Ross Beal
with drilling crew
and showing two
water well drilling
rigs.

Left:
Anthony Carollo

Below:
Frank Piazza

Left:
Donald Smith

Below:
John Kelly (left)
and Behrend Goossen
(right)

Left:
Malcolm T.Beal

Below:
Frederick L. Goossen

Above:
Robert C. Rapp
(KIA)

Below:
Edward G. Roth

Robert C. Rapp (KIA) (upper left), Richard Rapp (upper right), Frederick Rapp (bottom)

Feb. 1945 – Duren, Germany
Prior to crossing the Rhine River

Standing left: Leo Brennan
Standing right: Joseph Foster
Kneeling left: Robert E. Palmer
Kneeling right: Michael Green

Left: John J. Foster
Right: Joseph Foster

Left:
Anthony Vanaria

Below:
H. Crosby Wells

Henry H. Wells Jr.

Tomlinson Wells

Alexander Vanderburgh M.D.

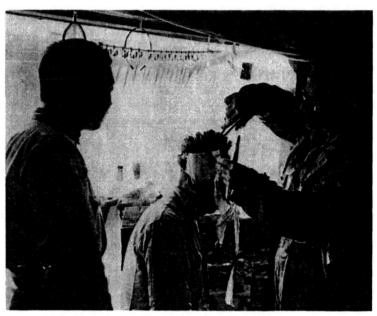

Capt. Vanderburgh treating a Chinese patient.

Air Force

Bernard Brandon

While in high school I had a job at the Cameo Theatre sweeping the floors. The kids were messy. Sometimes I would only sweep into the center so it looked as though I had done a good job. But on Saturdays I did a good job. Our class was the last one to be able to have a Washington trip and included in the class trip were Les Garnsey, Earl Pinckney and Eddie Brady. In 1941 I graduated from Brewster High School a year behind "Bunky" O'Brien, Fay Pinckney, Dick Donley – that bunch. After graduation I went to work for the New York Central Railroad in the Signal Division.

I wanted to be in the Aviation Cadets of the Army Air Force, so I enlisted December 9, 1942, took the test and got into the program. First I went to San Antonio, Texas for pre-flight, then to Sikeston, Missouri for primary school. It was my first time flying. I was there for six months, then washed out, and it was the biggest disappointment of my life. It might have saved my life, because I have the world's worst sense of direction! I was sent to Sioux Falls, South Dakota, Radio School for sixteen weeks – then to Gunnery School in Yuma, Arizona. That is where I had the most fun while in the service, shooting skeet. I knew I'd be a radio operator, but had to know how to operate the gun in case anything happened to the gunner. But I never had to shoot a gun on a mission.

After Gunnery School, I went to Chatham Field, Savannah, Georgia. That is where the crew all got together. We were assigned to a four engine B-24 heavy bomber. We trained at two or three other fields and then finally took off for Ireland flying in the B-24. We were the lead crew, but just before we took off our bombardier deserted, so that ended our lead crew days and I never heard what happened to that fellow. We trained for a couple of weeks in Ireland, then we were sent to a base in England - the 446th Group, 705th Squadron.

When enough repaired planes were available, the Group usually had about thirty-six to forty planes. This was called "maximum effort".

When flying missions, going over a target, it was my job to open the bomb bays. I had to jump down into the bomb bay carrying a screwdriver in case any bombs got hung up in the bay. I would have to trigger it with the screwdriver to drop it, and that was pretty ticklish, because I was 30,000 feet up without any parachute. There wasn't a lot of room for a mistake. It was a very narrow passage to get through to the bomb bay. Let me tell you, I held on. I always watched them loading the bombs to make sure they were loaded properly.

I had to do oxygen checks in the plane every five minutes while on a mission. The youngest crewmember was our mechanic and gunner. He was fairly nervous and was constantly swinging the turret, shooting or to check for fighters, and he would often catch the oxygen tube without knowing it. He would pass out, and every time he didn't check in I'd look up and find him passed out. I'd hook up his air again, and he would come back. The oxygen check was important.

I flew thirty-three missions over Germany and France, but on the thirty-third mission by the time we got back our field was socked in, so we couldn't land there. They were giving us a different field to go to and try to land, but there was no field open where we could land. We ran out of fuel. Our pilot climbed to 7,000 feet, aiming the plane for the channel so as not to crash on any homes. We were anxious, as it would be the first jump for any of us. We bailed out. One crewmember couldn't jump and had to be thrown out of the plane. When my chute opened my shoe was jerked off my foot, and I landed in the muddiest field in England. I dragged my parachute out to the nearest road and started walking. A civilian car passed me without stopping. An Army jeep finally came along looking for me. I was the last one to be picked up. The plane didn't crash in the channel but ended up landing on a field, flying empty, never hitting a soul. There was a picture of the crashed plane, and there was really nothing wrong with it except for the bent propellers. The plane wasn't wrecked at all.

They grounded the entire crew. Originally they were going to ground only the pilot, co-pilot and two or three gunners. Some of the crew had battle fatigue. They wanted me to go back and complete my missions because I passed my health exam with flying colors. But I said I had been with the crew for all those missions, and if they're grounded then I'm grounded. I was superstitious. So I was grounded. That was the end.

They sent us back home on a liberty ship by way of the northern route. While on the boat (April, 1945), I heard that President Roosevelt had died. We hit four days of storms, and those ships heaved like corks; the waves came over the decks. The flyers were so sick they wanted to die. We carried about one thousand German prisoners on board. Because my name began with B, and I was the ranking non-com on the boat as a Tech Sergeant, they put me in charge of making up all the American guard details for the German prisoners going to the U.S. These guards had been through the North African Campaign, Italian Campaign and the Normandy Campaign, and they put a 19 or 20 year-old flyboy in charge. I told the lieutenant that these guys had much more experience than I had, but he said not to worry, as they were so happy to be going home they would do anything I wanted. And that was the truth. I've always said the flyers didn't win the war. They helped, but it was the foot soldiers who did.

My father tried to get me into the Air Force Rest & Rehabilitation Center at the Pawling Prep School, because it was so close to Brewster. His friend however didn't have enough pull to get me out of Atlantic City where I had been sent for R & R., but it was great there, nice and warm in the springtime.

I was shipped out to St. Louis where I became a Radio Instructor. That was a joke, because I became a Navigational Instructor, and I didn't know my ear from my elbow. I talked a good game – I could read a book, so that helped, but I wasn't experienced. When I was flying over Europe, I actually only used the radio four or five times. We kept radio silence, except for sending an SOS. Otherwise, the enemy could take a fix on us and follow us in.

The only time we got hit was when the Germans came out with the jets toward the end of the war. They went through the group so fast, not one fellow got a shot off at them. That's how fast they were compared to our planes. I 'm glad the war ended before they came out with faster jet planes. We would have been in big trouble.

On September 29, 1945 I was separated and went home. I enrolled at Pace Institute using the G.I. Bill attending there for one year, followed by a year at NYU. While I was going to school, I was using the railroad having been given free transportation and time off to go to school. I went to work for Siebold Ink Company and stayed with them for forty years.

In 1949 I met Alice Gorman at the Tonetta Lake pavilion. She and her family had been Tonetta Lake summer residents for ten years. We were married on July 8, 1950. We have six daughters.[41]

Arthur D. Jenkins

In 1917 Arthur was born in Croton Falls but was a Brewster resident when he was drafted in March of 1940. He was sent to Fort Dix for basic training and spent a year there in the Medical Corps. He re-enlisted in the Army Air Corps. and was sent to Shaw Field, South Carolina to work on BT-13's (bomber/trainer). From there he went to David Monthan Field, Tucson, Arizona and subsequently to Harlingen Army Air Field, Texas where he attended gunnery school. His training included practice with every sort of gun including the .50 cal. Browning, tearing them down and reassembling the weapons while blindfolded. Practice also included shooting at targets being towed by training planes and medium bombers. It was at Harlingen that he became a Flight Engineer, earning his Technical Sergeant stripes. From there he went to Keesler Field, Mississippi to attend mechanics school.

He flew in a new B-24 bomber to Scotland. From there he was flown to Flixton Bomber Base in England and was assigned to his mission plan. Sgt. Jenkins flew two missions pre-Normandy from England dropping bombs over Sangatte, France in the Calais area, bombing gun emplacements and pillboxes. On June 6, 1944, D-day he was in the first group and second plane in the formation of the Eighth Air Force, 446th Bomb Group, 705th Squadron, leading the attack. Using the Norden Bomb Sight he would take over the steering of the plane to the mission sight. The airplane was being hit and the glass bubble of the top turret in which he was located was struck, shattering the glass, which hit him in the eye. He was heard yelling over the intercom, and crewmembers pulled him down, gave him oxygen and patched his eye.

On June 7th the 446th Bomb Group bombed Alençon, France, on June 10th pillboxes at Wimereaux, France, and on June 11th they bombed Beaumont Air Field near Paris. There were days when the weather would not permit flying. On June 12 Rennes, France was bombed, on June 14 Orleans/Bricy Airfield in France. Every plane returned. On June 16 their 9th Mission, being escorted by P51's and P38's the group bombed Hamburg. On June 19 there were no missions, so he, his pilot Frank Douglas, his co-pilot Hank Gancarz and Ray Sampsons bought bicycles and rode on the grounds of Flixton Hall.

The next day, Mission #10 on June 20, 1944 the target was an oil refinery in the Stettin Bay area of Politz, Germany. Escorted by P-51, P-47 and P-38 fighter planes, the 446th B-24 bombers could not drop any bombs, because a group of B-17's flew under them. The secondary target was Bibinitz Airfield near Rostok and the Kiel Canal. As they approached the target, they were on two engines after being hit by a German fighter. They dropped their bombs, and an antiaircraft gun knocked out the third engine. At that point they had two options: land in Germany and be taken prisoners of war or head for Sweden, a neutral country, on one engine. They chose the latter and landed in Sweden with no brakes and one engine. The pilot cut the engine and crash-landed into the fence that surrounded the airfield.

Arthur got out of the plane and kissed the ground. Swedish soldiers surrounded them with guns and took the crew's pistols. They were taken to a building where they were interrogated. They had a short stay at a hotel and were then taken to Stockholm where a member of the American legation questioned them. Because all of their identification had been discarded when their B-24 was disabled flying over enemy territory, they had no identification to show the Swedish authorities. He was eventually issued a document signed by the Vice Consul of the U.S.A. stating "That he is unable to submit evidence of his American citizenship for the reason that he was forced to land in neutral territory and had to destroy all evidence of his American citizenship" and "they had not been naturalized in or taken an oath of allegiance to a foreign state nor has he done anything else which to his knowledge and belief, caused him to lose his nationality of the United States," ... From there he was sent to an internment camp for 8 or 9 days; after a month they were broken into smaller units and Arthur was sent to Granna Internees where he was given a three-day pass each month to visit Stockholm or any of the large cities. Once a week they were allowed a 24-hour pass to tour the vicinity. They played baseball between the crews of the B-24's and the B-17's.

Upon their release they were given a dark green, unarmed B-24 with no identification markings, one which had been converted into cargo and passenger use. The planes left at about eleven p.m. flying over Nazi-held Norway to England. From there they went to Scotland

and flew to Washington, D.C. in a C-54 where many questions were asked of them at the Pentagon about their experiences in Sweden.

Sgt. Jenkins was married on Sept 16, 1945 to Jeanette Barnum of Danbury, CT., and his wife was with him at Fort Dix while office personnel hunted down his papers. After almost ten days his papers were found being used as a booster cushion by a short WAC at her desk. Arthur was honorably discharged on September 24, 1945 with a Good Conduct Medal.

The Jenkins lived in Danbury, Connecticut, and Arthur was a self-employed general contractor, retiring in 1989. They had one son and one daughter. After retirement he spent a year in California with his son building his house. They subsequently made their home in Salisbury, N.H. near their daughter and family.[42]

Harrison Lane

In 1935 Harrison graduated from Brewster High School. His family, including two sisters Marjorie and Shirley, had a year round home at Tonetta Lake. He was working for the Packard Motor Car Company in New York City when Japan attacked Pearl Harbor.

Harrison was inducted into the Army Air Force on May 15, 1942 and subsequently trained at Lowry Field and Buckley Field in Colorado. During this time he met and married Arlie Mae Jackson of North Dakota in August 1943. After training to be a member of the ground maintenance crew and spending one year, 5 months and five days in this country, he was sent to the Asiatic Pacific Theatre where he worked on B-29 bombers in India. Every night after working as member of a ground crew, he would go to the hospital and spend the night. He had serious asthma and in the hospital could get oxygen, which kept him going. He might have been a good candidate for being returned to the states, but apparently they felt too much had been invested in him to let him leave. He was a Staff Sergeant in the 20th Air Force, China Burma India Theatre.

Sgt. Lane was transferred later in the war to the island of Tinian, and worked on the Enola Gay, not knowing it would be carrying the atomic bomb to Japan. Nevertheless, the crew suspected something unusual was about to happen.

Harrison received the following medals: Asiatic Pacific Theatre Medal with 6 stars, Good Conduct Medal and Distinguished Unit Badge.

Having used the G.I. Bill, Harrison graduated from Montana State College in 1950 with a degree in Applied Sciences and English, followed by an M.A. from the University of Minnesota and a Ph.D. in American Studies from the Univ. of Minnesota. He taught high school for two years before being offered a position in the Department of Social Studies at Northern Montana College teaching Western and Montana history and American Studies until he retired in 1981. He was chairman of the Department of History for 20 years. He apparently loved Montana and teaching young people about the state and its natural wonders, each year taking a class and others for a float trip down part of the Missouri River.

Harrison and Arlie Mae had three daughters.

Note: In George Schneider's story, he tells of being on board ship about to go through the Panama Canal and noticing a familiar face. It was Harrison Lane. They were both headed for India and eventually Tinian Island where they were members of ground crews working on B-29's. Harrison spent time at a Rest and Recreation Camp in the Himalayan Mountains, and Sgt. Schneider details his experiences there. On his return to Brewster, Harrison went to George's home to visit with him, mentioning he would be going to college. [43]

William Macomber

Although I was a member of the Brewster High School Class of 1944, I enlisted at age 18 in 1943. It was necessary to go through the draft because of the Putnam County quota; when my father picked up my "war diploma" I was already overseas. My oldest brother Harry was in the Army stationed in Hawaii, but had left there before the attack on Pearl Harbor. He switched to the Marine Corps and became an instructor. My middle brother Myron was in the Navy on a Destroyer Escort, which sank a German U-boat.

I was able to get into the Army Air Force and was sent to Fort Dix, N.J. for basic training. From there I went to Miami, Florida where most men went for pilot training. There were so many signed up, they took around 20,000 guys who were supposed to be in pilot training and put several thousands into the infantry right there and sent them overseas where they took their infantry training. I was picked to stay in the Air Force, and went to Gunnery School at Tindall Field which was also connected to the Apalachicola Base. Gunnery training took place from January to March 1944; when we finished, they sent us to a distribution center in Lincoln, Nebraska, where they assigned us to a crew. There were ten men in a crew – four officers and six enlisted men. The pilot, co-pilot, navigator and bombardier were officers. The engineer was usually a staff sergeant or better, and the radio operator was usually a staff sergeant. It was the rule in those days in the Army Air Force that as soon as we got overseas, we all became staff sergeants. There were two waist gunners, the ball turret gunner, the nose gunner and the tail gunner; the flight engineer had two duties - that of flight engineer and when in combat, top turret gunner.

We trained as a crew, and stayed with our crew as long as possible. Each person continued his training, the navigator more navigation, the bombardier more practice missions, target shooting for the gunners, etc. From El Paso we went to Topeka, Kansas and were assigned to a plane to fly overseas. Some of the crews went overseas by ship. Other crews took replacement planes over. I was in a crew that took the northern route to Gander, Newfoundland, the Azores, Marrakech, French Morocco, continuing on to Italy. I landed on a base just outside of Foggia-Castaluccia Air Base set up for the 451st

Bomb Group, which I was then assigned to. They had been overseas, and we were a replacement group. I flew all my missions out of that base.

The Germans were still in northern Italy. We were pushing them up through the Alps. I went on bombing missions to Trieste and Bologna in northern Italy to bomb bridges and railroad yards near the Brenner Pass. I flew all over Europe, France, Athens, Greece, and our longest flight was to Ploesti, Rumania and Oswego, Poland to hit the Nazi-controlled refineries. Everybody was running out of gas on that one. It was one of the longest missions I think I was on – over eight hours – four hours up and four hours back. On that raid up in Poland, the group flew in four squadrons. I was in the 451st Bomb Group, 725th Squadron, 15th Air Force. There were also the 426th and 427th- sometimes not that many. Each squadron tried to put up at least seven planes. Sometimes there were as many as 28 planes in a squadron. We flew missions to Lyon, France, Lenz, Austria and Prague, Czechoslovakia.

There was no heat in the plane. We wore heated flight suits. You'd put your pants on, then the jacket. There were wires through them; you would plug the jacket into the pants; then you'd put your boots on, plug them into the pants, then put the gloves on and plug them into the sleeve of your shirt. Before that, all we had were sheepskin jackets and pants. They were so bulky, and then they came out with the heated suits.

On that raid to Poland, our groups had four squadrons – I was in the 725th. We flew wing tip to wing tip. You could almost jump from one wingtip to the other – maybe not quite that close. I was the tail-gunner, and if I was in the lead or center plane I could see the pilot below me smiling. One would be a little right; one would be a little bit off, but all flying formation to the target. The worst part of the run, if we didn't run into fighters was when we'd get to where the i.p. (initial point) was turned on. We would get to a certain place, make a turn and follow the i.p. straight to the target. The plane would stay at one level, and that was when they could track us. That is when the bombardier took over using the Norden Bomb Sight and flew the plane to the target. Everybody followed the lead bombardier. If the lead bombardier was wrong, everybody was wrong. When we had hit the target and were headed home, we could take evasive action – as much as we could in B-24's and all in formation. We had pretty good success; we got all their refineries and all their rail yards.

In the course of the missions I saw a lot of planes shot down. I saw a whole group behind me going to Oswego, Poland; the whole group of 28 bombers was shot down right behind me. They didn't have much fuel left. The Germans went after the last group, and they got them. There was a difference between the B-24 and the B-17. The B-17 when out of fuel could float down, whereas the B-24 was tough to float down. We were always tight on fuel on those long missions. If a plane had to crash land, it was best not to have any extra fuel. When we were that far away from our home base, there was no fighter escort. The fighters extended their range by using wing tanks when I was there. Sometimes one group of fighters would come up; then another group of fighters would come up. But as soon as we got on the i.p.the fighters left. They didn't want to go through the flak. The Germans knew we were coming, and they would bring their AA guns in on railroad cars. We would throw chaff (cut up pieces of tin-foil) out the windows to foul up their radar. That was the duty of the waist gunners. Often we would see a German fighter plane flying right off our wing, flying our speed, our altitude, far enough away so we couldn't shoot at him, and he wouldn't get the flak. He would radio our speed and altitude. They had ways – they were smart people.

Guys were going home having finished their 35 missions. I finished mine sometime in February 1945, but somehow the paper work got messed up, and I finished with thirty-six missions. I was fortunate, because I had a good pilot – especially on landing and taking off - Clark Nelson from Idaho and then Kentucky. My co-pilot was from Carlisle, Pennsylvania. The other crewmembers were from Florida, Arkansas, Ohio and Washington. I was the youngest. We got pretty close. I saw some nice country - those were the good parts.

I was on my way home, went down to Naples and got on a luxury liner, the *Miraposa*. It only sailed one trip in the Atlantic; it was built for the Pacific and didn't ride the Atlantic too well. I was in mid-Atlantic when the Germans surrendered. Before we got to the states, a German submarine surfaced off our shipside and wanted to surrender. They wanted to come into the harbor with us, but they weren't allowed to do this. Bobby Enright from Brewster was on the same troop ship, and I ran into him. He was in the infantry.

It wasn't until I was on the ship returning home that a physical reaction occurred. It must have been because it was the first time I could relax. My whole body started to shake. You might say it was like the d.t's. All my feelings must have been pent up over all those months; now they were coming out physically. I spent five months in the hospital in Atlantic City, and then I went to North Carolina. After a while I was sent to a rest center at Fort Logan Army Hospital, Denver, Colorado. With the help of psychiatrists, I started to talk about the experiences, and it helped. I was discharged from Fort Logan Hospital with a Disability Discharge. But the shaking continued even when I was home. Guys would get together, and sometimes they would start talking about their experiences in the war; then that feeling of shaking would come over me. It got so that I wouldn't shake, but the feeling would come. That lasted four or five years. Most of the guys didn't want to talk about the war. My Honorable Discharge was on May 6, 1945 with European African Middle Eastern Service Ribbon, six Bronze Battle Stars, Distinguished Unit Badge 15th AF, Air Medal and 3rd Oak Leaf Cluster, 15th AF, American Defense Service Medal, Good Conduct Medal and World War II Victory Medal.

At first I worked in my dad's tool and die shop, but I found I couldn't work in the close tolerances of a machine shop. In my condition I couldn't handle that fine work. I'd be working on a machine, and I'd start shaking. I took the end of one finger off and then another; it was time to move on. After running into a guy in a refrigeration company, I started working in that business. I went to a refrigeration school in New York City on the G.I. Bill. At the same time I took a night job at the New York Central roundhouse in Brewster. Fran and Henry Palmer did that also after their return from the war. I worked as a boilermaker's helper on steam engines. Then I started my own refrigeration business, Bill's Refrigeration. Fran Palmer was doing plumbing during the day. Some oil companies were doing plumbing work as well as selling oil. So Fran and I said why don't we go into the oil business? Dick Palmer, Fran Palmer and I became partners and had the business for twenty years, Palmer & Macomber. He did his plumbing, and I did refrigeration, but we would help one another. My son runs the business now.

On August 17, 1946 I married Carol Ekstrom of Brewster. We have six children, and we are a close family.[44]

Donald B. McLagen

I don't boast about my four and a half years in the Air Force, because I was one of the more fortunate ones who did not see combat, and in fact spent about three years in Miami Beach, teaching in the OTS and working in Redistribution.

In 1940-1941 I was teaching in Brewster (known as Mr. Mac) and was drafted from Brewster in August of 1941. At that moment I was counseling in a camp in Great Barrington, Mass. I think it was about August 21st that Willis Ryder of Carmel and Gordon Foote of Mahopac and I got on the train (Put. Division) in Carmel, with Mayor Wells waving an American flag at us as we steamed out of the station. We ended up that night in the Army on Governor's Island. I won't detail that first night's experience, but Gordon drank too much beer, and it was not a pleasant evening for Willis and me – especially Willis who cleaned up after Private Foote. God bless him!

From Governor's Island we were off to Camp Dix. There I joined the regular Army, chose the Army Air Corps. and was shipped to Biloxi, Mississippi. It would be warmer there, I thought, than in some of the other places I could have chosen. The new barracks were not heated and the water for showers was cold, and because the Sergeant liked me, I chose to lead the five a.m. exercises rather than run around the barracks in pajamas.

Biloxi was a good place, and the oyster bars were wonderful - horseradish, ketchup, Worcestershire sauce, and then you dip ém and yum! yum! I still like ém. In February I got into Officer Candidate School 42A at Miami Beach. I graduated May 10th, and was assigned to Special Services at Scott Field in Illinois. I married Mary Alice Truran of Brewster on May 14th and was at Scott Field by that Saturday. After spending three months at Scott Field, and because they were looking for teachers, I was sent back to Miami Beach in August to teach in the Officers' Training School until it closed in 1944.

I was reassigned to the Redistribution Station there, until I was shipped out to San Antonio, Texas. We had two babies by that time. I bought a 21-foot trailer so we could stay together, but blew two tires on the way because we were overloaded. We were not supposed to be in Texas but in Greensboro, North Carolina. On the way there we blew another tire and almost lost our second child to dehydration due to a spasmodic stomach.

By this time I was a Captain in the Air Force and in charge of Officer Classification at Greensboro. Well, the war ended! I passed up promotion to get back to teaching and guidance counseling at Brewster under the great leadership of principal Herman H. Donley, whom I admired.

I retired in 1974, and the good Lord has given me 26 years of wonderful experiences in New York, Georgia and here and there. We had three children.[45]

John R. O'Brien (KIA)

John R. O'Brien ("Bunky") was born in Danbury Hospital on November 26, 1922. He played football for four years at Brewster High School under Coach Sterling Geesman, playing quarterback on that untied, unscored upon and undefeated team. He attended George Washington College in Chestertown, Maryland on an athletic (football) scholarship.

With a letter of permission from my parents, Jackie enlisted in the Army Air Force. In 1942 he trained in Atlantic City, New Jersey. Joan Beal and I went down to see him there; the trains were in darkness, and New York City was dark. His training continued in North Carolina, then at Curtiss Wright Corp., Robertson, Mo., U. S. Army Air Force, Fort Myers, Florida and Mount Home, Idaho. On his 20th birthday he went to Casper, Wyoming and then to the Air Force Base at Topeka, Kansas in February 1944.

The squadron flew from Natal, South America across the Atlantic to Dakar, French West Africa. Jackie was an engineer and top turret gunner on a B-24 Liberator (known to the Air Force as the "pregnant cow") whose name was the "Gypsy Queen".

I remember a letter from Jackie on his way from South America to French West Africa while flying east into the sunrise in which he remarked about hearing "Sunrise Serenade" on their radio – and said how beautiful it was. After Africa the squadron flew to an air base in England.

His last letter was dated April 24, 1944. On the third daylight raid over Berlin, Germany on April 29, 1944, the Gypsy Queen was shot out of the sky (on the return trip to the airfield in England) just a short distance from the Belgian border. The plane came down in Osnabruch northwest of Berlin.

Newspapers that day reported on the raid stating that there was heavy German antiaircraft fire and enemy aircraft in large numbers over Berlin. One tale gunner was reported having seen over a hundred Luftwaffe fighters.

According to a letter to Mrs. Eleanor O'Brien from Brigadier General Leon W. Johnson, Headquarters, Army Air Forces dated 31 August 1945, "...your son's airplane sustained damage in an encounter with hostile fighters and shortly thereafter eight parachutes were seen to open from it. His bomber then went into a steep vertical dive and disappeared from the formation. The crewmembers of aircraft returning from the mission were unable to furnish any other information. ... I extend my heartfelt sympathy in your great loss, and I wish to assure you that Sergeant O'Brien's great contribution to his country will long be remembered." The crew reported the last they saw of Jackie, he was headed to the cockpit, where the pilot, Lt. Ponge was injured. It was believed that Jim Hines had been shot and was pinned in the plane, and Jackie went up to help him. Both lives were lost.

His remains were brought home to Brewster and buried in St. Lawrence Cemetery in June of 1949.

Staff Sergeant John R. O'Brien received the following medals: Good Conduct Medal, Air Medal, EAMET medal with star, World War II Victory Medal, Aviation Badge (air crewmember), American Campaign Medal, extra ...... and the Purple Heart whose certificate reads, " for military merit and for wounds received in action resulting in his death April 29, 1944." Also: Citizen of Brewster Honor Roll, Citation of Honor – H.H. Arnold, George Washington College – post-war Reunion Memorial Service.[46]

THE UNITED STATES OF AMERICA

TO ALL WHO SHALL SEE THESE PRESENTS, GREETING:

THIS IS TO CERTIFY THAT

THE PRESIDENT OF THE UNITED STATES OF AMERICA PURSUANT TO AUTHORITY VESTED IN HIM BY CONGRESS HAS AWARDED THE

PURPLE HEART

ESTABLISHED BY GENERAL GEORGE WASHINGTON AT NEWBURGH, NEW YORK, AUGUST 7, 1782

TO

Staff Sergeant John E. O'Brien, A.S. No. 12182452,

FOR MILITARY MERIT AND FOR WOUNDS RECEIVED IN ACTION

resulting in his death April 29, 1944.

GIVEN UNDER MY HAND IN THE CITY OF WASHINGTON
THIS 27th DAY OF June 1944

_____
SECRETARY OF

OFFICIAL:

_____
MAJOR GENERAL,
THE ADJUTANT GENERAL.

Henry H. Harding O 'Hara (KIA)

Harding was in the Brewster High School Class of 1941. He was a talented musician who played several instruments. He played the clarinet in the high school band and orchestra for four years, and he also had his own orchestra. He later became solo clarinetist in the band at each base where he was assigned in the Army Air Corps.

As a boy of eight or nine, he became one of the first mascots of the Brewster Fire Department, wearing a fireman's uniform. He had loved to tinker with cars and learned to drive the family automobile up and down the driveway of his home by the time he was nine years old. He became a very good driver and later as a fireman was asked to drive Chief Morehouse's car as well as the Brewster ambulance.

Harding enlisted in the Army Air Force Reserve hoping to become a pilot in the Army Air Corps. He was inducted September 7, 1942 and was amongst numerous others from Brewster who went into the military that same day: Roland Burdick, Robert Palmer, Arthur T. Ashby, Alfred Dahm, Lafayette Pinckney, Patrick Carlone and Kieran O'Neill.

Harding had passed the test for pilot training, but when he was called up there were no openings for pilots. Gunners were needed on the B-24 Liberator bombers. He went from Fort Dix to the U.S. Air Corps, 989th Technical School Squadron in Atlantic City and from there to Fort Myers, Florida where he started his training in the aerial gunnery school. This consisted of study of the mechanisms of .30 and .50 caliber machine guns, instruction in methods of estimating the speed and distance of an airplane, etc. He received his diploma, his gunner's silver wings and his promotion to sergeant. He was given the choice of staying there as an instructor, but elected to continue his training.

From Florida he went to Lowry Field, Denver, Colorado for further training and then his training continued for two more months at Davis-Monthan Field, Tucson, Arizona. When he reached Salinas Army Air Base at Salinas, California, he was attached to the 391st Bombardment Squadron and was promoted to Staff Sergeant in July 1943. In August of 1943 while the Liberator Bomber "Sack Time" on which he was the armorer-gunner and photographer was being prepared for an overseas flight, he spent a short week at home with his parents and sister Rita O'Hara (Rapp).

Sergeant O'Hara was assigned to the Eighth Air Force in England and flew missions over Germany, Ploesti oil fields in Romania, Danzig, Gydnia and Norway. On one mission his plane was badly shot up by antiaircraft and managed to come in on one engine. His sister Rita saw a picture on a newsreel of that badly damaged plane showing "Sack Time" painted on its side. That plane had to be abandoned, and another B-24 Liberator took the name "Sack Time 2".

According to several news reports American Liberator bombers attacked Norway going through frigid weather, and without escort to inflict damage on the Kjeller depot where German fighters went for over-hauling. Another target was at a power station, Rjukan, about eighty miles west of Oslo, a steel hardening molybdenum mine hidden in the mountains at Knaben. It was on the longest flight made by a British-based bomber in October lasting ten hours that Sergeant O'Hara's plane was lost. He was considered missing in action as of November 19, 1943, the date of the mission having been November 18, 1943. After full investigation it was determined that Harding was killed in action and although the actual date of death was not known, "The records of the Department of the Army are being amended to show that Staff Sergeant O'Hara was killed in action 18 November 1943 when his plane crashed into waters between England and Norway while on a bombing mission to Oslo, Norway." Henry Harding O'Hara received posthumously the Air Medal, which was sent to his parents. The citation read: "For exceptionally meritorious achievement, while participating in five separate bomber combat missions over enemy occupied Continental Europe. The courage, coolness and skill displayed by this enlisted man upon these occasions reflect great credit upon himself and the armed forces of the United States".[47][48]

Lafayette Pinckney

The beginning of World War II found me in Herkimer, N.Y. working for the New York Central Railroad, signal construction division. It was there that I received my letter of greetings from Uncle Sam to report to Governor's Island for induction on August 21, 1942. I could have turned the invitation down, because my three brothers, Remington, LaVerne and Earl were already in the service, so it was optional for me to remain home or report for duty. I chose the latter. On Sept. 21, 1942 I went to Fort Dix, N.J. to begin my basic training. In the meantime I had the opportunity to play the trumpet in the Army band. I had played the baritone horn and the trumpet in the Brewster High School band. I was informed that I could stay at Fort Dix to be a part of the band. However, I chose to move on to Robbins Field, Macon, Georgia to finish my basic training. While in Georgia I was assigned to the 46 Air Depot Group – a part of the 8th Air Force.

From Georgia our outfit was sent to Camp Shanks, a port of debarkation. There we were put on a ship headed for England. At that time the German submarines were active in the Atlantic. Because we were in a convoy with other troop ships, we had to change direction quite frequently, resulting in our arriving overseas in 10 days, not the usual 5. The convoy was surrounded by battleships to protect from enemy U-boats. When a submarine was spotted, an alarm was sounded; everyone proceeded to the upper deck with their life preservers on, remaining on deck until the all-clear signal was given. Needless to say, many tense moments were spent on upper deck, and we were thankful to be safe.

We were about three-fourths of the way across the ocean when a severe storm came upon us. The Captain said he had been crossing the Atlantic for 30 years, and this storm was the worst he had been through. Again, we were thankful for God's protection.

After 10 days we arrived in Greenwich, Scotland at midnight. The sun was just setting due to clocks being set ahead. We boarded the train and traveled throughout the night, arriving the next morning at the RAF Base outside Norwich, England, July 27, 1943. I served as a Dental Technician with Dr. Harvard D. Jacobs, who had been head oral surgeon at Mass. General Hospital in Boston, Massachusetts. It was a great experience working with such a talented man.

Conditions in England at the time were not good. The Germans were still doing some bombing, mostly at night. There were planes in the air around the clock. Over Europe the RAF did night bombing, and 8th Air Force bombers operated during the day. There were many casualties. I had made contact with a Brewster school friend, Harding O'Hara; we were to meet in a hotel in Norwich on Saturday at 1:00 p.m. I went to the hotel as planned and waited. Harding never showed up. He had to go on a special bombing mission. His plane was shot down in the North Sea.

Another school friend, John O'Brien (Bunky) was based at another field in England, but we were never able to get together. John had been our class president and quarterback of the famous Brewster High School football team that was undefeated, untied, and unscored upon. John wasn't in England six months, and his plane was shot down over Berlin, Germany.

John Green, another friend from Brewster, was injured in the Battle of the Bulge and ended up in the hospital on our base. He was serving in a tank division when he was injured.

Leslie Garnsey, another Brewster boy and I had the opportunity to get together in London for a time of reminiscing.

My brother Earl and I met in Cambridge, England a month before the invasion of Normandy. Thirty days passed and no word from him. I spent many anxious moments waiting to hear from him. I finally called the Red Cross, and they were able to track him down. What a relief to receive word that he was fine.

After the war ended in Europe, Earl was stationed at a base near LeHavre, France. His letters revealed some of his wild experiences in the city. Then one letter came through with some startling news. He was converted and was going to study to be a minister when he got home. It was hard for me to believe that, so I didn't think any more about it.

In the meantime our organization was scheduled for the South Pacific. We were sent to the States and given a 30-day furlough. It was nice getting home to see family and some of my Brewster friends again. One Saturday night several of us went to the Green Gables on Rt. 22 in Patterson, N.Y. We were there until closing at 3:00 a.m. I ended up riding with Jim Collins, who was using his dad's new car. Joe Carollo was the other occupant. Recognizing Jim's condition from too much alcohol, I offered to drive, but he said no. He had had his driver's license about two weeks. So away we went down Rt. 22 about 70 miles an hour. Because of Jim's condition he failed to make a turn. We went off the highway, grazed a tree two feet in circumference and ended up down a 20 ft. embankment with the car on its side. It so happened that a car coming northbound saw our car go off the road. He stopped at the scene. The driver was hesitant about coming down to look in the car, because he didn't hear any sounds. But he finally did, got up on the side of the car and was able to open the door. We were able to get out of the car and climb up the bank to the road. We thanked the Lord for coming out of that accident alive. In fact, six months after that accident I made the decision to become a minister.

At the end of the 30 - day furlough I had to report to Tinker Field Air Base in Tulsa, Oklahoma. Because the war had ended after the atomic bomb attacks in Japan, I was sent to Rome, N.Y. Air Base and was discharged November 7, 1945 at 24 years old. What a day of rejoicing that was!

I married Carol Deacon whose first husband had died and who had an 18 month old child. She was a cousin of the Howell girls in Brewster. We had a son. She passed away. I married Geneva Daniels Savrey and we had four children. In 1965 I graduated from Houghton College having used the G.I. Bill and subsequently became a Baptist minister.[49]

George W. Schneider

In 1941-1942, as a student in Brewster High School, I was an air raid warden with an armband patrolling on my bike Carmel Avenue and the back road going to the farms. I mostly told the people to put out their lights when the air raid whistle blew. We would go to Lou Blaney's house in Sodom district and learn about air raid procedures on his console television, one of the earliest in town. The screen faced upward with a mirror slanted for viewing the picture. Dr. Ritchie taught us first aid at the old firehouse across from the Baptist Church.

I started working on the N.Y. Central RR section gang with Italian men who couldn't speak English. Temperatures got to be 10 degrees below zero and lots of snow. Tony Ercole, foreman, let the others cut brush, and we took the put-car to White Plains to look at a switch. It took all day to go down and back, as we pulled into sidings and let trains go by. I earned 54 cents an hour and lasted two weeks, before I went back to school.

November 1942 I received greetings from Uncle Sam and went down to White Hall, New York City for a physical and swearing into the Army. I chose the Army hoping to get into the Air Force.

Early in March of 1943 the Palmer family gave me a ride to the Carmel railroad station. There must have been 50 or 60 guys leaving at the same time. We were given coffee and donuts, and the politicians made their speeches. We went to Penn Station where we boarded a train to Fort Dix, arriving there in the late afternoon. We received all our clothing and shoes and were assigned a barracks. I was put on K.P. the first night, and all I had to do was put coal in the cook stove. At midnight the cook asked what I wanted to eat. "I'll take a big T-bone steak and french fries"; to my surprise he made it for me. I thought the army wasn't so bad after all. I never saw a dinner like that again.

We stayed in Fort Dix for a couple of weeks; then went by train to Florida for basic training. We sweated it out all the way to Florida before we knew we were in the Army Air Force. Henry and Ed Palmer were in basic with me.

They had a boxing ring behind one hotel, and as I was walking by, I saw a man shadow boxing. As I stood there and watched him, he came over and said, " I need a sparring partner, would you be willing? I won't hurt you." I agreed. A couple of other guys were passing by and put the gloves on me. We got into the ring, and I popped him on the nose so hard, he fell flat on his back - end of fight. I told the other guys, get these gloves off me fast before he realizes what happened.

After we were there two weeks, I got prickly heat on my body. The medics said I had measles, so they put me at this big estate that had been owned by Al Capone, the gangster. I stayed a couple of weeks in the darkened room and missed the daily exercise.

Easter time we had a choice of turkey or ham; I took turkey. Everyone who had ham got food poisoning. Basic training was coming to an end, and it was time to get on another train, this time for Denver, Colorado. Ed Palmer was still with me, and I met a few others from Brewster including my school teacher Donald McLagen who was a 2nd Lieutenant.

My next assignments were two armament schools – one was at Buckley Field for six weeks for fighter planes, and the other was Lowery Field for heavy bombers. These courses included machine guns, cannons, electrical and bombing equipment.

We got the weekends off after about a month. We would go into the city and ride the trolley cars out into the foothills of the Rockies, where they had a big amusement park and big bands of that era. After returning from a weekend pass, every bunk bed in the barracks was turned over. It seems an instructor and a student were drinking and thought it was a big joke wrecking the place. The joke was on them; the instructor's S/Sgt stripes were ripped off, and they were both put in the guardhouse.

Back at school a bunch of soldiers were examining a 4-engine B-24 bomber. Unknown to them there was a soldier resting underneath the plane with his eyes closed. When too many men went in the tail section, the plane came down and rested on his chest. It didn't hurt him, but they had to take him to the hospital for shock. The plane was so well balanced it acted like a seesaw.

After graduation in August 1943, a few of us were sent to gunnery school in Kingman, Arizona. I lost track of Ed Palmer at that point. We rode first class on the train, were served at a beautiful dining table and given whatever we wanted for dinner. We traveled down the Santa Fe Trail, past Colorado Springs and on to Albuquerque, New Mexico. That afternoon we boarded the train for Kingman.

About 2 a.m. the train stopped, and the conductor told us to get out and not to go anywhere, because someone would pick us up. After the train left we sat on the tracks and watched the shooting stars. After a while we were picked up. Where we had been sitting there had been a tragic accident. A train in broad daylight hit a bus full of soldiers. You could see for miles each way. I guess the bus driver thought he could get the stalled bus going again before the train hit.

We went to the firing range to learn how to stop runaway 50 caliber machine guns. When we were through, the lieutenant and tech. sergeant would put the guns back on the truck. This time the lieutenant threw the gun on the back of the truck, and it went off, killing him instantly, also wounding the sergeant. Flags were half-mast that day.

One Sunday I was standing by the field watching a B–17 four-engine bomber starting its engines and wishing I were on it. The side door opened and a sergeant waved to me and said come on if you want to go. I ran over and climbed in. He showed me how to put the parachute on and told me we would be gone for four hours. I wasn't supposed to leave the base, and we were flying to California, Nevada, Grand Canyon, and Yuma, Arizona near the Mexican border. I rode in the tail and got a bird's eye view. Another B–17 came up along side us, and the pilot was trying to talk to me on the radio. I shook my head saying I don't know how to work the radio. We couldn't fly over the Boulder Dam; they had orders to shoot down any plane that tried. The pilot showed me all the controls and explained what they were for. Back at the barracks, I told the guys where I had just been... lucky for me.

I met a few guys from Newburg, NY who were wise guys. They were going to gunnery school, but they had no respect for anyone. The small one was the mouthpiece and his big friends did his dirty work. But they liked me, because I was from Brewster. It was time to keep distance from them. If they didn't like you, they would beat you up. You could go to the guardhouse hanging around them.

One day the colonel came to the skeet range and asked the sergeant where Schneider was. He told me to hop in his command car. We went back to camp, and he told me to get ready to leave in a couple of days. I only had a week or so before graduating as a sergeant. I figured he knew something that he wasn't saying. Two days later fifteen of us were on a bus going to Boulder City, Nevada where we stayed for a week. Next they put us on a Pullman train with civilians, stopping over at Las Vegas, another little cowboy town, and then back on the train to Salt Lake City and Ogden, Utah. It was a desert land where they trained atomic bomber crews. We stayed two weeks and were processed for our permanent base.

Time to go again; this time we stopped at Cheyenne, Wyoming, another small cowboy town. We left Cheyenne for Denver, then Pratt, Kansas. By this time I had seen a lot of the U.S. Little did I know I'd see a lot more before I finished. The next morning, I saw rows of B-26 medium bombers parked in long lines. We figured we were in that kind of outfit, but in a few days they all flew away. Now we wondered what kind of plane we would be working on. One day an officer told us we would be in a B-29 outfit. What's that? He said he didn't know; he'd never seen one.

I thought that everybody who came to the field was experienced, but I soon found out differently. I was a corporal by then; they gave me a tech sergeant (five striper) for a helper. It worked out well. When we went to different parts of the field to show people how to use electric hoists; they thought I was a master sergeant. He was in the army fifteen years before I got in. All he liked to do was get drunk after work. He slept on the top bunk and almost turned the bed over when he came in, so I told him to sleep on the bottom after that. They put me in for sergeant after September 1943, but the officer thought I had lied about my age to get in, so he turned me down.

I liked going to town on pass. It was like Brewster; people were friendly and would help any way they could. It wouldn't be like that later on when a few thousand guys would show up. October was a beautiful time of the year. All the waterfowl were flying south; the sky was full. The planes didn't fly much that month.

When the first B-29 came to our field, everyone stood in awe, because the plane was so much bigger and streamlined with pressurized cabins and computerized gun turrets and radar. It had a tunnel that went from the front to the back, and it was well insulated from the cold. It had a 6,000-mile range with a ten man crew. One fellow I knew from Idaho was blown out the side window at 26,000 feet over Texas. The gunner on the other side said all he saw was a pair of feet going out the window like a bullet. Luckily, he had his parachute on. He told us it took fifteen minutes to land in the desert. It took quite a while before he was rescued. His wife told him to quit flying.

We had to use B-17 flying forts that they used over Germany, so the aircrews could practice long-range flights. We were told not to mention the kind of airplanes we worked on, the B-29's. On the B-

17's we had to wear heavy flying suits, not like the B-29's with heated and pressurized cabins. On one occasion we were working on a B-17 and the mechanics tried to start the engines; one got flooded and the gas drained onto the snow. When the engine started, a ball of fire went by us. Luckily we weren't hit.

Christmas time, 1943 everybody was going home on leave, but unfortunately I waited until Jan. 1. An officer came to the barracks and told me he wanted me in an outfit that was ready to go overseas. I told him I hadn't been home yet. It didn't matter; I had to leave all my friends and go. A couple of days later we left for Hampton Roads, Virginia. They kept us there about a week before we boarded a freighter. Once we left the harbor we formed up with a hundred-ship convoy. We had destroyers and Canadian Corvettes protecting our rear. That's what the German subs were looking for. We had to wear our life vests twenty-four hours a day – no chance to look for one if we needed it.

I had a pimple on my head next to my ear, so I went to the army medic that was with us. He squeezed it, and the next day it was like a balloon. I was in trouble then, as there was no doctor on board. A sailor and the medic put hot patches on my head for three days to no avail. They finally told me they couldn't help me any more. People started to come in and visit me, and I wondered why. The next night we hit a terrific storm. I got so seasick; it felt like my head was going to blow off. All of a sudden everything blew out the side of my head and hit the wall. A day later I walked out of the infirmary in good shape. They told me they visited me, because they were saying good–bye. A sailor stopped me and asked if I was the one who was in sick–bay and where I was from. I told him Brewster; he said he was from Pawling. Small world.

We had a safe trip across; it was some sight to see one hundred ships around you; some were barely visible because of the curvature of the earth. After about ten days when we started seeing sea gulls and albatrosses, we knew we were getting close to land. Our route had taken us down the coast of South America through mountainous waves that battered our ship, across to Africa. We sailed up the coast of Africa to the Rock of Gibraltar, Spain to Oran, North Africa where we spent two weeks to rest and wait for another ship. They never told us what our final destination was.

The posted guards were spending all their time chasing the Arabs away, because they'd steal everything they could get their hands on.

In the daytime we would go into the city, but we would still be on our guard; the kids would throw mud on your shoes so they could polish them, or they would grab your watch and run. When you caught them, they would scream and holler; then you'd have a bunch of Arabs surrounding you.

After two weeks we boarded a British troop ship, converted from an old luxury liner. As we were passing by to board the ship, American troops on another ship hollered down: "you want us to carry your bags, Air Force?" We were 'love to hate guys'. You could tell the ship must have been beautiful with all its furniture in place. Now all it had were bunk beds. I slept in a hammock fastened between two steel posts. We would look out the porthole, and the guys would say there's the island of Capri, what are we doing here? Later in the afternoon we pulled into Naples harbor. Ships were sunk all around us.

At the pier all the big ships were on their sides including a big Red Cross ship. Up on deck you could hear all the big guns blasting the Germans at Monte Cassino a few miles up from us. About two a.m. all hell broke loose; the German bombers were trying to blow us out of the water. We were three decks down. The ship was bouncing up and down with every explosion, and all the guys were trying to get out. I never heard so much screaming and hollering. The British MP guards wouldn't let anyone out the exits. I stayed in my hammock and swayed back and forth. The guys in the gun turrets were blasting away with tracers at the twin-engine planes. Next morning I went up on deck and surveyed the damage. All the windows were broken, and shrapnel was everywhere. The captain was going to have the gun crews court-martialed for leading the bombers to the ship. B-25's from Sicily were flying by to bomb Monte Cassino. The gun crews said the planes laid a string of bombs across the ship and missed hitting it in the middle, luckily for us.

When night time came, I went up on deck and was talking with a British MP, when they started dropping flares to see what was in the harbor. I got scared and told the MP I was going down below. Later the ship started moving, so I went back on deck. To my surprise Mt. Vesuvius was erupting, and the lava was running down the side of the mountain. We sailed south going between Italy and Sicily and the steaming Mt. Etna, a 10,000-foot volcano. Before we got to Port Said, Egypt, we went past barrage balloons fastened to big cables to prevent the planes from bombing the ships that were anchored underneath.

The ship docked at the pier for fuel and food. We watched them load the meat on board with a native standing on the meat in his bare feet. Our guys refused to eat the British food. The cereal had big white grubs in it. We pushed it away and ate K- rations.

The next day we started through the Suez Canal. Walking on the deck, I stepped over a bunch of guys sunning themselves. When I looked down I saw a familiar face from Brewster. It was Harrison Lane, brother of Marjorie Lane. We agreed it was a small world. He was with the B-29 maintenance crew as well.

Going through the Red Sea was like riding on a glass mirror; the only things that moved were the flying fish. The mountains looked oven-baked. We sailed across the Arabian Sea to Bombay, India. After disembarking, one of the soldiers heard that the ship we had just left a few hours before was destroyed at the dock along with the buildings along the waterfront. A fertilizer ship had blown up in the harbor and set off a munitions ship. The ship had survived Naples but met its doom in Bombay. Luckily we got off in time.

Half way across the center of India, we stopped at a place called Nagpur where we rested up for a couple of days. It turned out to be a British prisoner of war camp for Italian P.O.W.'s. All the guys of Italian decent from our outfit had a ball speaking with them. Later that night some of our guys started hollering across to the British soldiers, "come on over, we'll kick your ass". They hollered over, "we were in Montgomery's 8th Army", trying to scare everybody. Lucky we didn't have a riot that night.

It was time to leave this camp before things got out of hand. We boarded the train again for a couple of days more travel. At lunch time the train stopped and our guys took out the cans to make coffee. The boiling water was taken from the engine, and they opened up the tinned cans of ham for lunch. We finally reached our destination, Chakulia, 100 miles from Calcutta and Jamesapour, a steel-making complex.

It must have been a couple of months since we left the U.S. Our camp was a few miles from the airfield for safety reasons, and Burma wasn't that far away in case they decided to come after us. Tents were set up for us, but there weren't enough cots. I happened to be the unlucky one, so I slept on the ground the first night. If I had known there were poisonous snakes around, I wouldn't have done it. All night long the Indians would pound on their drums, and the jackals and hyenas would howl along with them. We had to start using mosquito nets at night. One guy caught malaria and died. We were actually living in a jungle. Wild elephants ran through the officers' camp. I was in charge of quarters when they ran in the orderly room, and I had to call the M.P.'s.

Tokyo Rose spoke on the radio and told us not to get too comfortable, as they were going to send the Japanese commandos after us. The officers said if they come, grab your guns and run for the mountains in the background.

All of us went to the airfield to wait for the B-29's to come in from the states. Mountbatten, the Supreme Commander of the British and Indian forces was on hand to witness the event. M.P.'s were put on every plane that landed, so nobody would sabotage them. I took a ride on one that day. We couldn't work on the planes during the day; the temperature was 110 in the shade. Everyone worked for 36 hours straight to get the planes ready for the first mission to Rangoon, Burma. Everything looked good, until one of the last planes took off. Its left engine failed, and it went down past the end of the runway with a terrific blast. The heat could be felt a couple of miles away. Ten tons of bombs and ten thousand gallons of one hundred octane gas went up. The co-pilot was the only one to survive in real bad shape. All our hearts dropped into our shoes, and we knew it wasn't going to be the last.

Shortly after that, the same outfit had a bomb-loading accident, which happened to be across from us. The cable must have snapped while hoisting it up in the bomb bay. The bomb went off setting off 10 tons of fragmentation bombs meant for enemy troops. I told my helper to run for his life, as the shrapnel was whizzing around us. I grabbed my camera and took a picture of the plane standing next to it. It was riddled full of holes and ended up in the junkyard. The firemen who tried to put out the fire also lost their lives. There was nothing left but a big hole in the ground and wreckage all around. Eighteen men lost their lives that day. My helper and I finished loading the plane and hoped we wouldn't make a mistake. A fellow across from me asked if we were down at the field when it happened. I said yes. He asked where I was from, and I told him Brewster. He asked if I knew Dr. Cleaver who was his uncle. Small world again. After that accident no other ground crew would come near the plane, until it was loaded. One radioman was fooling around with the gun-sight in the tail when the guns started firing. We later learned he mowed down a bunch of Army Engineers who were eating their supper miles away.

They never knew what hit them. They didn't think much of us after that

A British plane came over our field without permission; needless to say our fighter planes surrounded him and forced him to land. Our colonel chewed out the pilot and radioman and said next time we're going to shoot you down.

It seems they did the same to us. One of our bombers was off course coming back from Burma in full moonlight, when a British night fighter shot them down. They said they thought it was Japanese. No way! I had lost my plane the day before over Rangoon, so I helped my friend out that day. Both of us waited for planes that weren't coming back. My plane was lost due to a mixed load of 500 and 100 lb. bombs. They unloaded them over the target, but because of the mixed sizes and air resistance, as they were dropped they collided, blowing the planes out of the sky. The enemy didn't have to do anything that day. The crewmen of my B-29 were taken prisoners and held for a year in Rangoon, and the radioman lost his hand due to infection. The Japs didn't treat his wounds very well. I saw their pictures in a New York newspaper after the war.

Though the Russians were our allies, they confiscated one of our B-29's that had engine trouble over Muckden, Manchuria. The fighters led the plane to Vladivostok, Russia and interned the crew. They finally were released after U.S. demands. The colonel gave strict orders not to land on Russian soil but to let the plane crash. The Russians copied the plane and made their own fleet after the war.

One night we were walking through the woods from the outdoor theatre and came upon a big snake. We grabbed bamboo sticks and started beating it to death. It escaped in the dark, so we had to look for it with our flashlights; we finally found it near a tree. The next day they told us it was good thing we weren't bitten, as it turned out to be a deadly Blue Krait, a member of the Cobra family.

If the planes weren't going on a mission, we'd go to Calcutta for the weekend. It wasn't a regular stop, but the train would stop and pick us up. We would always try to get a first class car; because the others were like cattle cars. We tried to get in one first class car, and the voice coming through the shutters said, "Go away". We said, "No way". Finally the door opened and a British officer let us in. The voice turned out to be an Indian officer who commenced to chew us out. We had some nerve. When he was finished, the British officer laid him to waste. He said wait 'til you get back to camp. These

Americans are here to help keep the Japanese away from your doorsteps. Sometimes you'd have to settle for the second or third class cars. That's when you would have to watch out for phony conductors. We got clipped once, and when we got to the Calcutta station, the American MP's and Indian police said we hadn't paid our fare. We told them what the guy looked like who took our fare. Their reply was, Oh, that one! We've been looking for him. Proceed on your way.

We visited many beautiful temples in the city, ate in the best restaurants, and visited the "Black Hole of Calcutta", where they crammed all the prisoners in the basement where many died. We had a chance to go to the crematory by the Hooghly River where they stacked the dead from the streets over logs, then lighted the fire. Later they shoveled the ashes over the wall into the river.

Friends and I went to a fancy hotel where they had an outdoor theatre and where they played excellent jazz music. While we were there, we met a gunner from our field. He was downhearted, and we asked him what the problem was. His reply was that he didn't want to go on the next mission because they wouldn't be coming back, and he asked one guy to please tell his mother he saw him and not to worry. It's ironic, the tail gunner told his friend the same thing, and if anybody wants his job they can have it. Three days later the plane ran into the Himalayan Mountains. All were lost. That hit us below the belly.

As a sergeant and Armament Crew Chief, I had to go to the airfield and stay all night in the armament shack in case they had trouble before they took off for a mission. One night I was sleeping on a cot where I heard a great commotion outside. I looked out the window and saw a double tractor-trailer that was fueling a bomber and was on fire. I made a quick exit out the door and stood a safe distance away. The plane caught fire, and after about an hour all that was left was a big puddle of metal and the steel shell of the truck and trailer. There went one million dollars plus the truck.

I was called into the office one day, and the Master Sergeant told me that since I had never been home on leave since being in the air force it was time to go to a rest camp in the Himalayan Mountains for thirty days. I told him I had already sent my money home, so how could I go now. His reply was, you're going whether you like it or not. Here's thirty dollars, pay me when you get back. We got on a narrow gauge railroad train to Lucknow, first stop. We wouldn't dare eat any food from the vendors, so we brought our own K rations and water. We didn't know this was going to be a 1,500-mile ride to the foothills of the Himalayas. You couldn't go from car to car, so there was nothing to do but look at the desert for three days. In some of the cars ahead the guys brought their rifles and were shooting out the windows like the Wild West.

Before we had left, we found out the British rifles use 30/06 ammo for big game. Five of us had a hundred rounds apiece, since we found out from returning men that they gave you only five rounds for hunting. We arrived at the foothills of the mountains, boarded the old 1920 buses and zigzagged up the mountain roads towards the camp 50 miles away. By this time it was getting dark. Looking over the stone-walls that paralleled the road, it looked like a 10,000 foot drop. The driver did a lot of shifting to get us up to 6,500 feet where the camp was located. It was pretty late when we arrived, and the first thing the British soldiers did was give us heavy blankets and show us to our rooms. Each room had a small fireplace just big enough for one big pinecone. It gave off a terrific amount of heat.

The next morning we got up early and washed up in ice-cold water – then it was off to the mess hall for chow. Now we really had a chance to see the 28,000 ft. mountains in front of us. We were near the border of Tibet, in the Kashmir section of India in a place called Raniket. The British had built a golf course on the side of a mountain. It's a good thing we were young and healthy climbing up and down to each hole. It is the highest course I ever played on.

It was time to get ready for the 5-day hunting trip into the mountains. They could only take five people at a time. The guides picked us up in an army truck and headed towards Nepal. There was only one man, a guy from Oklahoma who knew how to hunt. The gunner from Michigan shot a monkey on a cliff; the poor thing dropped down in front of us dead. The other monkeys were mad as hell. I thought we were going to be attacked, so I threw it over another cliff. All the monkeys went down to look at it. We hollered at the gunner. Why did you shoot that monkey, we're after big game?

Next to the last day I went hunting by myself and roamed around looking for a tiger. I saw footprints in the dirt on the mountain trail but never saw one. I had more courage than brains. They weigh about 500 lbs. and sometimes like people for dinner. I came upon a small mountain stream with crystal clear water. Was I surprised when I saw all these trout! Nobody ever fished for them. Since we had run out of food, I remembered about shooting in the water, and the concussion would belly them up. I blasted away with the 30/06 and sure enough, they started floating down stream. Unknown to me a native was downstream and started picking them up as fast as they floated down. The real big ones were in deep pools, but I didn't try for them. Everybody had a fish that night, and there were enough for the natives too. Our hunting was coming to an end; we were going to sleep outside the last day, but the natives said it was too dangerous to do that – a tiger might get us, so they let us huddle up in a tool shed; it was a miserable night. On the way back to the main camp, we stopped in a mountain town where they had many tiger skins hanging in front of their stores. They had a big opium pot where the town's people puffed on hoses to get a big high.

We spent the last day getting ready for our three-day trip back to our airfield. On the way back through the mountains a tragic accident happened to the next bunch that was coming up to the camp. The driver must have missed a gear while shifting; the truck rolled backwards, went through the stonewall and over the cliff. No one survived. One fellow was from Danbury, Connecticut. Our thirty-day trip was over, and it was time to pay the sergeant and thank him for the wonderful time.

One day I had to check the bombing equipment on a practice bombing run. I was in the back in contact with the bombardier, looking through the window into the back bomb bay. He asked me if the bombs had fallen. I told him it's a good thing they didn't, because a B-29 flew directly underneath us. He was looking in his bombsight and never saw the plane coming.

Working around airplanes was a dangerous job. One mechanic was on a stand, working on the propeller hub, when someone in the cockpit hit the switch. He went flying to the ground - luckily he wasn't injured. Another mechanic forgot to tighten one of 36 spark plugs. After the plane took off on a test flight, the plug blew out, and they lost power right away, so they came back to the field. The first thing they did was look for the person responsible. They could have killed him. It's a good thing it wasn't loaded with gas and bombs.

Almost everyone in our enlisted quarters caught yellow jaundice, and was sick for two weeks. I was lucky enough to go to the hospital; everyone else stayed in the barracks and got treatment.

They started phasing out the Chinese bases as it was too much trouble getting gasoline; everything had to be brought in from India over the Himalayas (the Hump). The missions from India to Japan took four days round trip. It was tough on crews and planes.

On Christmas Eve the Japs came on a suicide mission from Burma with their twin-engine planes. We were all sleeping when the antiaircraft guns started firing. Everybody jumped out of bed and ran outside and hid wherever we could. I hid in a ditch. We couldn't see any lights, and it was pitch black outside. I was more afraid of jumping in the ditch with a snake than worrying about the Japanese. They hit most of the bases between Calcutta and us doing minor damage and were all shot down.

We started winding up operations in India after ten months and got ready for the next move. The officer told us we were going on a Navy troop ship out of Calcutta to a small island in the Pacific that had just been captured from the Japanese. After we left Calcutta, we headed down the Indian Ocean, past Burma, Thailand, Sumatra, Singapore to Melbourne, Australia, 2000 miles from Antarctica. All the small boats came out to greet us. It seems it was the first American ship to stop by in a year.

After the week was up, we waited for the tide to go out; then we set sail. We stopped at Townsville, then on to Port Moresby, New Guinea. We were getting near the equator, so it was hot and humid with palm trees and jungle. Once we left New Guinea, we picked up a harbor pilot to guide us through the Coral Sea where the Japanese lost all their big battle ships. We passed by all the South Pacific islands we had taken from the Japs. We passed Guam and a few smaller islands still occupied by the Japanese, until we arrived at Tinian in the Marianas, which the Marines had captured. It was pretty much of a mess. The Sea Bees made new runways for us, plus the water system and new mess halls. We went back to living in tents again.

We went through the Japanese homes which we thought must have been beautiful but now were in ruins. These people were living on these islands for years and preparing for war they knew was coming. There were hundreds of soldiers hiding in the caves all the time we were there; we had to pull guard duty at night so the camp was safe. The Sea Bees were always bugging us to go for a plane ride. One day one of the pilots said okay. Eighteen of them got in the plane; everything went fine, until it was time to come back and land. That's where the pilot made a mistake on landing. They crashed in flames; no one survived. After that no Sea Bees were allowed near the planes.

We were now within range of Japan, 1500 miles each way. One good thing about Tinian was its weather. It was about 75 degrees year round with a beautiful sea breeze to keep the heat down. Day after day we would load the planes with 10 tons of bombs; sometimes we didn't have enough fuses to put in all of them. The pilot wondered if they would go off. I told him they're supposed to go off, if you drop them five feet without a fuse.

On the north end of our island facing Saipan there were about twelve runways next to each other. They needed that many to handle the traffic coming back around the same time. Many ran out of gas and went into the ocean. I heard a plane overhead and happened to glance up; the outboard engine was on fire with flames shooting back over the wing. I could see all the guys jumping out and a couple of minutes later their chutes opened. The pilot headed it back out to sea and jumped. A few minutes later the plane crashed into the sea in flames. There were so many planes flying, it was no wonder there were accidents happening all the time.

The war in Europe was over, and our war was starting to wind down. With extra technicians they gave us extra help loading bombs. The one fellow I got had thick glasses. He hooked the bombs on one side of the plane, and my regular crew the other. All went well 'til the last bomb. We had electric hoists, and I controlled the switch. I asked the new guy if it was hooked securely, and he said yes. So I told him to unhook the cable. I was standing underneath and just touched the tail. The bomb came down about a foot and hit me on the head. I still had my hands above my head at the time, so as it hit I gave it one big push. It hit the bomb bay door and wrecked it. I had a big gash on my head and had to go to the hospital. All I could think of as I pushed it away was: is it going to go off when it hits? It was a 500-pound bomb, and if I hadn't gotten hit with the tail end, forget it! I relieved the guy and told his sergeant he is too dangerous to work with. He couldn't see well enough.

The next day I had to work with the carpenter who was building a ramp down to the water over the coral rock. The colonel happened to stop by and noticed the patch on my head. He said, oh you're the one that got hit with a bomb; boy you're lucky you are around. Two weeks later my luck started to run out. I couldn't blame it on the guy I canned. The plane had just come back from a mission over Japan, and I got a report from the crew that one tail gun stopped firing. I told my regular man to get on a ladder, and look in and see if he could see anything. He couldn't, so I went into the tail compartment, took off the armor plate in back of the guns and removed the back of the faulty gun. Usually when you pull the inside of the guns out the back to clean them, they pull right out with no trouble. This time it was different. It wouldn't come out. It was so cramped in the compartment it was impossible to see anything, so I gave it a push forward. That's when it exploded. All the parts blew out back and smashed my hand against the armor plate. I knew I was in trouble then, even though it didn't hurt at all. I looked at my hand and saw that it was badly injured. I had to turn around in the cramped corner and crawl out through the back of the plane and climb down the ladder. My buddy almost fainted when he saw my hand. We flagged down a jeep going by and asked the lieutenant to take me to the hospital. My buddy and I waited two hours in the waiting room before I was taken care of. They told me to take off my cap and climb on the operating table. This was early afternoon. When I woke up it was two or three o'clock the next morning. I wound up with a cast on my hand. Little did I know I would be spending two months in the surgery ward recuperating from my injuries. While I was in the hospital, I was resting on my bed, and as I turned my head I thought I recognized a lieutenant walking by. He didn't return, but my mother wrote me that it was Lt. Arthur Elliot from Brewster who had been stationed there. All the marines from Okinawa and Iwo Jima were in the same ward. I felt sorry for them. Many of them had body parts shot off.

I kept busy during the day helping keep records for the nurse, and other times I would help the surgeon, a major, put casts on patients with my one hand. He wanted to get me in the medics – no problem, same army, different patch on shoulder. I told him I liked the air force better. I think the officers back at my camp suggested it to the surgeon. They told me later if the war hadn't ended when it did, they were going to ship me home on a medical discharge. They figured I was getting accident-prone. I was promoted to Staff Sergeant when I was 20 years old.

The nurse that I worked with was twenty-one and I was twenty. I was her boyfriend. We weren't supposed to fraternize on a personal basis, as she was an officer, and I was a non-commissioned officer. The army didn't approve of that. There were only a few hundred nurses on the whole island and about 100,000 guys. Everybody was falling in love with them. I couldn't have a minute's peace with her.

They would pretend to have some medical problem, or they would try to fight. I told her I could get killed knowing her.

Near the end of the war we had to watch everything we owned. We had a bunch of crooks in our midst that were stealing everything when we went to eat. We had to have written permission to drive the jeeps or other vehicles, because they were even stealing them. The Navy used to hoist them aboard ship and paint them blue, their color. No one was ever caught.

At this time the underside of the airplanes were painted black so the searchlights couldn't spot them over the target. We were on alert to watch for captured American transport planes. The Japs used to land on our fields and shoot up our planes. Each armament crew had to stay with the plane all night. They gave us "grease guns"- what we called submachine guns. Thank heavens we didn't have to use them.

We loaded the planes up one more time in August 1945. They took off for Japan, but they called them back and said the war was over. We unloaded the bombs and taped the gun barrels for the trip back to the U.S. The next day they dropped the bomb on Hiroshima, then Nagasaki. We were shocked that they did that after they had told us the war was over.

October on Tinian was beautiful, until we were hit by a typhoon. I had just left the mess hall after eating breakfast, when the winds came up unexpectedly and tore the big roof off. I couldn't believe what I was seeing. The wood was flying all over the place. The winds were 180 miles an hour. We had to hide in the wooden shower for ten hours until the storm died down. All our tents were flattened to the ground with all our clothes. What a mess! One fellow went over to look at the mountainous waves when one grabbed him and pulled him out to sea. After eighteen months overseas, he had to meet his end that way.

I grabbed my camera and took off for the atomic bomber field to take pictures of the Enola Gay, the B-29 bomber that bombed Hiroshima the day before. It was a stripped-down B-29 with just the tail guns left. I was stopped by M.P.'s at the gate, so had to settle for pictures from the fence.

Before we left for home we had to take all our tools to the dump. We couldn't take them home. Bulldozers pushed all the vehicles over the cliff into the ocean. If I had known at the time, I would have taken home a beautiful flying jacket and a big pair of binoculars. Everybody who had seventy-five points got to fly home. I had seventy-four, so I had to take a ship back to San Francisco which took two weeks. We heard some of the planes crashed on the way home. What a way to go after all that time overseas.

Crossing the equator for the second time meant every one on board was initiated into the Kingdom of "King Neptune". On the second deck, they removed a hunk of hair, mixed it with dough and rammed the mixture into our mouths. After they dunked us a few times, they tossed us out choking where we were met by a long line of paddles working us over. Then we got in line and did the same. It was better to go through early – not as many to work us over

From California we went to New Jersey. It was an enjoyable trip, because we knew we were going home at last. Thirty two months without coming home was a long time for me. It's a good thing I didn't get homesick. This completed our trip around the world. When I went in at 18, I believed everything they told me; by the time I reached 21, I didn't believe anything they said.

We arrived in Fort Dix, N.J. five days later, and were processed out of the Army. We took a bus to Trenton Railroad Station and jumped on the first train heading toward New York City. I arrived in Brewster late at night. Prisco Bros.Taxi gave me a free ride home. I had to wake up Ma and Dad to get in. After I was home for a few weeks, I built a chicken house behind the house and bought a few ducks and chickens. Later on when they got bigger, we had one for dinner.

My dog Brownie looked at me for quite a while before he remembered me; then he jumped all over me. Later I had to take him to the vet and have him put to sleep, because he was pretty old by then. While I was away, my brother Bob had his eye put out playing Cowboys and Indians. My parents never let me know; they figured I had enough trouble.

One day, Harrison Lane came to my mother's house, and we hashed over old times in India and Tinian. I walked with him back to the village. He said he was going to college.

I divorced in 1970 and raised three boys and three girls, having lost two children in infancy.

After getting home I attended the YMCA Trade School in New York City. I worked in refrigeration in Carmel and then in Mahopac. I did sheet metal work for fuel companies in our area. After twenty years I had my own sheet metal shop in Carmel, then Patterson. My brother Johnnie was my partner and Bob a worker. [50]

Charles Stefanic

For my first year of high school I went to Danbury High and then in 1939 I started at Brewster High.

When the European war started, I was at Brewster High School and lived with my parents in Sodom, northeast Brewster. I had a wonderful family. My mother and father were hardworking down-to-earth people, and I had four great sisters and one brother. I played the trumpet in the high school band and sang in the school chorus. I also was in baseball, track and basketball. It was a good time in my life. My graduation was in June of 1941, and I was seventeen at the time.

On December 7, 1941 several of us were playing pool upstairs at the local pool hall when we heard the news of Pearl Harbor. I was drafted, but for some reason they didn't send my draft card. So I finally called them, and I had it within a few days. I entered the service in March of 1943 and went into the Army Air Force. I was sent to Fort Dix and then on to Miami Beach where I had my basic training. I met my English teacher from Brewster High, Donald McLagen who was teaching at the Officers' Training School, and he urged me to apply. He had Clark Gable in one of his classes. I also played in the marching band while I was there. From there I was sent to A & E School at Love Field. During an athletic period, I just about had my knee broken. Every time I would run after that I would fall down.

From there I went to Sheppard Field to try to become a pilot. During the physical they discovered my depth perception was off, so that ruined by chances. After that I was sent to a place in Utah close to Salt Lake City, then on to Oakland to board a Liberty Troop Ship. The trip was quite scary. I had never been on the open ocean and never got sick. We ran into one bad storm. We landed at New Caledonia in the South Pacific not too far from New Zealand, and from there I flew to Guadalcanal. It had been secured by then. I ended up on a small island off North West New Guinea called Biak. All that was on it were three airfields. My time there was pretty uneventful, working on several different types of planes. From one of the other airstrips, almost daily you could see B-24's taking off in the mornings. They had a skull and X bones on their tails and were called the Jolly Rogers. There were ten to twelve take-offs in the mornings, and sometimes there were missing planes when they returned.

I was sitting in an airplane cockpit listening to the radio, when I heard of President Roosevelt's death. I cried; he was a good man.

One evening we were playing basketball, and I came down on my knee. It went out again, so I had to come home to San Francisco on a hospital ship. From there they sent me to Utica, New York, where they operated on my knee. It didn't do much good. My mother, three sisters, Irene, Ann and Sophia plus Joe, my brother-in-law came from Brewster to visit me. It was so good to see them after almost two and a half years. After the operation I was sent to Coral Gables, Florida to recuperate. I was discharged from there in February of 1946. Shortly after, I received ten per cent service-connected disability for my knee. In 1973 and 1975 I had two osteotomies and received thirty per cent disability after that. Because of further medical problems, I later received one hundred percent disability.

On my return home I worked as a carpenter with my father, and for a few years I worked at the Lee Hat factory in Danbury, Connecticut.

My sister Sophie introduced me to a real pretty Irish girl named Virginia Lee. We were married in August of 1946 and had one son in 1948. She divorced me in 1961. I met my second wife not too long after that. Her name was Elizabeth Ann Myers, and she had a daughter named Jackie from a previous marriage. Elizabeth was a joy.

After moving to California I sold cars in Burbank, and Chevies in Modesto. Later I moved to Livermore where I was a manager for used cars and then Sales Manager for a Dodge dealership in Monterey Co. In 1969 Elizabeth and I moved to Wichita, Kansas to be with her folks. In 1991 we moved back to California to be with her daughter Jackie. Elizabeth died in 1995 after about thirty-eight years of marriage.

In 1991 we had a 50th year reunion at Brewster High School, but I only recognized about six people. Knowing that I did some singing, I was asked to sing the Star Spangled Banner at the graduation. I was proud to do it.[51]

Willis H. Stephens

On Sunday, December 7, 1941 I was playing gin rummy with Sidney Chaplin at The Lawrenceville School – it was my first year there – when we learned of the destruction at Pearl Harbor.

On June 7, 1943, my eighteenth birthday, I graduated from Lawrenceville. I was in the College Air Corps. Cadet Program and had flown in planes at Danbury Airport. Before that my mother had found out I had gotten a ride in a plane at the airport, and instead of being angry with me she gave me flying lessons for my sixteenth birthday. I never did solo, because I was going to school and didn't get around to it.

In October of 1943 I went for training at the Army Air Corp. Basic Training Center #10 in Greensboro, N.C. After about a month I was sent to Wofford College, Spartanburg, S.C. which was a women's college taken over for the duration of the war by the college training detachment of the U. S. Army Air Corps. I had flown light planes and had some flying lessons. After a few months there, having done well, they released me a month or so ahead of time, but the release turned out to be something that I really wasn't looking for. I was sent out to Cortland Army Air Force Base in Cortland, Alabama, and all I did was put gasoline and oil into basic training planes, BT 13's, never even getting a ride in a plane. I spent two or three months there. I had a friend there who was a cadet. He said if I could possibly get help in transferring out, I should do so, because I was in a dead end job. So, I told my dad about it in one of my weekly collect calls home. Apparently he spoke to our congressman, Hamilton Fish and not long after that I was transferred out. My friend - I think his name was Doug – who had made this recommendation to transfer out, went on to advanced training on multi-engine airplanes. He became a B-17 pilot with the 8th Air Force based in England. We corresponded, and one-day a letter came back unopened, and it just had stamped on it *DECEASED*. I always think gratefully about that fellow who certainly was very helpful in the advice he gave me.

So I was sent out to the Western Flying Training Command at Santa Anna, California for pre-flight and went from there to Army Air Corps. Contract School run by Ryan Aviation for primary flight training. We had civilian instructors. We flew Stearmans, which were bi-planes. That was in Hemet, California. Then I went to Marana Air Force Base in Marana, near Tucson, Arizona. We were the first class

– 45B – to fly AT6's, the advanced trainers instead of the old BT 13's. I went to Luke Field (named for a World War I pilot) in Phoenix, near Scottsdale and graduated April 15, 1945 as a pilot, 2nd Lieutenant. May 1945, the war was over in Europe, and they didn't know what to do with us, but I was fortunate enough to be sent to Basic Flying Instructors School in Waco, Texas. I remember our graduation day; they had Jack Teagarten's Orchestra.

The war with Japan was over in August 1945, and I got shipped back to Luke Field to instruct combat returnees awaiting discharge. Some had been combat pilots, and some had been POW's. They needed four hours flying/instruction time a month to get their 50% extra flying pay. One guy was a B-24 pilot, and I couldn't get him to fly an AT 6 right to save my neck, because one is like driving a truck, and the other is like driving a mini-car.

I was discharged in October of 1945 and started college in November of 1945. I had passed my college boards and had been accepted at Princeton.

In 1951 I married Daphne Dunbar. We have four sons.

In 1952 I ran for the New York State Assembly and spent thirty years representing the people of Putnam County as well as holding the office of Chairman of the Ways and Means Committee from 1969 to 1974. In 1959 I started the W. H. Stephens Coal Company brokering coal and oil, retiring in 1990.[52]

Edward Vichi

Eddie, as everyone called him, lived on Carmel Avenue perhaps a mile and a half from the Brewster High School, which housed kindergarten through 12th Grade. In his teen years he was very concerned about the war news even before Pearl Harbor. His sisters went to California to work in defense factories.

In 1942 he graduated from Brewster High School, and after receiving a draft notice, was inducted on March 18, 1943. Choosing the Air Force, he was trained at Lowry Field, Colorado on flexible gunnery and Harlingen, Texas on a B-17 bomber. Trained in the U.S. as a waist gunner, he was transferred and made a crewmember on a B-26 Marauder after being sent to England. He was a Staff Sergeant with the 9th Air Force, 391st Bomb Squadron.

Over Luxembourg, his Marauder was shot down in flames. All of the crew reached the ground safely, one crewman landing in a brook. The airmen could have been easily shot by the German airplane crews, but they merely waved to them. The nearby prison camps were full to capacity, and after interrogation the airmen were marched all the way to Barth, Germany on the Baltic Sea. Elderly German men accompanied them, and very often the American flyers would help them – especially when the American planes were hitting targets. One time in particular their shelter was hit, and they were covered with concrete. Ed thought his leg had been broken, but it was not. This camp, Stalag Luft #1, was actually an officers' camp. There was little or no food at the camp, and it wasn't long before government issued pants had to be tied to keep from falling off. On one occasion while in the barracks a stray bullet came through and knocked the cup and grazed the finger of his buddy.

Staff Sgt. Vichi was in the German prison when the war ended and was freed by the Russians. He was sent to an Atlantic City Hospital to recuperate. His nerves had been affected, and he developed a rash, which made it impossible to sit through a movie. He had served 1 year, 5 months in the states and 1 year, 27 days stationed in England. His combat missions took him over Normandy, Ardennes, Northern France and the Rhineland. His decorations and citations included the Air Medal with 2 Oak Leaf Clusters (9th Bomber Command), the

Purple Heart and Distinguished Unit Badge. Ed thanks God every day when he thinks that his life could have ended at such an early age.

On August 6, 1949 Ed married Doris Johnson. They have two sons.[53]

Donald R. Von Gal

The house Don grew up in was very large, and his mother closed it for the duration of the war, as it was too large to heat, and her sons were in military service. It later burned down and arson was suspected.

Donald graduated from the Wooster School in Danbury, Connecticut, but he had no desire to go on to college. He wanted to be a pilot, and so he enlisted in the Army. To be a pilot it was a requirement to have a college degree, and that he did not have. He was given a six-hour college equivalency examination, passed that test, and went into the Army Air Force as an officer. Advanced training was at Pampa Texas Central Instructors School, Waco, Texas and Gunter Field, Alabama.

He was sent to England in March of 1944 to fly with the 9th Air Force and participated in the European Air Offensive over Europe, Normandy, northern France, the Ardennes and Rhineland. First Lieutenant Donald Von Gal was pilot of a twin engine 1082, a B-26 bomber and was attached to the 397th Bombardment Group. At times he co-piloted the plane. Although he was based in England, he also spent some time at a base in France, as he talked about the pilots landing and being sent up again and again. They were scared, and they drank Calvados, the local apple brandy. There were a couple of times when he had to land his crippled airplane with only one engine. One time he made a crash landing, having lost an engine, and before he could get out of the plane, he saw a French farmer coming toward his plane with a lighted cigarette. Don frantically screamed at him in what Don called his barroom French to stay away, not to come near the airplane. The gas fumes could very likely reach the lighted cigarette causing an explosion. Don walked away from the airplane.

…"For extraordinary achievement while participating in aerial flight against the enemy in the European Theater of Operations. On 7 August 1944, while he was serving as co-pilot of a B-26 type aircraft attacking a heavily defended railroad bridge, First Lt. Von Gal's aircraft suffered severe damage from enemy gunfire. Although one of his engines was badly damaged, he nevertheless continued on to bomb the target with the formation. The damaged engine continued to operate with less and less power and subsequently the remaining engine also began to lose power. Lt. Von Gal demonstrated great tenacity of purpose and flying ability in maintaining his aircraft and bringing the crippled aircraft back to base. His devotion to duty and determination are in keeping with the highest tradition of the Army Air Forces." It is not clear in which crash he sustained his fractured spine. Some years later it was necessary to have an operation, subsequently receiving partial disability.

For one planned mission from England, Don was pulled aside and told that he could be excused from flying that day, as on the mission his ancestral Von Gal castle in Bonn, Germany would surely be bombed. He did not want to be excused, and he flew the mission.

Don flew 68 or 69 missions, the Air Force having increased the total number permitted to be flown. He received the Distinguished Flying Cross, Distinguished Unit Citation, the European African Middle Eastern Theatre Campaign Ribbon, Air Medal with 11 Oak Leaf Clusters, the Purple Heart and the Victory Medal. He was relieved from active duty in August of 1945.

When he came home, he weighed 124 lbs., and he loved to drink milk shakes. Don was a Brewster fireman. He stayed in the Air Force Reserve becoming a Reserve Lieutenant Colonel. He loved to fly.

In 1948 he married Lizette Jung Borer who was a widow with two children whom he adopted. Her first husband, Harold W. Borer had been a Navy pilot who was lost and later declared killed in action. Don and Lizette had two more children. They later divorced, but remained good friends. Donald Von Gal had three brothers who served in the military during World War II: George E. Von Gal, Jr., Herbert V. Von Gal and John C. Von Gal. John married Gay Martin, a Brewster girl.[54][55]

Left:
John R. O'Brien
(KIA)

Below:
H. Harding O'Hara
(KIA)

Above: Arthur D. Jenkins

Right: Edward Vicki

Above: Donald R. VonGal
Right: Charles Stefanic

Coast Guard

Frank R. Genovese

I was born on February 25, 1921, the second baby delivered by Dr. Robert S. Cleaver. Robert Blaney was the first. Our house was at 2 Eastview Avenue. It was originally a church and was located across the reservoir from the Electro-zone Field and then moved to 2 Eastview Avenue. How they did it, I can't imagine. They didn't have trucks then, only horses and wagons. At some time an addition was built across the back of the house, as it now stands.

I loved sports. When I was thirteen years old and in first year high school Dr. Ritchie examined all students. I was told I had heart trouble – a murmur and enlarged heart, and could not play sports anymore. When baseball season came around I told Coach Geesman that my parents said it would be all right to play baseball because it wasn't so strenuous. I lied (only child – a spoiled brat). I played three years on the first team. After high school, I went to N.Y.U. for a year. I commuted from Brewster to N.Y.C. six days a week, signed up for R.O.T.C. and was issued an Army uniform. I wore it one day to school and saw my name on the bulletin board to report to the doctor's office. I was told, because of heart trouble, I wasn't allowed to be in R.O.T.C. and should return my uniform.

Around 1940 my father purchased the bowling alley and poolroom above the Studebaker garage next door to the movie theatre. I worked with my mother and father to run the place. I loved being with the people who came in.

In 1942 I was waiting for my number to be called to go into the Army. John Santorelli, home on leave from the Coast Guard, was telling me about being aboard his ship doing escort duty across the Atlantic Ocean to Europe. (John was also in many invasions.) I asked him about the physical exam he had to take. He said there was nothing to it: you get in line with everyone, and when you get to the doctor, you're examined and you're in. So, I decided to enlist in the Coast Guard and reported to New York City. The doctor told me to come back in two weeks. Another doctor told me the same thing. Come back in two weeks. Evidently they didn't want to make a decision. Two weeks later the third doctor said, okay, I guess you're in. I reported July 8, 1942 to Manhattan Beach for duty.

After four weeks of "boot" training, I went to Miami, Florida with about 150 other "boots". I put in for radio maintenance school and was told I had to be a radio operator first. I was sent to Key West and finally after a couple of months I left for duty at Radio School in Atlantic City. After six months I was sent to Hollywood, Florida. Within a week orders came for me to go aboard a lightship anchored thirty miles off Florida – sixty miles from Cuba. The reason for the light-ship was to stop any ship going to Key West and to radio in to Key West for an officer to come out and guide them through the mine fields.

At the time I made about $50 a month. We stayed on duty for twenty-one days and then got a ten-day leave. It cost $27 for a round trip ticket to N.Y.C. and took two days to get home and two days to get back. For the six days at home, I helped my parents take care of the bowling alley and poolroom.

After about a year of duty off Florida, we got notice to relocate to Boston, Mass. after Boston was hit with a hurricane. A lightship in the harbor had broken its anchor and was carried out to sea. The ship and all its crew sank and were never heard from again.

While waiting in Boston Harbor to get new supplies in December of 1944, I received orders to report to the lighthouse off Cape Cod at North Truro, Mass. After a month of duty there I received orders to report to the *USCG Cutter Taney,* at Boston Harbor. It was being converted to a flagship. They were rebuilding it to hold more people and added a two-story super-structure atop the main deck. The *Taney* was the first ship to fire back at the Japs in the attack on Pearl Harbor.

From Boston we went through the Panama Canal to Pearl Harbor where we got a two-star admiral aboard as well as twenty officers to assist the admiral, twenty Marine radio operators, ten Navy operators and twenty steward mates to take care of the twenty officers. There wasn't enough room for everybody, and the twenty Marines and five of the ten Navy operators were sent off the ship.

The invasion of Okinawa took place on April first, and we arrived four days later. The first night we were sent to battle stations. I reported to the radio room and saw my name on the bulletin board to report topside to the radar room. I ran up one flight of stairs to the Main Deck, then back to the rear of the ship and up two flights of stairs to the doorway to the radar room. I lifted the latch on the side of the door, swung the door closed and then turned into the radar room. There were two steps down to the main floor. As I swung around I bumped into someone and knocked him on his behind. I looked down and saw the two stars on his collar and didn't know what to say. He laughed and said, "that's okay, sailor" and held out his hand and asked me to help him get up.

Inside the Radar Room they had a radio that you talked into and didn't have to use the Morse code. It was used to talk to the pilots of the airplanes. The officers did all the talking, and I did nothing. When at battle stations we would be at Code Red which meant all our pilots should be out of the area. Code Red Flash Yellow meant no ship could fire any guns, even if you saw a Japanese plane, because our planes were in the area. The officers took charge of the voice radio, and we never had to go there anymore.

In order to copy all the frequencies that the admiral wanted, we had to stand watch six hours on and six hours off. On the 30th day at Okinawa, we were told we had been to battle stations for the 100th time. They lasted between two hours and twelve hours. I only got two hours of sleep for over a month. Finally, we were told we did not have to go to duty while at battle stations. We could lie in our bunks. But with our ship shooting machine guns, a bigger bullet called pom-poms, and the 5-inch cannon, plus all the other ships in the area shooting at the Jap planes who could get any sleep?

While at Okinawa a cyclone was approaching Buckner Bay, and the admiral decided to go out to sea instead of going around it. We were caught in the middle with waves fifty feet high. I never got seasick and went to lunch. With over 250 men aboard ship, there were only ten men around one table eating lunch that day.

I would copy code from Honolulu for one hour and then get relief to copy other signals for one hour. Sometimes I would assist the chief petty officer and decode the heading of the messages to and from. The chief got sick, and I took the messages to a small room where the admiral's officers took turns taking the messages into another room at the very front of the ship where they had special machines to de-code the text of the message. The second time I went there all of the messages were still there. We were not allowed to go into the coding room. I knocked on the door and no one answered.

Although against the rules, I opened the door. There was a step about six inches high to go over. Inside in about four inches of water full of vomit washing back and forth was the officer lying on his back, unconscious with the water turning his face from one side to the other. I got down on my knees, lifted him up, set him in the corner, ran to the radio room and sent for the medics. They came and put him on a stretcher and left. I went to take a shower, put on clean clothes and went back to the radio room where I copied code for thirteen hours before anyone came to relieve me.

All the ships had generators aboard – not to make electricity, but to make smoke. They made so much smoke, the Japs would pass overhead and could not see us.

Near the end of the war the Japs would approach Okinawa flying close to the ocean and then swoop over the island and crash into our ships. We were at Flash Red, Control Red, when a plane came at us – and we shot it down. As it was falling into the sea, we saw it was one of our own pilots. We believe his radio must not have been working and didn't know we were in Flash Red, Control Red.

A Jap plane hit the battleship *Missouri* and disabled the controls of all the ships' guns on the port side of the ship. The *Taney* was ordered to go to the port side and be its protection if the Japs struck again. We only stayed two days, and they fixed the controls.

It was only a couple of weeks before the war ended when I received a letter from my mother that my father could no longer take care of the bowling alley and sold out the alleys. I was devastated.

They sent sixty-five radio operators to our ship to help us out. In school we learned to copy 20 words a minute. Hawaii sent the code out about 26 words a minute, and not a single one could copy the code. All 65 were sent out to other ships.

The night the Japanese surrendered and it was announced over the loud speaker, all the ships in the harbor started shooting off their guns. The admiral called everyone to battle stations. We heard the next day that five sailors had been killed in the wild shooting.

The battleship *U.S.S. Missouri* was tied up at Tokyo. Our admiral brought us to the opposite side of Japan. While on radio duty, I heard Honolulu calling a ship with an operational priority message. I checked with another operator and was told it was for the *Missouri*. The *Missouri* didn't answer, and I was given permission to receive the message and then relay it to the *Missouri*. The treaty was signed on the deck of the *Missouri* the next day, September 2, 1945 in Tokyo Bay. All my life I have wondered what that message said.

Thanksgiving Day of 1945 I was aboard the *U.S.C.G.C. Taney* on the way home from San Francisco to Charleston, South Carolina.

The Coast Guard vessel, *Taney*, is on display in Baltimore. I hope to be able to go there and maybe finally learn what was in the message to the *Missouri*.

I married Jeanne Mattioli, a Brewster girl, and we have seven children.

A card was given to me stating that I am entitled to the following medals: the American Area medal, the Pacific Area Medal (1 bronze star) and the Amphibious Insignia. The medals were never sent to me.
56

John Santorelli

In October 1941 I left high school and joined the Coast Guard. It was before the draft was instituted. At eighteen years old, I enlisted in order to pick my own service. I went to the Brooklyn Naval Yard, then to Newport News, Virginia for amphibious training. The Coast Guard was basically amphibious using smaller boats. In 1941 they were called Higgins boats and were thirty to forty feet long, each holding twelve men and a tank or armored vehicle. They were invasion boats that would be picked up by APA transport ships with davits. These transports carried 36 small boats and 4,000 to 5,000 men. We would practice landing. On the day of the invasion the Higgins boats were dropped by davits from the transport. They would hit the water, line up in formation and go into the beach they were assigned to.

We were part of the North African invasion, and in November 1942, D-day, we went in at Fedala Beachhead about nine miles north of Casablanca. We lost our boat at this beachhead because the terrain was so rough with such big waves. We didn't capsize, but we were banging into each other, going from port to starboard. It did a lot of damage. The hardest part was getting in. They had breakwaters on the side. They'd let five or six rows of these small Higgins boats get in, then they (the French) would turn the lights on, and we were like sitting ducks. There was ground fire directed at those going in. Everybody in the small boats concentrated on the breakwater to shoot the lights out; in about twenty minutes they hit four or five lights, so we could get in. But my boat never got in. The waves were turning the boats sideways, and they were just backing up. They had beach masters stationed on the beach, and they would tell us what to do. We were to get the men and supplies in. They'd say leave it – get out of the boat, go! They ran the beach; it was their job. The boats were piled up all over the place. The supplies, everything was left. They'd call out the orders. I was in the 4th Wave. I never got in. The boat had holes in it already. They told us to get to the beach. We were about 60 yards out. We had to jump from boat to boat and into the water. It was chaos. The contributing factors to the chaos were weather conditions and inexperience, North Africa being our first invasion. We had to get on the beach, and that's what we did. From there on I joined up with the Army Rangers and stayed with them walking the nine miles to Casablanca.

Before I got to Casablanca, one of the largest French battleships, the *J.B.*, was tied up at the dock. It was huge with 16-inch guns; it never got touched. We went over to look at it. I believe it was to have been commissioned for warfare, but it was too late when the invasion started. They left it there. It looked so beautiful, and it never got scratched.

The nicest thing was that we had so many supplies for the men. It was unbelievable. If you had to get out of one boat, they had ten others to take you in. The American people did a good job in getting the stuff over there. The men had everything. If you had a gun and you didn't like it, you could most likely throw it over your shoulder and get another issued. They had a lot of transports, a lot of men-young guys like me, regulars from the Army and Navy, and Rangers. They had to mix the older experienced men and the younger men.

It took about nine days walking most of the way to Casablanca. From there I went back to the states and was assigned to another transport, the *USS Delta* and went back to North Africa. Isn't that something? I ended up in Bizerte, North Africa, which had already been taken by our armies. It was one of the busiest places, getting ready to go the rest of the way. I was assigned to LST-327 (3 davits and small boats on each side) and stayed about a month and a half. Lake Bizerte is a huge, calm lake with breakwaters that allowed all the landing barges in where they could get supplies. There were air raids all the time, because the Germans knew the next push would be Sicily. There were hundreds of ships there. The English had antiaircraft all around this lake. We couldn't shoot down any planes unless the Germans broke through their umbrella of fire. That's how we could see that every fifth bullet was a tracer with searchlights. Every now and then you'd get a plane that broke through the searchlights beyond the lake and then would come down around the ships; that's when everybody else opened up. The poor guy never got back up out of there. He'd get down in there and try to get back out, but that was a big mistake. The English had some beautiful AA guns. You had to see it with your own eyes. When I say every fifth tracer you could see all around the lake, and it looked like an umbrella of tracers up and down. We stayed there until one night when we sneaked out and went to Sicily. D- Day was at Licata. It wasn't a big battle, but some men were hurt. We got in, did what we had to do and got back out. When we banged into another LST and put a hole in our side we had to go to a dry dock at Palermo and stay there two weeks for repairs. The American government had taken over the dry docks.

I knew Eddie Brady was on 290LCI, and I kept looking, wondering what he was doing. All of a sudden they started picking up the small ships and putting them on the LST. They picked up his LCI with a six or seven man crew and put it on our LST, so we had a nice reunion. It was really something getting together with him. We spent about three or four days together. Then we went to Swansea, England where we stayed until it was time for the Italian campaign (Salerno and Anzio). The whole fleet went to different ports in England after the Sicilian invasion. Eddie and I made a couple of liberties there together, and that was nice.

During the Salerno invasion, we had on board the Irish Guards (infantrymen) wearing their kilts. We delivered them to the beachhead. They were big and tough. While there I kept my binoculars on Eddie Brady's LCI, tied up to a pier. I told him he better get out of there.

Our biggest problems were unloading with air strikes and German 88's. They were tough and they were accurate. If you were within 50 or 70 yards of them, you'd better drift away, because the next barrage would be a lot closer or direct. They were tough. They did a lot of damage. We pulled back and went to Anzio, south of Salerno. We were there quite a while taking in men and supplies. We also took about 250 wounded on our tank deck and took them back to England. We took prisoners out too, and they were well guarded. They were taken to England.

After Anzio we were picked to go to the Isle of Capri for a 15-day rest period. But we had no money, so we went to the Red Cross and borrowed money, which I later paid back. Four LST's were picked to go there. Because we carried explosives and fuel for army vehicles on board and could be hit and blown out of the water, they figured we deserved a rest. The rest period was supposed to be 15 days, but they took us out after four days. We went back to England, and tying up there was a break.

In London we went to Piccadilly Square. I heard three or four V-rockets going over. It was scary. You didn't know what direction it was going, or where it would land. It looked like a torpedo going along. When it ran out of fuel, that's when it would come down. The poor English people took some beating from those things. Up and down their coastline they knew it was coming, but nobody knew when. If they had a pint of beer they were jolly as hell. They took a beating, but they were tough people and determined. I got along with them during the time I went on liberty.

My LST 327 was involved in the Normandy invasion making numerous trips into the beach with men and supplies over a period of weeks. On August 27, 1944 after making our thirteenth trip to the Normandy beachhead, we were last in a line of ships leaving Normandy heading for England when an explosion occurred tearing apart the stern of the ship. Those of us who had been standing on deck were thrown into the air and out into the water. On the way my legs caught the railing, fracturing them. They were useless to me in the water. We were about two miles out. The explosion threw men into the sea, fracturing limbs and narrowly escaping drowning. Many lost extremities. One of them had been thrown up on deck. Helping one another to find floating life jackets they "kept yelling to each other to keep up our spirits". One Navy shipmate didn't make it. "The Navy LST 346 swung around and came back to help us. They didn't waste a precious minute, and I know we owe our lives to the men of that ship. They rescued us and gave us the best care anyone could possibly have received under the circumstances. Some of them even gave blood transfusions before we got ashore." There were many acts of courage during the rescue. We didn't know what hit our LST. We thought it was a mine.

After all those years, with the benefit of a computer, a German WWII buff found information showing that LST 327 was hit by a German U-boat firing a single torpedo aimed at the last LST in the convoy of several ships. A German captain did the damage to us. He must have been resting on the bottom of the ocean and finally took a shot from there. There were so many English and American tin cans going in and out picking up sonar that once he revved up, our tin cans and ships would have picked up their sound waves. They would go closer and closer to it, get it pinpointed, and then they'd start dropping depth charges. That captain is still living.

The fibular bones of both my legs were fractured, and as a result of the explosions I lost 80% hearing in one ear and 20% in the other. I owe my life to Jack McCollum, a motor machinist mate. He found a life jacket, and gave to me. I spent at least two months in England having operations on my legs. From England I went to Ireland and spent a couple of days on an airfield in a tent. They wanted to give us more food than I could eat, and I'm a good eater.

We were taken down to the waterfront and put on a Pan American Air Clipper. We were four stretchers high on each side, and I was at the window. I thought the plane would never get off the water. As I watched the water splash up against the little window I asked when the hell was it going up. The plane was vibrating. I said you better give me another life preserver. I was told to watch. As we went along the vibrations became less and less, and it finally went up.

We landed at St. Albans, Long Island. They had big long barracks with beds up each side and double rows of beds down the middle. I'm sitting there with only the emergency lights on to make it dimmer overnight. The lights were going on and this WAVE corpsman walks past me and gets about four bunks by me. I said it can't be. She went up the other side walking fast; then she came back by me in the center, and I could see her face and was eyeing her up and down. I called out "Joan". It was Joan Beal, and she came right over. I never knew she was there. It was great to see somebody I knew. Anything I wanted extra she got for me. She was really something. She worked hard there. She was a good person; you could bet your bottom dollar on it. She'd be working and some guy would want something, and when she came back later she always remembered the things she had to do. I stayed two and a half months.

From there I went to the Coast Guard Academy Training Program in New London, Connecticut. The war was winding down. Since I was going for treatments, and they figured I was a good guy to get rid of, I was discharged from there on September 12, 1945. I was in the Coast Guard three years, ten months and twenty-four days.

It took a hell of a toll. When I talk to my friends, you can see that their lives have all been changed through their experiences. They see things differently.

The medals earned were for the campaigns of North Africa, Sicily, Salerno, Anzio beachhead and Normandy with five stars - and the Purple Heart.

After spending some time in my own business, I went to work for the New York Central Railroad. On September 22, 1946 I married Lee Zerbato of Mahopac. We have one son.[57] [58] [59]

John Santorelli

Marines

Kenneth J. Brennan

Kenneth Brennan, second from the youngest Brennan brothers, graduated from Brewster High School. He enlisted in the Marine Corps and according to a Brewster Standard article of the time was believed to be on Bougainville in the Pacific. A photograph from the same newspaper shows Kenny Brennan with another Brewster fighting man, John J. O'Hara before the battle of Iwo Jima. Another Brewster Standard article as quoted from one of Kenny's letters written while fighting on Iwo Jima: "The battle here now is well in hand. It has been a rough, hard fight, but we made it o.k. So far old Tojo hasn't caught me. He's been closer than he ever has before. However, in this game close doesn't count...the weather here is very cold compared to what I have been living in. I'm telling you I damn near froze my (deleted) several times...me and my buddy, which is my foxhole, see a lot of one another day and night. Occasionally a piece of shrapnel will pay me a visit but hasn't been able to touch me... must go now, things are getting a little hot, so I'll have to dig a little deeper... my regards to all. Drop me a few lines. As always, Kenny." He retired after spending thirty years in the Marine Corps.

He married Ann Cox, and they had two children, a boy and a girl.[60]

Robert Lawrence Collins, Jr., (KIA)

Bob was born in Troy, N.Y. on February 1, 1921 but came to Brewster with his parents when he was a boy. When his twin brothers Eddie and Jimmy were very small, their mother died. In Brewster High School Bob excelled in football, baseball and basketball and was elected president of his class of 1939.

At 5 ft. 81/2 inches tall, he enlisted in the Marine Corps. on the 7th of May 1942. He was in the Asiatic-Pacific Area from August 31, 1942 to July 21, 1944. A letter from Capt. Josephus Daniels Jr. U.S. Marine Corps states that: "he participated in action against the enemy on Bougainville, Solomon Islands, November 1, 1943 to November 24, 1943, consolidation of Northern Solomons December 23, 1943 to December 25, 1943 and Guam, Marianas Islands July 21, 1944."

According to another letter to his father, Robert Collins, from Headquarters U.S. Marine Corps, "Robert L. Collins, Jr. U. S. Marine Corps Reserve, sustained a gunshot wound of the left arm in action against the enemy on 24 November, 1943. He has been evacuated and was admitted to a U. S. Naval Hospital for further medical treatment on 1 December 1943". This communication did not tell on what island this wound was sustained, but according to the dates above, it was on Bougainville, Solomon Islands.

Almost eight months later Sergeant (OW) Robert Collins was killed in combat. Under the Great Seal of the United States, with the signature of President Franklin D. Roosevelt is the following statement: "In grateful memory of Robert Lawrence Collins, Jr., United States Marine Corps who died in the service of his country at Guam Island, Mariana Islands, 21 July 1944. He stands in the unbroken line of patriots who have dared to die that freedom might live, and grow, and increase its blessings. Freedom lives, and through it, he lives – in a way that humbles the undertakings of most men." Robert L. Collins, Jr. received the Purple Heart with Gold Star; Asiatic-Pacific Campaign Medal and World War II Victory Medal and was greatly mourned by the people of his hometown, Brewster, N.Y.[61]

IN GRATEFUL MEMORY OF

Robert Laurence Collins, Jr

United States Marine Corps

WHO DIED IN THE SERVICE OF HIS COUNTRY AT

Guam Island, Marianas Islands, 21 July 1944

HE STANDS IN THE UNBROKEN LINE OF PATRIOTS WHO HAVE DARED TO DIE

THAT FREEDOM MIGHT LIVE, AND GROW, AND INCREASE ITS BLESSINGS.

FREEDOM LIVES, AND THROUGH IT, HE LIVES—

IN A WAY THAT HUMBLES THE UNDERTAKINGS OF MOST MEN

Franklin D Roosevelt

PRESIDENT OF THE UNITED STATES OF AMERICA

Howard E. Dingee, Jr.

Howard Dingee was inducted into the Marine Corps at Carmel, N.Y. in late 1943 and traveled by bus and train to Parris Island, S.C. for training. After three weeks of drilling, he went on to the shooting range. Private Dingee was then sent to Tent City, 49th Replacement Battalion at Camp Le Jeune, N.C.

In the summer of 1944 he became part of the First Marine Division, Company C, Third Armored Tractor Battalion. This battalion, organized on Pavuvu, was specifically for the invasion of Peleliu, an island in the Pacific. It was to be a rugged coral beach landing with many complications. They were given only two weeks of training with their new tanks and their guns on the Russell Islands as well as Guadalcanal which was then in American hands. Howard said that temperatures got to be between 110 and 120 degrees. The convoy spent time on Guadalcanal to practice landings before heading to Peleliu. Howard wrote to his parents in Brewster just before leaving. (Many of his letters are printed in the book, *Before the First Wave* by Larry L. Woodard).

One of 800 men of the Armored Amphibian Tractor Battalion, Howard Dingee would take part in the fierce landing of Peleliu on September 15, 1944 "and would land before the first wave of infantry." This invasion came at a high loss of American men. Howard said, "We were all between 19 and 22 years old. We had to fight in thick jungle after going about three miles in from the beach. I lost a lot of good friends. The reconnaissance had not shown the extensive amount of caves dug along the beaches." Getting beyond the beaches and the caves was only the first leg of the fighting.

The Navy pounded the island "with round after round of high explosives and soon Navy and Marine fighter aircraft were working it over with their strafing and bomb runs. A thick cloud of smoke and debris arose from the quivering island."

The Japanese were defending the island with grenades, mines, artillery and mortar fire, and the heavy tropical vegetation made progress extremely slow. Destroyed or disabled tanks could be seen along the coral shoreline, and dead comrades were everywhere. "On September 22, 1944, D+7, the men were dog-tired. Lips were cracked and bleeding. Anyone who had crawled in the coral for over five yards had the elbows out of their dungarees. The sun came up once more in the eastern South Pacific sky to beat down on the warriors of the 1st Marine Division. The men didn't feel like warriors that day. They were slowly being bled and burned to where all thoughts turned to just one cold drink"..."Then there was that smell of death that permeated the entire island-a sickly smell that offended the nose and affected the taste - the smell of rotting Marines and Japanese soldiers. Accompanying the smell was the swarms of large, blue blowflies. Men of the 3rd Battalion began calling them the 'blue bombers,' after the Navy bombers supporting the action on the ground."

"Finally, the rains came and men stood bare-chested in the open to allow some of the grime and sweat of battle to wash off in the pleasant tropical downpour. The rain felt good, but men actually shivered from the sudden drop in temperature - probably down to 80 degrees..."

"No Regiment in the history of the Marine Corps had bled and died in the way the 1st Marines had on the coral ridges of Peleliu...As the 1st Marines straggled off the ridges back to the beach, one soldier hollered, 'Are you guys the 1st Marines?' "A Marine responded, 'There ain't no 1st Marines, we're just the survivors.' This wasn't quite true, but the casualty figures for the Regiment were the highest of any unit in the entire Pacific campaign...the 3rd Battalion...55 percent." Howard said that the battle lasted 60 days, and they lost 20,000 men.

The battle went on and "by Sept. 24, D+9, the 3rd Armored had its companies scattered around the fringes of the island..." "C Company was on the small island of Ngabad, just about a quarter of a mile north of the island." The end of the battle to take Peleliu came on Sept. 28 when the 3rd Armored started to move out. But mopping up was taking place, flushing out more Japanese from their bunkers, and this didn't end until October.

Howard Dingee's Company C "received a counter attack one night by a few Japanese, who were quickly dispatched. "By mid-October the battered 1st Marine Division left for Pavuvu. Men of the 3rd Armored Tractor Battalion came down off Bloody Nose Ridge on October 16, D+31 and continued as stretcher bearers for the 323rd Regimental Combat Team"..."On October 20, 1944, the first large contingent of men from the 3rd Armored Battalion left Peleliu"..."for Pavuvu"..."To go back to the dampness and mud of Pavuvu was a real disappointment to most men, because the rumor had circulated among them that they were going to get a break and spend some time in New Zealand or Australia"..."they knew they would never be the same." They were refitted at Pavuvu and after six months with new men who were well trained, they were ready to participate in the invasion of Okinawa. Company C was needed for the beach landing there.

During the last days of March 1945 bombardment of Okinawa took place, and on April 1 the 3rd went ashore. "The new Commanding Officer, Williamson,"..."was to get a second Bronze Star for his leadership of the 3rd Battalion on Okinawa." It was during this time that the men found out about the death of Ernie Pyle, the correspondent who was killed by a Japanese sniper. "He had talked to several of them before their landing on the small island of Ie Shima."

During one of these battles Howard Dingee was struck in the face by shrapnel from an exploding bomb. Howard needed surgery, but refused to go to a hospital, which would mean leaving his unit. He was bandaged and continued to fight. He was awarded a Purple Heart.

One of the missions of Company C was to take a number of tanks "by LST to Kume Shima, (an island about 50 miles west of Okinawa in the China Sea)." Kamikaze planes were being directed from this island. After about ten days of fighting approximately 200 planes were destroyed by a Marine rifle battalion.

Howard Dingee participated in the landings and battle of Okinawa, which ended in late June. "On July 8 the 3rd Battalion left the rain and mud and the island that took three months to capture at the cost of over 100,000 U.S. casualties." At this point the 3rd Armored Amphibian Battalion was dismantled and the men in various companies were reassigned.

On August 8, 1945 the first atomic bomb was dropped; surrender took place August 14. No longer did the men have to look forward to an invasion of Japan. On that date Howard Dingee was in Hawaii with his unit for much needed rest.

In a letter to his mother written August 24, 1945 Howard said, "I had about a 7 day liberty and what a time I had. I was drinking rum cokes - not bad! So I spent all of my money, excepting a few dollars. I won't be able to send any money home. After all, that was the first liberty we have had in 16 months." He was subsequently assigned to duty with the occupation forces in Japan.

When he returned home, he returned to P.F. Beal and Sons where he worked in the pump installation and repair department until his retirement. Howard married Margaret Zenobia; they had three children.

Note: When I contacted Howard at his home in Florida, he was very willing to help me in obtaining his story, but was very reluctant to talk about his difficult experiences. So, he sent me the book, *Before the First Wave: The 3rd Armored Amphibian Tractor Battalion* by Larry L. Woodard, and said, "it's all in there." I couldn't find exactly where Howard was at a given time, but wherever Company C of the Third Armored Amphibian Tractor Battalion was, I reasoned Howard was there, somewhere.[62]

John F. Larkin, Jr.

John graduated from Brewster High School in 1934 during the Great Depression. He started at Columbia University but didn't like it, so he quit and went back to B.H.S. to play football as a post-graduate student. He took a class with Kay Hubbard the first year she was teaching in Brewster. (Kay later married Bernard Waters). Jack went to Fordham University in 1935 and graduated in 1939. He came back to Brewster after graduation, but there weren't any jobs available. He started working for the postal service as a mail carrier on the rural route, and in 1940 he married Joan Fenaughty of Brewster.

In February of 1944 Jack enlisted in the military, choosing the Marine Corps. He trained at Parris Island, subsequently studied Aerology at Lakehurst, New Jersey, and in the fall he was to go to San Diego, California.

The entire outfit shipped out from San Diego except Jack. He was in an air squadron and went to school in San Diego. At night and on weekends he worked in a hot dog stand so that he could send money home. His son had been born before going into the Marine Corps. Jack was in San Diego two Christmases and then was sent back to Quantico in 1945, where he was trained to teach others the process of discharging. He spent all his time in service going to schools and ended up a Private First Class.

Jack developed an allergy in the south and was discharged earlier than expected. He arrived home just before Christmas, 1945. He went back to his job with the Postal Service spending his working life there.

Jack Larkin had a twin brother William H. who was in the U. S. Army. [63]

Louis R. Prisco

While I was in my second year of high school I was drafted on August 2, 1943 and was sent to the recruiting center in New York City for my physical. I was taken into the Marine Corps and sent to Parris Island for boot camp and then to Camp Le Jeune where I trained for light antiaircraft gunnery. From there we were shipped to Camp Pendleton, California where the Fifth Marine Division was being formed. We went through the necessary training for combat and then were shipped to Hilo, Hawaii where there was more training at Camp Tarawa up in the hills.

When we were put on a combat ship, we didn't know where we were headed. Once on board we were told our destination was Iwo Jima. Approaching the island we saw many ships, landing crafts, battleships and others. For days the guns were firing on Mount Surabachi, and then finally we got orders to disembark from our ships onto landing craft in order to get to the beach. Wave after wave of ships went in unloading combat troops. The Japanese let us get to the beach, but once on the beach we were pinned down by mortar and heavy weapons fire. The casualty rate was very high. When we finally reached our destination, we set up our machine guns and waited for our 105 Howitzers, the big guns, to get into position.

We were in a place where we could see the American flag being raised on Mt. Surabachi, which was a great sight. We moved forward pushing the enemy back and securing the aircraft landing field for our bombers. Airplanes, which were shot up or for other reasons could not get back to their original base, could now be flown to this airfield. On the 16th of March 1944 we left Iwo Jima having been there since February 19th. We boarded ship and were taken back to Camp Tarawa, Hilo, Hawaii where we were given a few days of R and R on the big island of Hawaii, then back to Camp Tarawa. We had lost so many men that we were given fresh replacements to fill our ranks.

We were on board ship on our way to Japan when the atomic bomb was dropped on Hiroshima. We could see how the bomb had leveled the city, and we could see bodies on the land and floating in the harbor. We left the ship and moved into a garrison, as the Japanese were moving out. It was quite a sight. Inside the barracks you could look out into the harbor cove and see all the suicide submarines the Japanese did not get a chance to use against us. While we were in Japan, all we did was guard duty at the Japanese warehouse that they had built into the hills. After we were relieved in Japan we were again put on a ship for the long trip back to the United States. We were sent to Bainbridge, Maryland, where we were discharged on May 16, 1946. The following medals were awarded to me: Good Conduct Medal, Certificate of Satisfactory Service plus ribbons for Asiatic Pacific Theater. I came back to Brewster, N.Y. and went back to work for my family.

I married Regina Ludington on October 3, 1954. We have a daughter and a son. About three months ago I received my diploma from Brewster High School. (Brewster High School awarded diplomas to all the Brewster veterans in the spring of 2001.)[64]

Above:
Kenneth J. Brennan

Left:
Robert L. Collins Jr. KIA

Navy

Ernest Adam

Ernest Adam was born in Cornol, Switzerland in August 28, 1913. He came to the United States when he was a young man and lived on Long Island. He worked as the projectionist at the Cameo Theatre in Brewster and stayed at the Red Brick Tourist House in Brewster. There he met and married Iola Dutcher whose parents ran the business.

In 1937 they had a daughter they named Gail, and in 1938 Ernest became a United States citizen. On October 28, 1943 he enlisted in the Navy. After boot training and other specialized training, he sailed on the SS *President Johnson* as an Electrician's Mate to the Admiralty Islands. On the day he left home, his wife Iola kept her six year old daughter home from school explaining where her daddy was going and why.

In his letters home he told about Brewster men he met overseas and a friend from New York City who was killed a few weeks after the two men had visited.

Ernie was honorably discharged on December 16, 1945 as an Electrician's Mate 1C CB. He earned Expert Rifleman's Badge, the Asiatic – Pacific Ribbon and Victory Medal. He was discharged at Lido Beach, L.I., New York.

Gail Adams Manente, Ernest's daughter said, "I only wish my father could tell you in his own words how he felt about the war and some of his personal stories of WWII.[65]

Philip F. Beal, III

I was in the class of 1943 at Williams College where I majored in chemistry. Because of the war we were in an accelerated program, and as a result I graduated mid-December 1942. Prior to graduation I interviewed for jobs. Amongst my interviews one was at the Winthrop Chemical Company in Renssellaer, N. Y., and one was at Columbia University. The job at Columbia was so secretive I couldn't tell much about it. It later turned out to be The Manhattan Project (the development of the A-bomb). The one in Renssellaer sounded much more interesting to me. They were producing penicillin and had just won the Army-Navy E for Excellence for their production of the new anti-malarial drug, atabrine. After working at Winthrop for about a year, it appeared that many of the chemists were going to be drafted.

I went back to Brewster, took the train to New York and enlisted in the Navy. When I went back to Brewster, I found that Jimmy Smyth and Matt Fisher were also going into the Navy. We took the Put (a short-run spur of the N. Y. Central Railroad) over to Carmel to report to the draft board and show them our enlistment papers.

We all then went back to N.Y.C. and were inducted into the Navy. We were put on the Erie Lackawanna Railroad and shipped to the U.S. Naval Training Center at Sampson, N.Y. outside Geneva on Lake Seneca. After about two months of boot training as an apprentice seaman, I was granted a commission as an Ensign and ordered to Officer Training at Fort Schuyler, N.Y.

After two months of officers training I was ordered to join the USS LST 49 as the Gunnery Officer. The ship had been constructed at Dravo Shipyards in Pittsburgh, Pa. and was an older LST. It was returning to N.Y.C. after the invasions of Normandy and southern France. It had been part of the invasion flotilla going into Utah beach and made twenty-one runs carrying wounded to England and supplies and ammunition back to Normandy. In New York the ship was extensively upgraded, including new antiaircraft guns and fire control systems. After about two months of updating and repair work we left N.Y. for Pearl Harbor, where we joined the convoy and left for Eniwetok, Saipan and then the invasion of Okinawa. After passing through the Panama Canal, we had a memorial service on our main deck for President Roosevelt.

We took elements of the Second Marine Division into Okinawa. After unloading the marines, we anchored in Buckner Bay (Nagagasuha Wan) next to the battleship *Tennessee*. It was comforting to see that we were surrounded by battleships, cruisers and aircraft carriers on the way into the beach. A few mornings later a Kamikaze plane flew into the harbor entrance right down the middle of the bay and very low, right over our ship. Everyone thought he was going to hit us, but he continued on and struck the *LST 534* next to us. That incident was described on the History Channel and is on a videotape- "Onto Rugged Shores". They never mentioned us, but we sent a Fire and Rescue Party to help fight the fire which burned all day.

We left Okinawa and returned to Saipan where we re-supplied. It was really neat to see the B-29's take off to bomb Japan every night. We received our preliminary orders for the invasion of Japan and were to be converted into a post office on our tank deck. We were to beach on the second wave of the invasion, send our small boats out twelve miles where they would meet amphibious aircraft bringing us mail. The mail was to be processed in our post office and then delivered out through the bow doors to marines on the beach. Our landing site was very heavily fortified with Japanese artillery. Kyushu is a volcanic island, and since the shores drop off abruptly, there were only a couple of spots for an amphibious invasion. The Japs were aware of this, and this allowed them to heavily concentrate their defenses. I honestly was convinced that we would never survive.

We were on our way back to Pearl Harbor when the first A-bomb hit Hiroshima. When we got to Pearl, we received over one hundred mail specialists and two naval mail officers, and they made our tank deck into a post office. While we were in Pearl, the second bomb was dropped on Nagasaki. A few days later peace was declared, and there was one hell of a celebration in Honolulu. All the pyrotechnics on the ships in the harbor were fired off – a real 4th of July display.

Any bleeding hearts who claim that dropping the A-bomb was a war crime were not in the Pacific at that time. Needless to say, I was mightily relieved. We left Pearl Harbor for the orient and dropped off mailmen to establish post offices in Olithi, Singapore and Okinawa.

None of the mailmen who had been flown out to us from Fleet Post Offices in New York and San Francisco had been on a ship before. Just before we arrived back at Okinawa, we were hit by a typhoon. You never saw so many sick sailors in your life. We headed for Shanghai and established a post office there. We then hauled relief supplies up the Yangtze to Hankow. After we arrived back at Shanghai we were sent to Taku Bar, the seaport for Tientsin and Peking. We were anchored about ten miles offshore and processed military mail for all north China brought in to us by aircraft and merchant vessels. After over six months at Taku Bar we were then shipped back to Shanghai and thence to Subic Bay, Philippine Islands to decommission our ship.

While at Subic Bay, I applied for admission to graduate school at Ohio State U. where I met Martha and received my PhD in organic chemistry. After we were married and after graduation I accepted a job at Upjohn and moved to Kalamazoo where we have been since February 1950. I had a great job and was very lucky. I was the first to synthesize hydrocortisone, and Upjohn used that process for about 40 years to become the world's leading producer of steroids. Martha and I have three daughters and one son.[66]

Edward Joseph Brady

Edward Brady graduated with the Brewster High School Class of 1941 having participated in the school band, three years on the baseball team and four years on the football team. Eddie enlisted in the Navy on February 19, 1942 and went to the Naval Training Station at Newport, R.I. for boot training.

On September 1, 1941 S2nd Class Brady completed sixteen weeks of radio school at Bedford Springs, Pa, qualifying as striker for radioman. He was transferred to the Receiving Station at Norfolk, VA.

He left New York on an LST, which carried his LCT 290 and arrived in Oran, North Africa approximately 30 days later. He went across North Africa with the Army to Lake Bizerte, a very large, calm lake where the landing barges could come in and get supplies. They were subject to constant air raids from German planes. It was also the steppingstone to the Sicilian invasion of July 10, 1943 in which Boatswain's Mate Second Class Brady took part. The larger LSTs were picking up the small ships which had a crew of six or seven, and Brady's LCT was picked up by his friend, Machinist Mate John Santorelli's LST. Santorelli had watched Brady's boat, and they had a fine reunion. Friend John Santorelli, a Coast Guardsman, and Edward Brady were sent to Swansea, England where they enjoyed several days together on liberty. After more training, they were on the ocean again headed for the invasion of Salerno, Italy on September 3, 1943. Again his friend John kept a watchful eye on Brady's small boat when it was at a pier.

After the invasion of Sicily, Brady was given some R & R time. On January 22, 1944 the hard-fought Allied invasion of Anzio took place. After that battle he took the long trip back to England where there was more training in preparation for the Normandy invasion June 6, 1944. Back at Falmouth, England, he was assigned to Flotilla 26 on August 21, 1944. In November of 1944 as BM 2/c, Eddie received instruction at Night Lookout Vision School at Norfolk, VA. On March 13, 1945 he reported aboard *USS LSM 434*. Eddie Brady received his Honorable Discharge at the Separation Center at Lido Beach, L.I., New York.

His records show the following ratings earned: AS, S2c, S1c, Cox, BM2c (T). He earned the following medals: Good Conduct Medal, Victory Medal, American Theater and European Theater with 4 stars.

Edward Brady married Marie Destino of Brewster on September 5, 1948. Serving as ushers in their wedding were three other Brewster veterans, John Santorelli, Larry Enright and Robert Folchetti.[67]

Daniel A. Brandon

Dan graduated from Brewster High School in June of 1940; then worked as a grocery clerk for one year. On September 16, 1941 at 90 Church Street, N.Y.C. he enlisted in the Navy, spent the war years as a hospital corpsman and later went to the Naval School of Hospital Administration becoming an ensign a year later. He retired a Captain June 1, 1984 after forty-two years and nine months and says he never regretted a day. About his hometown, he says, "All of my life Brewster has been, is now, and will be HOME!" His words follow:

On September 16 the Navy put the 50 new recruits enlisted that day on an overnight steamer to Providence, R. I. From there we went to Newport for recruit training. I remember that trip well, my first night in the Navy at sea. The steamer had gambling on board, because part of the time we were outside the 3 mile limit. After nine weeks of training I got a week or so of leave. From Newport I was sent to the Naval Hospital, Brooklyn, N.Y. on 15 November 1941. The war started on December 7 while I was in Brooklyn. On 16 January 1942 I went to Naval Hospital, Washington, D.C.; stayed there for three weeks when we started moving the hospital and patients to the newly completed National Naval Medical Center. Left on my own at 19 years old to get to Foggy Bottom, I was carrying a sea-bag, hammock and a mattress. Getting to 23rd Street I walked up the hill to the entrance of the naval hospital. By the time I got there I was totally exhausted. The personnel office was in the basement of Building Two (Old Conservatory). As a "fresh-caught HA duce", which was the expression they used for us at that time, I was treated rather well and sent down to the barracks in a truck.

As an "HA duce" I was given a bunk in a ward-like atmosphere with everybody else. It was just about liberty time when I arrived there, and up until then you did everything in uniform. My first sight was to see somebody come down the middle of the barracks in riding jodhpurs. I asked if that was a corpsman; it turned out that it was, and that was how I was exposed to civilian clothes in Washington, D.C.

The following morning I went to the surgical ward. We had one patient in critical condition who died while I was there. He was a young marine corporal with cancer. It was almost impossible to believe that this guy was so young and dying of cancer. The corpsmen did all the AM and PM care, and we also were responsible for feeding the patients. We picked up tureens of food in the galley, took them to the patients, serving the food on trays. I worked somewhere between 80 and 90 hours a week as hospital corpsman, but that wasn't bad. I was also in charge of laundry - collecting it, bundling it up and getting it ready to be placed on a truck and taken to the laundry on Constitution Avenue.

When we moved to the National Naval Medical Center in Bethesda, those who could walk were put on buses and those who couldn't were prepared for movement by ambulance. After the feeding and preparation of the patients for movement, we stripped the beds and left everything there. That day we didn't have to go down to the laundry hole. We cleaned up the galley and the food preparation area and got ready to move. Dr. H. Lamont Pugh (who later served as Surgeon General of the Navy from 1951 to 1954), some other corpsmen, two nurses and I moved the bedpans and urinals from the surgical ward of Naval Hospital Washington to the surgical ward of National Naval Medical Center, Bethesda in Dr. Pugh's old car. Ordinarily, I never had any communication with him of a personal nature. It just wasn't done.

At the new hospital we no longer had to go to the galley with tureens to pick up the food, but would go there to get these monstrous-looking food service wagons that had tureens in them. Everything was new; nothing was used. We never went anywhere without our own blanket.

On September 1, 1942 I made hospital apprentice first class, then pharmacist's mate third class in January of 1943, second class in April of 1943 and first class in September 1943. It was a time when the needs of the service were such that you got promoted rather rapidly if you passed a test and put in the time.

From Bethesda I went to Pier 92, Mobile Hospital No. 5 in N.Y.C. Within a month I was moved to the receiving barracks in Brooklyn (near the Brooklyn Naval Hospital). After two months we were brought together as a unit. Our officers joined us, and we began our activities. Mobile hospitals were built by the corpsmen, doctors and a small gang of artificers led by one Civil Engineer Corps officer. We didn't even have an electrician, just a CEC officer. We were then shipped out as a unit from Brooklyn to San Diego to New Caledonia, arriving in late August of 1942. The battle of Guadalcanal was underway. In the opening parts of the war, the sea forces were under considerable stress even before we had our hospital built. Our first casualties were burn cases off the destroyer, *Porter(DD-356)*. Two sleek-looking cruisers *San Juan(CL-54)* and *San Diego(CL-53)* had gotten into some sort of skirmish. There were also casualties from an aircraft carrier. That hospital had no nurses until Christmas of 1942.

The hospital on New Caledonia had to be set up from scratch, built in a cow pasture. The first part of the hospital was 250 beds in small Butler huts, and we had our own food service. There was no electricity; later on we generated our own power. Fortunately the Army had been there a month or two before us and had provided us with some logistics support. Initially, they fed us for a couple of days until we could get our galleys going. It was rather primitive at first, and when I was ill with dengue fever, we didn't have a building.

We were able to get the buildings up without bathrooms. We had tents on the end of each ward with facilities for bathrooms, but all that changed as time went by. We were able to construct permanent operating rooms, but we had no air-conditioning. Several months later another operating room was built, and it was air-conditioned. I was an OR corpsman at the time so I was able to enjoy it.

For treating our burn cases we used Vaseline and gauze. I don't think we had a thing called pre-made Vaseline gauze at the time. We had to make our own. Another treatment was with tannic acid, which almost crusted up, but apparently it worked.

When we arrived on New Caledonia we had one anesthesia man who was not a board-certified anesthesiologist even though he had experience in anesthesia. He trained a nurse who could administer gas and ether. We also had corpsmen who were acting as anesthesiologists who gave spinals, pentothal and ether. I even did spinals. We trained using surgical packs. Using the spinal needles, you could go through the packs and feel yourself going through the various tissues until you were in the spinal cord. That's how we trained to be able to feel the passage of the needle into the spinal column, and it was very effective. In those days there were no nurses who would scrub for surgery. We would do suturing but never anything else except hold retractors. When the nurses came, they didn't do more than supervise, never scrubbing. The surgical nurse for the OR made the schedules, assigned people to cases, etc. In late 1942 when they got there, they didn't have khakis or greens. They did everything in whites, long sleeved whites – that was the only uniform they had. The nurses came on the scene around Christmas 1942. They took over very quickly, and the shift from an all male atmosphere to nurses and corpsmen was not difficult at all for us in the OR. We had three nurses in our OR, and they were very well accepted.

Noumea, New Caledonia had a beautiful harbor, and we were right on the beach looking at the seaway into the harbor. We had at least one hospital ship down there. We received our patients by ship, not by air. As time went by, we got more and more gunshot wounds, mine wounds, etc. We also got a significant number of neuro-psychiatric patients. Our hospital grew from 250 to 2,000 beds in the 18 months I was there. We had two or three buildings of patients with NP difficulties. We received small drafts of 10 or 15 people from places like Bougainville or Rendova or other battles. Sometimes 600 patients would come in one day, and we could handle them. We had a large staff, and they could handle that number of casualties.

Shortly after my arrival in Noumea, New Caledonia, Fred Burdge (Brewster), a gunner's mate in a destroyer, the *USS Mahan*, visited me in the fall of 1942. His ship was truly in the war at sea in the South Pacific – the battle of the Coral Sea in particular. Never did see him again during the war. The following year Larry Enright (Brewster) was a USMC patient in the hospital in Noumea. He was evacuated soon after arrival, and I never saw him again during the war.

Surgical patients hadn't had much surgery before arriving, although they had been seen and stabilized. Not too many died at our place, although we had some deaths. We acted more like an evacuation hospital in the sense that they would be treated for a while, and we would ship them out on hospital transports, not hospital ships, and send them back to the States.

I was there 18 months when orders from COMSOPAC (Commander South Pacific) advised that six corpsmen from Mobile Hospital No. 5 were to accompany the patients back to the United States. They would be six original corpsmen, and they would be taken alphabetically from the top, so within an hour or two I was on my way.

In Noroton Heights, CT. there was a small communications school where they taught basic and advanced radiomen techniques. The building had been a VA hospital. We had two doctors, no nurses, one chief, and maybe 10 to 15 corpsmen, and we had a ward of about 8 to10 beds. I made chief in April of 1945 the day I left there, and I was paid a certain amount of money for a new uniform and other things.

My next assignment was the pre-commissioning detail of *USS Sanctuary (AH-17)* before it was built. When I got to the ship I was the only slick-armed chief on board. That was a guy who didn't have a hash mark, which meant he had less than 4 years in service. Therefore I was the junior chief. My duties were very sketchy because they were still constructing the ship. The decks had not even been completed. It was a fully air-conditioned ship, one of the first in the Navy. The deck surfaces were made of some sort of composition. I happened to be one of the Hospital Corps chiefs responsible for the security of that material when it was delivered to the yard.

The ship was commissioned on June 20, 1945, and I went to sea on the *Sanctuary* en route to Okinawa and Guam when the war ended in August of 1945. Our first job was to go to Japan to a place called Wakayama to evacuate POWs. Our ship was very good for that because we had 802 berths on board for patients alone. But the eagerness of people to get out of there was such that we took over 1100 on board. They slept on the decks, in the yeoman's office, and anywhere we could put out cots. The POWs were marvelous. Every one of them was malnourished. You would stick your finger into the fleshy part of their leg and, and your fingerprint would stay right in there, like a hole. I think they had beriberi. They were very hungry, and we fed them anything and everything that they wanted to eat. We had a few deaths. On this trip, the ship was overloaded, and then we hit a typhoon that drove us 5 or 6 days off track from where we were going. We had many seasick POWs.

We brought the first shipload of POWs from Japan to San Francisco. We were well received, to say the least, and it was thrilling. We left that load off and took a shipload of military wives to Hawaii en route back to Japan to pick up more POWs. That was in late 1945. We picked up another load of POWs in Nagasaki. While there, we were permitted to go in and take a look at what the atomic bomb had done. This was in September or October of 1945, not long after the bomb had been dropped. The people were still walking along the roadside of the bombed out area with masks over their faces, and they were still dying in the hospitals at the rate of 100 a day. What an unbelievable, unbelievable sight! You can't imagine such a thing. I remember seeing a barber chair standing upright in the middle of a totally devastated block. The site where Mitsubishi had built submarines was near the site of the explosion. There were steel-framed buildings, and they were all bent away from 'ground zero' and completely gutted; there was nothing on the outside of the buildings. It was devastating.

The only POW casualties we took from Nagasaki were the ones that were hit by food or clothing bundles that our people had dropped by parachute. Many POWs had been injured trying to catch them.

The men at Nagasaki also had beriberi, and we were able to handle them a lot differently than the ones at Wakayama. By then, we had become experienced in this thing. We took over a hotel when we moved into Nagasaki. We got a schoolteacher and several Japanese students to help us herd the POWs through a screening area, so that we could pick out the ones that were seriously ill and still walking. We also had to send out teams into the surrounding country to round up the guys who escaped from the POW camps. Of course that was no problem because the word soon got around, and in a matter of 3 or 4 days we had found all of the POWs. They all suffered from malnutrition but were of good spirit and of course glad to be aboard that hospital ship. They were in an air-conditioned ship with all the food they wanted and clean berths. They didn't care whether they were sleeping on the floor. A few did die.

We took a second group from Nagasaki to Guam and dropped them there, then took another group of POWs from there and brought them back to the United States. About Christmas time of 1945 I met Eddie Collins (Brewster), a Navy man, by accident on a street in San Francisco.

In August 1946 I left the *Sanctuary*, lived on board the *Cascade* (AD-16), and with six chief petty officers still on board we were preparing the *Sanctuary* for the mothball fleet. I stayed in the Atlantic Reserve Fleet until Christmas of 1947 going to 90 Church Street in New York City for three years. I was the only enlisted man while I was there on the staff. I married the secretary to Admiral Thomas C. Kinkaid, the Commander of the Atlantic Reserve Fleet and the Eastern Sea Frontier. In 1950 my son was born, and he later became an Annapolis graduate, a USMC officer.

I became an ensign in 1954 at St. Albans, New York. In 1967-68 I was XO-AO in a large Naval Hospital near a place known as Marble Mountain in Da Nang during the TET and May offensive. In 1979 I went to Headquarters Marine Corps for about a year. In 1980 I became the administrative officer at the Health Sciences Education and Training Command and stayed there until I retired as Captain in 1984.

I married Barbara L. O'Hara in 1942, and we had two children. Anne M. Vrablic was my second wife, and we had two children. In 1955 I married Janet Slater, and we had three children. Three sons served their country in the military.

Using the G.I. Bill I attended the University of Maryland and graduated with a B.S. in 1987.

Frankly, my career was not too exciting. I never did hear a gun fired in anger during WWII – and the same goes for the remainder of my time in the Navy.[68] [69]

The following medals were earned as an enlisted man:
Navy Good Conduct Medal, American Defense Service Medal, American Campaign Medal, Asiatic-Pacific Campaign Medal, World War II Victory Medal, Navy Occupation Service Medal, National Defense Service Medal

The following medals and citations were earned as an officer:
RVN Civil Action Unit Citation 7-67/7-68 (NSA, Danang)
RVN Service Medal 7-67/7-68 (NSA, Danang)
RVN Campaign 7-67/7-68 (NSA, Danang)
Navy Unit Commendation 7-67/7-68 (NSA, Danang)
Navy Commendation Medal 7-67/7-68 (NSA, Danang)
Joint Service Commendation Medal 8-68/7-70 (COMCPAC Staff)
Meritorious Service Medal 9-78/10-79 (NSHS Bethesda Staff)

Frederick W. Burdge

Fred lived on Putnam Terrace, son of Jennie and Fred Burdge. He was born on March 9, 1920 and attended Brewster High School. One day Fred got a fishhook stuck in his finger, but he didn't tell his parents. The finger swelled to twice the size and he had to go to Dr. Vanderburgh. It had to be lanced and two guys had to be brought in from the street to hold Fred down for the procedure.

As his father had, Fred enlisted in the Navy at 90 Church St. New York City on August 13, 1940 and took boot training at Newport, Rhode Island. After a two week leave, he was sent by train to San Diego to board a destroyer, the *U.S.S Mahan #DD364*. His first day at sea was not pleasant because of seasickness, but that was the only time in his six years in the Navy that he became ill.

His ship went to Pearl Harbor which was his homeport while in the Pacific. He chose to study for a gunner's mate which proved to be a very busy rank, especially after December 7, 1941. He was due to have leave to go home for Christmas 1941, but that did not happen. That Sunday, his ship was in port at Pearl Harbor. The Japanese were targeting cruisers, battleships and aircraft carriers. The *Mahan** and many other destroyers were able to get out of the harbor without being sunk. Before December 7th, Fred and his shipmates had instruction on Japanese planes and ships and how to identify each kind. They knew the Japanese were going to stir up trouble, but had no idea they would attack Pearl Harbor. It was almost two weeks, December 20th,before Fred's parents received a telephone call that Fred was fine. His family and his girlfriend (since June of 1937) said many prayers for his safety. Communication was not fast back then.

Being a gunner's mate and gun captain, he slept most nights by a 5-inch gun. If General Quarters was announced, he was at his battle station for whatever action was necessary against Jap planes. A Life Magazine photographer took a picture of Fred with the commander of the *U.S.S. Mahan*, Roger W. Stimpson, next to one of the guns showing credits of enemy planes brought down and ships sunk. Unfortunately those at home didn't know about the photograph, nor did they know whether it was used in the magazine. Their ship went into many ports in the Pacific to get supplies, and sometimes supplies were brought to their ship by another ship. Talking about the engagements he was in still brings tears to Fred's eyes. Although he doesn't remember all of the dates he was in the Battle of Eastern Solomons, the Battle of the Coral Sea, the Battle of Santa Cruz Islands and the Battle of Midway. He went to Brisbane, Australia, New Zealand, Marshall and Gilbert Islands, New Caledonia, Guadalcanal and the Fiji's. Fred feels lucky to have come through all the battles safely. In his travels he came across two Brewster friends, Dan Brandon on one of the South Pacific islands and Bill Pitkat on Hawaii. He of course received many V-mail letters from home.

Fred's last assignment as chief gunner's mate was in Hawthorn, Nevada where the largest ammunition depot in the U.S. is located. He was made chief of the shore patrol at that large Navy/Marine Base.

He was married July 29, 1945 to Janet Anita McNeill, a Brewster girl. They had a son and a daughter. He was on leave at his in-laws' home when the war ended and received his separation papers on August 13, 1946.

After discharge from service, Fred and Janet made their home in Poughkeepsie, N.Y. Fred worked at IBM in the testing lab, retiring from IBM in 1983. They sold their home at Hyde Park and moved to Sterling, Virginia.

*The WWII *U.S.S. Mahan* was later struck by the Japanese, but not sunk. The US Navy had to sink it because of its damage. Six were killed, and the rest of the crew was saved. In 1998 the Burdges were invited to Norfolk for a trip of 18 miles out to sea on the present *U.S.S. Mahan* # DDG71, a larger ship than the original as well as being an advanced missile ship.[70]

James P. Collins and Edward A. Collins

Edward and James Collins, twin brothers, were in the Brewster High School class of 1943 and both joined the Navy that year and served in the Pacific.

Schoolmates will remember Eddie with dark hair and Jimmy with red hair. Jim was the class vice president. From the 1943 yearbook, *Resumé*, under Eddie's name: "noted for dry humor and good nature...Jim's twin, but you wouldn't know it." Under Jimmy's name, " distinguished by red jacket and red hair...apparently serious but humor lurks beneath the surface".

The Collins boys served in the Navy on the West Coast of the US and in the Pacific Theater. Their older brother, Robert, was a Marine who fought on Bougainville and Guam in the Pacific In a letter dated October 10, 1944, Jimmy wrote to his brother Eddie: "Our mail is still trailing behind us somewhere, so I thought I'd better write before we shove off again. Things are still the same with me, no further news concerning Bob's death, not even a letter from Dad. I can't understand why either...Well, Eddie, I hope things are o.k. with you. I'll be praying constantly that no harm comes to you. I think I will get to where Bobby is buried – are you out that way? I am sending you a package, Eddie, not much; hope you get it o.k. ...God bless you, Ed., Your brother, Jim."

From a very early age, their older brother Bob looked after them, seeing that they had new clothes, went to mass and generally cared about them. Their father, Robert Collins was an engineer on the New York Central Railroad. Their mother had died when the twins were very young.

Ed was separated from the service in April 1946. He worked for Assemblyman Mallory Stephens in Albany, in advertising in N.Y.C. and for the N.Y.C. Watershed until his retirement. He married and had two children.

Jim worked for P. F. Beal & Sons in Brewster and for Eastern Pumps Supply. He married Millie Buck of Brewster, and they had three children.[71]

Richard Joseph Harmon

Richard was employed at the New York State Electric & Gas Corp., and in 1941 he married Cecelia Radzevich. Although he could have gotten a deferment from military service because of the nature of his work, he felt he had to go; so he enlisted in the Navy in 1943. They had no children at the time.

His wife had been living in Brewster with Richard's parents but went back to Danbury to live with her parents and found a job with the United States Navy Inspection Service at the Barden Corp.

After training at Newport, R.I, he was assigned to the *USS Brough*, a transport ship. He traveled to Liverpool, England transporting troops and saw duty patrolling in the Mediterranean. As Storekeeper, Richard's duties were ordering and dispensing all supplies on the ship. During a stop at a North African port, the sailors sold their sheets to the people for clothing who would cut holes in the sheets and slip them over their heads. Since fabric was hard to come by at that time, they were glad to have sheets to wear. The seas were apparently rough, as Richard was seasick about every time he went out. His ship returned to New York occasionally, and he would get a weekend pass. Ceil would go to New York when he was in port. Once a year he got a ten-day furlough and would come home.

The V-mail letters she received would not say much, just that he was fine and hoped they were all fine. Sometimes the censor would black out what he wrote. At one point there were twelve weeks between letters.

Their son was born November 16, 1945. Richard was discharged February 5, 1946 with the rating of Storekeeper 2nd Class. He was given the African Theatre Medal, the European African Middle Eastern medal and the Victory medal. After discharge he went back to work for the New York State Electric and Gas Co.[72]

Herbert Hazzard

Herbert Hazzard was a third grader when his family came to Brewster from Central Valley, N. Y. He graduated from Brewster High School in 1929 and married Marjorie Wilkinson of Brewster in 1931.

Hap, as he was called by all who knew him, was 34 years old in 1943 when he was drafted and was considered by some to be old for entering the service. He entered the Navy as an enlisted man. It was also the year his third son, Dick, was born. The baby was one month old when Hap was inducted in February of 1944 and five months old when he left for active duty. He was employed by the Metropolitan Life Insurance Company at the time.

Hap was stationed in Puerto Rico on limited service because he had poor eyesight. He was in Communications, Codes and De-codes. After nine months he was re-assigned to New York City. With three small children, it was helpful that Hap could get home on weekends.

Being so close to Brewster he often brought a young navy man home who lived in California. He was from a large family, and he enjoyed being in a home with children. He brought another service man home who was from Sault Sainte Marie, Michigan, also a long way from home.

Hap, having been drafted, received promotions and was discharged a Lieutenant Senior Grade. On his return home he went back to work for the Metropolitan Life Insurance Co. He also became involved in local politics being elected in Brewster for two terms as Supervisor for the Town of Southeast. Two of their sons, Dick and Dave remain in Brewster and operate Beecher's funeral parlor.[73]

Robert Heinchon

As kids we didn't know a lot about what was going on early in the war. How much did we care? Everybody was against Hitler, but nobody was doing anything about it. We needed something to kick us into getting involved. The Japanese did that. On Sunday, June 7, 1941, when WWII started for us in the United States, I was working with my father fixing a house in Pawling that my mother had inherited. A neighbor came over about 4 p.m. and told Dad the news. We quit work immediately and went home to tell Mom and a couple of friends that were visiting.

At this time I was a very poor student. As a freshman I just wasn't trying. I started to study a little harder because I did want to be a pilot. I took the subjects needed for this, mostly math.

Early in September of my senior year I took a test given at Carmel High for Officer Candidate School. In October or November I received a notice saying I had failed. A week or two later I received another letter stating that although I had failed the officer training test I had high enough marks to qualify for flight officer training. I had to go to New York City for the test and passed. The catch though was that I had to have a high school diploma by the time they called. Eddie Polverari, Bill Ives and I passed the regents exam in January. If your parents would sign you could go in early, and that was the problem – my father wouldn't sign. He said he wouldn't sign unless I had a high school diploma, so I got my diploma in January and then he signed. He didn't like it. Bill went into the Navy, Eddie went into the Merchant Marine, and in March of 1944 I went into the Navy. That same month I was called for the officers' program. I didn't know that some of my high school class had been released early, and it bothered me that Henry Alfke stayed, then went overseas and was killed before I even got out of the states.

My Navy journey started at Dartmouth College in Hanover, New Hampshire. In three months I was released on "Quota Restriction". That term was used and meant that the lowest half of the class failed, no matter what the student's marks were.

From there I went to Opa-Locka Naval Air Station in Florida, just outside Miami, for training as a gunner in the TBF – Torpedo

Bomber. I learned to operate the turret gun on a stationary platform, with shotgun attached, and shot skeet from that.

I was then sent to a torpedo squadron in Virginia and assigned to Torpedo Squadron 98. Just before we were ready to go overseas we were given tetanus shots which gave me an allergic reaction, and I spent several days in the hospital. When I was released, my squadron was gone. I was then sent to Gross Island, Michigan for another squadron but only as an ordinance man. While there I was sent to a new squadron in Florida that needed an ordinance man and a gunner. On my way to Florida V E Day came, and I was still in the United States. The squadron from Florida was sent for more training on the island of Maui, Hawaii at an air base high in the mountains between two volcanoes. I was an Aviation Ordinance Man 3rd Class. I was supposed to fly in the back seat of a torpedo bomber flying off a carrier as I was trained in the use of guns, bombs and torpedoes.

We were later transferred to Barbers Point, Hawaii, near Honolulu to go aboard the aircraft carrier *Independence*. This made me happy, because I knew Ralph Zecker was supposed to be on that ship. At this point our squadron was de-commissioned, and we all went in different directions. While at Barbers Point I went to the beach for the Navy, and to my surprise the officer in charge of the beach was Sterling Geesman, our Brewster coach.

My next assignment was on the island of Hawaii on the opposite side from Honolulu, and I was assigned to a PBM-Flying Boat group. I was a test gunner in these planes before they went overseas. While there I worked hard to go into action but with no success. Then V J Day came.

A short time after that I was sent to the *USS Atlanta CL104*, a light cruiser. I was assigned ordinance man work on the two SC1 planes on the catapults. A full complement of ordinance people on the ship should have been three men, but I was the only ordinance man on the ship that was assigned to aircraft. On the *Atlanta*, I was all over the South Pacific. We went to Guam, and were chased away by a typhoon. We then went to Saipan and put on shore with the planes. I was amazed at how small Saipan was. It is about a mile wide and two miles long. I learned to dislike morning glory plants there, when I realized how they protected the enemy in ambush. I wrote a poem while on Saipan which speaks of how I was thinking:

Out on Saipan, where the palm trees grow

And now there are Quonset huts row on row.

There is a soft and refreshing breeze
Always whispering through the trees.

The trees are tall and the coconuts big
Beneath the trees some men did dig.

The holes were dug to protect their lives,
For they were fighting for their country,
Their homes and their wives.

Many died here that we might stay free,
So let's keep the peace, both you and me.

I lived to see the peace treaties signed,
But peace treaties were far from my mind.

Peace treaties were signed not long ago,
But peace on earth did not long flow.

Let's win the peace as well as the war,
So that peace can reign for evermore.

Let's raise Old Glory high in the sky
For a country at peace shall never die.

From Saipan our ship went to Sasebo, Yokasuko and Nagasaki, Japan, only about two months after the A Bomb was dropped. I was able to see Tokyo and a lot of military bases. I believe that the A Bomb was absolutely necessary. If you had seen how they were dug in, you would know they were not going to surrender. I went into a cave that had been dug. The caves didn't need any reinforcement because of the clay-like type of soil. Way in the back of the cave I could see little airplanes, only they just looked little. They could have been airborne in no time.

When we went into Nagasaki harbor, it looked normal except for the two bomb craters. Nagasaki is a twin city, and when I went to the city on the other side of the mountain, it had been completely obliterated. We visited other cities. Our final stop in Japan was Tokyo. We left on a small communications ship, the *Comet*, the same ship that Harvey Van Derlyn had been on. We went to Tsingtao, China and eleven days later to San Pedro, California. From there I was sent to Lido Beach, Long Island, N.Y. and then was discharged.

A friend of mine, Roy Skinka, lived at Tonetta Lake, Brewster before the war. He was the son of German parents. He was visiting his relatives in Germany when the war broke out and was actually put into the German Navy in submarines. It was either "fight for us or die". He came back to the U.S. after the war. His parents still live in Brewster, but he lives elsewhere.

I worked in the insurance business for 21 years. I married Mary Lambea of Brewster in 1947, and we have two children.[74]

192

George J. Hinkley

I lived in Towners, N.Y. in 1940 on a farm, a foster home. We milked by hand 35 cows twice a day. The owner was Howard Sprague. Our day started at 4:00 a.m. I was paid $5.00 a month and room and board. My dad had died suddenly in 1935 at age 39. It was a tough time.

Henry Alfke was a neighbor and friend. We walked to the railroad station (about one mile) and took the train to Brewster with others for high school. Some of the other kids were Peggy and Betty Perkins, Marion Flint, Gene Brandon, Ernie Lee, Frankie and Philamina Ercole and Betty Barker. Some were from Dykemans.

I thought Brewster and Brewster High School were great. Mr. Watson (history), Mr. Graham (shop), Miss Hubbard (commercial), Mr. Truran (science) were special. I was only able to attend part of the freshman year due to a working situation. I met Irene in high school and I was doomed.

On December 7, 1941 I was seventeen and went to a movie, Swamp Water in Danbury with James Gaines, Irene's father. We went back to Irene's home to a surprise birthday party for me. The radio was on and President Roosevelt came on telling us of the Jap attack on Pearl Harbor.

I joined the Navy in Poughkeepsie on December 9, 1941 with four other fellows who were from Pawling. What great names: "Peanuts" Capaldo, "Turk" Hollister, Arthur "Art" MacNamara and Charles "Buster" Hinkley who was denied entry into the Navy because of bad teeth. I was the only one accepted at that time. I was told to report to 90 Church Street in New York City on December 19, 1941 and was sworn in again December 20, 1941. Boot camp was the Armed Guard Center in Brooklyn, N.Y. Starting pay in the service in 1941 was $21.00 a month. Many people never heard of us. We were called the "dungaree navy". (The Armed Guard was part of the Navy; men were put on merchant ships and freighters to man the guns in an attempt to ward off attacks from enemy submarines and airplanes. Duty was rugged in all respects.)

In August 1942 I sailed to Murmansk, Russia carrying vital supplies aboard *JLM Curry*, a Liberty merchant ship. We arrived Christmas Day. The *CURRY* and many of the returning ships of

Convoy RA-53 were sunk by submarines and planes in early March 1943. The hull of the *Curry* cracked as a result of the bombs that exploded nearby. The rough weather contributed mightily to this situation, and the ship had to be abandoned. All 64 crewmembers were safely removed. My friend, Harold ("Harry" or "Schiltz") Schultz of Milwaukee was the main man in a motor whale lifeboat taking survivors off the *Curry* to the English rescue ship. He was a great guy. I still miss him.

"The Murmansk run was hard on ships as well as men. The *SS JLM.Curry* broke up and sank in a 40-knot gale en route home after having fought her way in and using Sherman tanks carried as deck cargo for defense against air raids while waiting to unload. Finally heading back after several months in that frigid port, the *Curry* ran into such a severe gale that the hull cracked with a sound like gunfire, a common effect in hull cracking. The break continued, and the captain ordered the crew to abandon ship. The *Curry* was finally sunk by an escort, *HMS St. Elston.*"

My friend Harry Schultz and I were in one of the 30 ton Sherman tanks on the deck of the *Curry* firing the 37 mm gun at the German planes. We had little firepower on ships in 1942, so we took advantage of everything we had.

In June 1943 my ship, the *SS John Woolman*, a freighter, was anchored in the Bay of Aden, Arabia where the *USS Cole* was blown up in 2001. We sailors stood constant guard on guns and would have blown any "Bum" boat out of the water that was coming straight at our ship. Of course, we had discipline in my Navy.

In July 1943, still on the *Woolman*, we were at Gibraltar. Enemy divers were coming out to the anchored ships and placing bombs on the ships' propellers, all underwater of course. Five or six ships were damaged while I was there. We did not allow any strange boats near us, or we gave a burst of machine gun fire to keep them away.

In 1945 I was aboard the light cruiser, *USS Savannah*, off Newport, Rhode Island and subsequently was assigned to the Scouts and Raiders. It was two months of real tough training with the Frogmen. We were all set to go when the Japanese surrendered. I was discharged on December 10, 1945, my highest rating being Gunner's Mate 3rd Class.

I have never gotten over my ill feeling for the Japanese. In February 1945 my brother was killed by a Jap sniper after having been in infantry combat for nearly two years. He was in the 152nd

Infantry, 38th Division. I had some bad times and a lot of good times –
saw the world and met some really great people.

I am very proud to be able to say, I was there and served. Thank
God for Harry Truman – my favorite President who had the guts to
drop the bomb and end the war.

Completing the A.M.I.A. Insurance Program and becoming claims
manager for a large insurance company in Poughkeepsie and
Syracuse, N.Y., I later worked for myself as an insurance adjuster and
investigator, retiring in 1997.

I married Irene Gaines of Brewster, N.Y. in 1946 and we have two
children.

I was awarded the Scouts & Raiders Amphibious patch, the
European-African-Middle Eastern Campaign Medal with one
engagement star, WWII Victory Medal, American Defense Medal and
American Campaign Medal and a certificate and medal from the
Soviet Union for convoy duty to Murmansk, Russia.

Note: In December 1991 George Hinkley received a letter stating,
"On behalf of President M. Gorbachev I am honored and pleased to
inform you that you have been awarded the Commemorative Medal "
the 40th Anniversary of the Victory in the Great Patriotic War
(WWII). This award is a token of recognition of your outstanding
courage and personal contribution to the allied support of the people
of the Soviet Union who fought for freedom against Nazi Germany."
Signed: Viktor G. Komplektov.

While visiting Brewster High School in 1943 George was asked
to address the senior class about his wartime experiences.[75][76]

AMBASSADOR OF THE
UNION OF SOVIET SOCIALIST REPUBLICS
1125 SIXTEENTH STREET, N. W.
WASHINGTON, D. C. 20036

Mr.George Hinkley
6250 Rosevelt Blvd., Apt.76
Clearwater,Fl.34620

December 2Y.1991

Dear Mr.Hinkley:

On behalf of President M.Gorbachev I am honored and pleased
to inform you that you have been awarded the Commemorative Medal
"The 40th Anniversary of the Victory in the Great Patriotic
War (WW II)".

This award is a token of recognition of your outstanding
courage and personal contribution to the allied support of the
people of the Soviet Union who fought for freedom against Nazi
Germany.

Please, accept our heartfelt congratulations and wishes of
good health, well-being and every success.

Viktor G.KOMPLEKTOV

Enclosure: commemorative medal, certificate.

„СОРОК ЛЕТ ПОБЕДЫ
В ВЕЛИКОЙ ОТЕЧЕСТВЕННОЙ ВОЙНЕ
1941—1945 гг."

УЧАСТНИКУ ВОЙНЫ

УДОСТОВЕРЕНИЕ

Хинклей

Джордж Д

ВРУЧЕНА ЮБИЛЕЙНАЯ МЕДАЛЬ

„СОРОК ЛЕТ ПОБЕДЫ
В ВЕЛИКОЙ ОТЕЧЕСТВЕННОЙ
ВОЙНЕ 1941—1945 гг."

Президент
Союза Советских
Социалистических Республик

12 августа 1991 года

Gaetano T. Lotrecchiano

Life in Brewster before the war was beautiful. I had great friends in Brewster High School, great teachers and played in all sports. My cousins Pat and George Carlone and I went to every dance we could. I worked at the First National Store after school and summers. We walked everywhere, even from school to my home at 71 Carmel Avenue with my sister Anna for lunch. I was in my senior year at Brewster High School when Pearl Harbor was bombed. When war was declared Anna and I were at home having lunch when F.D.R. was on the radio telling the United States about Pearl Harbor.

The first time I got thinking about a world war was with Hal Watson, a great teacher. When Hitler was invading Europe, he put on the blackboard: WANTED: A BATTLEFIELD – Hitler wants to fight, but is looking for a place to fight. He wanted to take over Poland, the Netherlands, and Denmark which he did, but he's looking for a battlefield, because he doesn't want to fight in Germany. He knew if he started fighting in Germany the buildings would be destroyed and the cities. Sure enough, where did they start fighting? In the Sahara Desert. They fought big battles in Northern Africa. Harold Watson said Hitler was looking for a battlefield. The worst thing Mussolini did was to team up with Hitler.

Hitler created the blitzkrieg in Europe, and nobody was prepared for the lightning strikes in countries like Czechoslovakia and Poland. We didn't know what was going on. Then Japan attacked the U.S. at Pearl Harbor, Hawaii, and everyone was ticked off about that. Some of our Brewster High School boys left school early to enlist. My cousin George Carlone was one. He enlisted and got an early diploma. Just last year (2000) they honored the veterans at Brewster High School and gave each one a diploma – 60 years after the fact.

A funny thing happened. I was walking up Carmel Avenue, and who comes walking on the sidewalk toward me in Navy uniform but Fred Dickinson who later became our District Attorney. I told him I was thinking of enlisting, and he told me to first finish school which I had planned to do. Then he advised me to go into the Navy because "as long as your ship is afloat, you have a place to sleep, a place to eat, and you can always take a shower. Once in the field fighting, you're in foxholes, eating K rations, running out of food and water". He qualified that by saying as long as the ship is afloat you can wash, sleep and eat. So that's what I did. I waited and graduated in the class of 1942 with Betty Cleaver, Gabe Blockley, Roy Garnsey, John Santorelli and John Ross. I enlisted on April 30, 1943.

My basic training took place at Sampson Naval Base on Lake Geneva, N. Y. I was given a battery of tests, and the fact that the teachers in Brewster school made me study hard along with math and science classes I took saved my neck. In the preliminary tests that 1200 of us took, only 3 were chosen to go to Electronic Technical School – Radar and Sonar. I was one of them – because of my grades in math and science. Once those kids left basic they went right to a ship, whereas I was sent to Wright Jr. College in Chicago. There they had refresher courses for three months in math and science that pertained to the Navy. After that I spent four months at Oklahoma A. & M. (now Oklahoma State) learning more about radar and sonar equipment as an electronic technician.

In Oklahoma I had my first experience with oppression against the blacks. There were signs – NO NIGGERS ALLOWED. Water fountains – WHITES – NO BLACKS. The blacks couldn't drink from water fountains, and I couldn't fathom it. It was an experience unto itself. I wrote home to my teachers in school telling them I was having a tough time watching this happen. I didn't go out and protest. I saw them treated like animals. "No niggers allowed!"

In those days in the Navy we had two black people; one was a chef and one was a steward who waited on the officers. For me the only black person I had known was Helen Butler in my class. Her brother who used to pitch was four or five years ahead of me. He was black, so what was his nickname? Crow. He was black so we called him Crow. It didn't make any difference to me. I have his baseball glove which he gave me. He used to pitch ahead of me, and Freddie Dickinson used to catch the balls. I was just a kid. I used to watch them. Crow Butler gave me his pitcher's mitt. Can you believe it? I still have it. Aboard ship my two best buddies were the chef and the steward's mate. The people from down south treated them terribly. I treated them like a friend of mine. So what would happen is, on my watch from 8 – 12 p.m. or 12 – 4 a.m., the chef would bake bread, and hot out of the oven he'd cut it in half with all the butter we wanted. (People back home didn't have butter.) He'd put the butter on it and bring it up to me. It was like going to heaven. Hot bread with butter! He was my buddy. The steward's mate wanted me to go into business with him in North Carolina after the war. He was going to open a restaurant.

Then at Treasure Island in San Francisco I worked on the sophisticated new radar and sonar equipment. My job was to repair them. Is there anything better than living in San Francisco for a year? Then the coup d'etat. I went to the amphibious base because they were getting ready to go into Iwo Jima and Okinawa. I became electronic technician for LCS – Group 13 which consisted of 36 landing crafts support - little gun- boats with twenty-five personnel. I was in charge of all the radar and sonar on the 36 ships. I trained for that in Solomons, Maryland not far from Washington, D.C. It was there that I met Ross Beal who was back from North Africa. I knew he was at Fort Belvoir, and one of my buddies and I were invited for dinner at their house on the post. Mrs. Beal, Dodie and her little brother were there also.

We went to San Diego, California, where we caught our ships – Group 13. From there we stopped at Hawaii. It was sad to see the Arizona; I just cried. The guys were still entombed. I liked Hawaii so much – gorgeous people, gorgeous island. I still want to take my wife there.

They were fighting on Iwo Jima. On Okinawa our boats gave gun support for the troop landings. Phil Beal might have been right next to me, because the LCI 's, the LCS's and the LST's were right together. The suicide planes went after the destroyers, cruisers and battleships. The ones that were dangerous were the suicide boats. The Japanese hid in the caves, and at night two Japanese in each boat would come out and ram our boats. All the small LCS's would form a fence around the battleships, cruisers and destroyers at night, so the suicide boats would hit us with fewer men, rather than the large ships with many men. They sank quite a few of our boats and hit a couple of the big ones too. The scariest thing was when they came in at night with the Kamikazes. They knew where they were going. So what we did at night was make a fog. Each ship had a fog generator, and on the bay would be a huge fog, and they couldn't see the ships. We're generating fog with diesel fuel. I'm out there, and I'm gagging. We figured we're going to die one-way or the other. Every night when we made the fog; it was terrible. You'd get to the point where you would say, if they're going to hit me they're going to hit me. If you were paranoid about being hit, you couldn't do your job. So, I didn't get sick, and I didn't get hit. I lucked out both ways.

The B-29 bombers took off every night for Japan, and we knew where they were going. When they came back, we'd all clap, but not all of them came back. After we secured Okinawa, we were getting ready to go to Japan. We knew what was ahead of us. They dropped the two atomic bombs, and it saved our lives. It was like New Year's Eve in Times Square. It was so exciting! War was over. Our commander on our flagship told us, "We're going to splice the main brace". He took the booze out of the cabinet, and we all had a drink.

We didn't lose anyone on my ship, but we lost ships in our group. A couple of men got hit. One got stuck and couldn't get out of the passage. The ships were small. One guy got stuck in the porthole trying to escape. He was in the radio room when it got blocked off. He was chunky and got stuck. Portholes were small. That was sad.

We went to Japan and visited Nagasaki. The only building that wasn't flattened was the hospital. All around it was debris. The Japanese people there were great. They didn't want to fight. Let the leaders work it out.

My discharge was on December 29, 1946. I figured if I didn't get involved in college right away, I wouldn't go. So I enrolled at Columbia University for the spring semester and commuted. While I was in Columbia who did I hear from but Coach Geesman, our coach from Brewster High School. One day I was down at the Electro-zone Field playing in a game against Mount Kisco, and Coach Geesman came to watch me play baseball. I spotted him and went up to him and asked what he was doing there. He told me he wanted to talk to me. We had both come out of the Navy. He was in the V-5 program, trained at Ohio Wesleyan University, and he said they offered him a job as line coach for their football team. He told them he had a kid who just came out of the Navy who played football at Brewster High School, and he should be playing at Ohio Wesleyan. I told him I was going to Columbia at the time. He said he knew and that he had checked on me, and if it were okay with me he'd like to have me switch over to Ohio Wesleyan and start the coming fall. That's how I got out to Ohio Wesleyan in Delaware, Ohio.

I had a job tending bar and waiting on tables. Two blacks walked in and sat at the bar, so I served them. The boss came out and said, "No niggers in here". It was humiliating to them and to me. This was just north of Columbus, Ohio. I couldn't get over that. I took off my apron and I left. That was that. I played football on the Ohio Wesleyan football team. Those who didn't have the money for a ticket would sit on the bank of the railroad trestle. They were my rooting section. The guys had told them about quitting my job over what they were called. I introduced my grandson when he went out there to school. This black friend whom I had stayed in touch with befriended my grandson. When my grandson got married two years ago, he invited him to his wedding. He came up to me and hugged me. He remembers what I did.

I played football and golf in college and made the Hall of Fame in both sports - a little guy from Brewster. I started college at age 22; I was mature, older, stronger and married, not like a 17 year old. I married Louise Veschi June 8, 1947 in my sophomore year. School was easier having gone to school in service. I was there to learn something. I did go on the G.I. Bill. It paid all the tuition and a ninety-dollar a month stipend to live on. Anyone who didn't take advantage of it missed the boat. It wasn't just for college, but for trade school or for any vocation. Out of our school only two boys in our class went to college. It's a shame.

I taught school for four years and then bought a printing business in 1953, retiring in 1988. I went back to work for the Mahopac National Bank, chairman of the business division and am still active. Louise and I have four children.[77]

Francis C. Palmer

My father Henry Palmer and my uncle Edward Palmer had an ice business, which they had bought from Mr. Willis F. Hine around 1914. This included the icehouse at Tonetta Lake. They took ice out of the lake during the winter and stored it for selling the rest of the year. I worked from the age of about twelve. The taverns had to cool the beer down, and when the summer people came up we sold a lot of ice. Liquor was legal, and we sold ice to all the bars and restaurants. People would be sitting drinking their drinks, and as the ice melted they would see cinders appearing in their drinks. The New Haven Railroad ran along one side of Tonetta Lake, and when the railroad started running more trains that meant more cinders. That is when we gave up cutting ice at Tonetta. An ice plant was built on Carmel Avenue in Brewster, and they sold it to us cheaper than we could put it up. When that ice plant broke down about 1941, we started buying ice from the plant in Mount Kisco. They could see refrigeration coming in a big way, and they weren't going to repair the plant.

Until my freshman year I had been attending school at St. Lawrence O'Toole School and then moved over to Brewster High School. I had been working from the age of twelve. I had no choice in the matter. I had to work. It was my brother's and my job to go to Mt. Kisco to pick up the ice before we went to school. I did it three days a week, and my brother Dick would go three days. Before refrigeration came, the Palmer ice truck made deliveries to all the people in Brewster, and the kids loved running up to the truck and helping themselves to a piece of ice on a hot summer day. We got out of the ice business in 1944 after thirty years.

Because we had the property at Tonetta Lake I had privileges to swim at the pavilion next door, but I never learned to swim. I was little and hadn't started working, but every time I would go in the water one of the bigger kids would duck me when I got far enough out in the water. It scared me to death, so I never learned to swim.

We had cows, and one day my dad told me to go down and milk the cows. I'd say I don't want to milk the cows, but he'd say get down there. We sold milk for ten cents a quart at our house. One night the cow knocked the pail over on me, and I said!!! As an example, if I usually got ten quarts of milk and five were kicked over, I put water in it to make up the difference. Low fat milk before it became popular! A neighbor came over the next night while we were eating dinner. She said, "Mr. Palmer, the last milk we got was awfully watery."

There were many farms in the area, and the boys had to milk the cows before going to school. Some schoolmates would come to school smelling like the cow barn. While milking the cow, if the milker rested his head against the cow that was all you needed; you'd smell like the cow.

The school was closed for two weeks over Washington's and Lincoln's birthdays in 1942 or 1943. So the two Collins boys, Weizenecker, Dwyer and I went to work on the New England Railroad section gang. There weren't men around to work, so we told them we had quit school to work. It was about 20 degrees below zero.

I was a member of the class of 1944, but in 1943 I enlisted in the Navy and went to Newport Naval Training Station for boot camp. My mother picked up my war diploma.

We were given swimming tests, and I passed by bluffing. I could swim only a little, and when I would get to the end of the pool I was walking but stroking with my arms pretending to swim. Otherwise, I would have had to go every night until I learned how to swim. It wouldn't make any difference anyway because if the ship went down we wouldn't make it fully clothed and in icy cold water.

I started in Radio School, but they didn't allow me to continue because I was tone deaf. I couldn't dance because the rhythm meant nothing to me. Coach Geesman was the first to discover I was tone deaf, although a name wasn't given to the condition that gave me more problems than hearing tones incorrectly. When I was a freshman Coach was going to make me a quarterback of the future. When I called out the play numbers the players got all confused, and Geesman asked me what I was doing. I wasn't calling the numbers out smoothly; they were up and down. Everyone was jumping off sides. Coach asked me if it sounded good to me. It sounded good to me. So he changed the way I gave the signals.

Well, in the Navy they were going to court martial me because they thought I was giving them the "raz-ma-daz" to get out. They kept me there twelve weeks. It was all Morse code. I could type, could get good marks in theory, but the sound meant nothing to me. I didn't know enough about my condition to tell the Navy that there was a physical problem. I knew the Morse code, so they sent me to New York Harbor, and I learned how to read the sign light and got a rating as a Signalman. We'd stand watch at Ft. Schuyler in the Bronx, and the guy would sit there and practice sending me the light. I got so I could read it better than the 2nd Class Signalmen. The Chief told me he was going to leave in a few weeks, and he would see that I made Signalman Third Class. From there I went to Staten Island where all the shipping went in and out. In the signal towers we would challenge all ships that came into or went out of New York Harbor. There were three or four convoys a day out of New York, and we would challenge every ship with flags and signal lights. There are 80 or 90 different flags, and they would get hooked on a rope on the cross-arm. We had decks of cards to practice with, or you'd forget. That is different than semaphore which I also knew.

On their way out to sea the ships went by us, then the gate ship, by Sandy Hook and then Far Rockaway. If they didn't answer or give us the right flag, the right response, the coastal artillery would fire on them. We would put the messages on the Teletype machine and send them to the other six signal towers around New York. There was a signal tower in the arm of the Statue of Liberty, one at the Whitestone Bridge – Ft. Schuyler for the East River, Ft. Wadsworth on Staten Island for coming into New York Harbor, Ft. Hancock at Sandy Hook and at Far Rockaway. Convoys were made up in all the rivers including New Jersey – the North River and Hudson River. There would be 80 or 90 ships in each convoy. It was some sight! Each one would have about six destroyers. The Germans would sit out there in their submarines and try to sink them.

One day Norm Donley, Joe Karaffa and I were at Peach Lake. We were on Vail's side and were planning to paddle over to Bloomer's side to see the girls there. We were in a canoe. I knew I should not be in a canoe with Donley and Karaffa. We go over, but on the way back they started fighting and tipped the canoe over. I go down, and I'm screaming. I had my Navy uniform on. I was yelling help! help! Norm said, "Stand up, you dumb bunny, it's only two feet deep". I would have drowned in two or three feet of water.

One night we were riding around with the Regents papers. They were in a locked box, and Norm couldn't find the keys in the old man's house (his father, principal). So we had to go put it back. I don't know why I was there – I was out of school and in the Navy.

One of the busiest afternoons while I was on duty was when a German submarine came along side a ship which started dropping depth charges. We didn't know whether he had been hit. They would send some oil up so we might think we got the sub, and then he would turn around and get away. If we saw a lot of oil, we'd know he had been hit. Around 1943-1944 we got a good handle on it because of the development of sonar, but prior to that they were sinking many of our ships. They were having a field day.

On V-E Day I was in New York standing on the island at Times Square with two buddies from Staten Island. Someone picks me up and starts twirling me around. I said to my friends, "Get this drunken so-and-so away from me." It was Norm Donley. There must have been 100,000 people in Times Square, and he spotted me. He was in the Merchant Marines. His eyesight was bad and later lost his sight. But he made the best of it and got a lot out of life.

As soon as the war in Europe ended they took us off those bases, so in 1945 I was sent to California picking up a destroyer at Mare Island. I was getting heavy winter gear to fight the war from the Aleutians down. Then the war with Japan ended, and they sent us back to New York to decommission the ship.

In November of 1945 I was aboard the *Augusta*, a heavy cruiser. That ship had carried Roosevelt and Churchill to the North Atlantic Conference. It also took President Truman to Potsdam out of Baltimore. They said Truman was a real nice guy. He would go up on the bridge every day. Every guy on the ship loved him. King George was also on that ship. The *Augusta* used to play hide and seek with the German battleship, *Scharnhorst*. The *Scharnhorst* was trying to get out from the Netherlands, and once she would start out of the harbor the Allies would send naval ships and aircraft with a lot of gun power. The *Scharnhorst* would go back in. It never did get out. It would have done a lot of damage had it succeeded.

We carried troops over to England; then we'd go to Le Havre and pick up American troops and bring them home to New York. Every space on the ship was converted for sleeping. We got down off the Azores in a big storm, which split the bow of our ship. So, instead of getting the troops into New York on Christmas Eve, we got them to South Hampton, England. They were very disappointed.

I was two and a half years in the Navy, being discharged off the *USS Augusta* in May of 1946. My father insisted I go back to high school to get the credits I needed to graduate. I would be at school at nine o'clock. Jackie O'Brien's father got me a job at the roundhouse, and I'd work from 4 p.m. to 12 making sixty dollars a week. My teacher was making thirty-five dollars as a college graduate. After I finished high school I gave up the job and went to work for Brewster Plumbing, owned by Henry Hughes and Louis Furio. Then I started my own plumbing business called F.C. Palmer Co. We still run it. Bill Macomber, my brother Dick and I had an oil business as well. In 1949 I married Helen Brandon, a Brewster girl. We have six boys.[78]

Joan Ross Beal Peckham

Joan loved Brewster, and of course that meant the people of Brewster. She had a good childhood, but like so many others it was spent during the Great Depression. She was the middle daughter of Florence and Ross Beal; these girls weren't aware of any deprivation. The children wore hand-me-down clothes as well as rompers and dresses their grandmother skillfully made. There were home movies of themselves swimming and ice skating, and then there was the radio. There were fresh vegetables from their Grandfather Beal's large garden as well as strawberries, apples of several varieties and grapes. Hoboes who came to the back door were fed. While at their summer cottage at Tonetta Lake they watched freight trains go by which often carried hoboes. But summer life at the lake couldn't have been more perfect for a child; and this particular child learned to love the water, playing games with her sisters and swimming three times a day in warm temperatures. She was a tomboy, and when the three girls wore their Sunday dresses she would have a large pink bow clipped to her short hair. Her mother thought this might help, but often found the ribbon askew after Joan ran outdoors. She was constantly moving.

When adolescence came, her mother wasn't prepared for all the issues that would present themselves. Joan was a very bright child and had to be challenged more than most in her classes. Rightly or wrongly she was made to skip a class in the fourth grade, putting her with older children. Her childhood sweetheart was Jackie O'Brien, a popular young man who was also one of the Brewster High School's finest football players and liked by everyone who knew him. Sadly, he was killed in action in April of 1944. Joan went to boarding school for her last two years of high school, and it is certain she would rather have remained in Brewster because that is where her heart was.

Joan wanted intensely to become a nurse She often sat in on medical discussions between her mother and grandmother MacLean who was a nurse. She started the nursing program at Danbury Hospital but after a few months was washed out, undoubtedly more to do with her way of doing things rather than her abilities or intelligence. Joan then studied at Katherine Gibbs and found an excellent position in New York City.

By this time World War II was on, and men and women were signing up or being drafted into service. Her father joined the Army in 1942 and in a short time was on a convoy to North Africa with the invasion forces. In a letter to her dad she told him of her wish to join the WAVES. His response was an emphatic request that she wait until he returned to the United States before joining. Having great respect and love for her father she honored his request.

Joan took a secretarial position at the Sikorsky plant in Bridgeport. She reported seeing an experimental airplane that she said looked like a wing and was undoubtedly an early prototype of the Air Force airplanes of the 1990's. She enjoyed her work there but was biding her time until she could "join up".

It was early 1944 when her father returned because of a back injury incurred while serving in Sicily. She then joined the Navy as a WAVE, took her training at the Great Lakes Naval Base and subsequently served at the St. Albans Naval Hospital on Long Island and Alameda Naval Hospital in California as a Corpsman.

She did nursing work, taking care of the badly burned and maimed Navy men who were fresh from battle. While at St. Albans Naval Hospital one of her patients was John (Butch) Santorelli who's LST had been struck by a torpedo at Normandy in June 1944. It was an annoyance to her that there were some sick sailors who complained, but as she said only had the sniffles, when there were so many seriously injured sailors who needed attention. While in California she ran into several Brewster boys, one being Edward Collins who was in the Navy. Joan was slated to be sent to the Pacific Theatre when the war with Japan ended.

After serving in the Navy, Joan worked at the Mahopac Emergency Hospital and later became the office nurse for Dr. Robert Eliot in Brewster. She became a member of The Polar Bear Club in Maine, served as chairman of The Putnam County American Cancer Society and later while living at Tonetta Lake taught canoeing, lifesaving and water safety for The American Red Cross. One of her great interests was the water safety of young children.

She married Paul E. Peckham who spent many post-war years in the Army. They had two children. Because of his assignments, they spent several years living in Europe. She spent her last years on the shore at her beloved Tonetta Lake.[79]

Robert Bernard Pitkat

Robert Pitkat was born on November 13, 1923 in a farmhouse on Drewville Road in Brewster, N.Y. to Mr. William C. Pitkat, Sr. and Mrs. Gertrude Meade Pitkat. The family moved to Hillcrest Avenue, Brewster in 1930 and Bob attended St. Lawrence Catholic Grade School. After graduation in 1937 he went to St. Mary's Catholic High School in Katonah, N.Y. and graduated June 21, 1941. "I reached my eighteenth birthday November 13, 1941 and became subject to the draft. The United States entered World War II on December 7, 1941 (Pearl Harbor Day)".

From January 7, 1942 to September 7, 1942 he was working as a brakeman for the New York Central Railroad after which he volunteered for service in the U.S. Navy. He took his boot training at Great Lakes Naval Training Station and upon graduation was shipped to San Francisco, California for assignment. "I was assigned to the *U.S.S. Rixey APH-3*. This ship was commissioned into the U.S. Navy on December 30th 1942. I was to serve my entire World War II service in the Communications Division of this ship".

The *U.S.S. Rixey* was a combination fighting ship and a life-saving hospital ship, which was "an experiment in naval ship types." She was designed to carry men into battle and to treat men carried from the battlefield who needed medical attention. Robert Pitkat participated in four invasions, the ship carrying fighting men ashore and then waiting offshore to treat those wounded men. Pitkat's ship carried patients, P.O.W.'s, ammunitions and other needed items of war.

After two years and three months Bob returned on the ship to the U.S., but before long they "joined the 5th Amphibious Forces for their first assault invasion" participating in the invasion of the Mariana Islands. The ship landed Marines on Guam and waited, treating the wounded. "For her work at Guam the ship was commended and Commander (now Captain) Philip H. Jenkins, USN of Annapolis, Maryland, skipper since November 1943, was awarded the Bronze Star". On October 20, 1944 Bob's ship successfully landed assault troops on Leyte, the Philippine Islands. The physicians and other medical personnel skillfully treated troops as the severely wounded men were brought aboard. The Japanese Kamikaze planes attacked, exploded and caused many burn patients. On October 22 the

U.S.S.Rixey left Leyte Gulf transporting patients to the Admiralty Islands, only to return to Leyte from New Guinea with units of the 11th Airborne Division aboard. More patients from the battle of Leyte Gulf were brought on board for treatment. The *Rixey* continued carrying invasion troops from various places to the designated South Pacific islands, treating patients and sending them on for further treatment elsewhere.

Apparently the *Rixey* was a lucky ship, just missing a torpedo here and a Kamikaze airplane there. When the Japanese put into operations a new form of suicide attack, a picket boat would patrol around the ship to guard against suicide boats and swimmers carrying explosives.

The *Rixey* joined a small force headed for Koram Retto "a group of small islands 20 miles west of the main target, Okinawa." The purpose was to secure "an anchorage and seaplane base for use in the battle for Okinawa." Koram Retto was taken from a small garrison of Japanese "three days after the Easter Sunday landings on Okinawa."

Robert Pitkat participated in still other battles while their medical teams continued treating the wounded and saving lives. After over two years, Robert Pitkat returned to San Francisco where the ship was to be overhauled. "Credit for *Rixey's* achievements goes to her skippers. And to all the officers and men who manned her...".

Robert Pitkat served as Radioman 3rd Class on the *U.S.S. Rixey* from the time of its commission to the end of World War II (3 years, 3 months, 6 days).

"I returned to work for the New York Central Railroad in January 1946. I married Shirley Lee Cunningham the daughter of Mr. Joseph F. Cunningham and Mrs. Genevieve Maroney Cunningham" of Brewster. "We had four children.... I retired from railroad service on July 1, 1987....and moved to Ocala, Florida. We celebrated fifty years of marriage." Shirley is no longer living. "I continue to live in Ocala." [80] [81]

William C. Pitkat, Jr.

I was born September 24, 1921. When I was eight years old, our family moved from the farm in Drewville (Brewster) to Hillcrest Avenue. The farm however remained in the family. During the summer my friends and I spent all our time at Tonetta Lake where the town park is now. We would walk up what is now Pump House Road and then walk the railroad tracks. Not having ten cents to swim at the pavilion at the other end of the lake we would swim at Brown's dock. Before I was old enough to work we used to go up there every day in the summertime. It was beautiful around here. At that time it was a hobo jungle. The New Haven Railroad tracks ran fairly close to the water, and the hoboes would ride the freight cars; sometimes we would see women, both black and white, carrying babies.

Near Brown's dock there was a big, flat rock anchored on the shore with a shelf. These guys used to wash their clothes there. Up in back they had a pretty good-sized fire and tin cans lying around. They used a couple of pieces of builders' marker line, a chalk marker, strung the twine between the bushes and hung their clothes on it to dry. They had holes in their shoes and would cut out cardboard to put inside them.

These men would talk intelligently to us and tell us stories of where they had been on their travels. Remember when you could buy Wings cigarettes? We had our own name for them, because they weren't the best. We'd go to the store on Railroad Avenue, down near Abe Diamond's place. We'd take empty bottles back to the store and get five cents and buy a pack of Wings for ten cents. When you bought a ten-cent pack of loose tobacco there was a packet of papers inside for rolling cigarettes. There were small cigarette-rolling machines, and we learned to roll a cigarette, and then lick along the edge of the paper. We'd give four or five cigarettes to the hoboes.

The New Haven Railroad ran through here with flat cars and coal cars. They used to come around the curve in north Brewster too fast, and the train would jump the tracks. The coal would spill out of the cars, and everybody would go down and fill up bushel baskets and bags with the blue coal. They picked up coal for the next ten years. There would be cops along the tracks. That was originally the old Putnam Division that ran from New York up to High Bridge, Westchester, Putnam, Crafts, Mahopac and Yorktown. When they built as far as Brewster, they ran out of money. The end of the line was at Andy Durkin's coal yard. The New York Central took that over. The old timers would come up from New York, be brought by horse and buggies from an old time livery stable and get on the New Haven which at that time had passenger service as well as freight service. This would take them to the Danbury Fair, an extravaganza.

When I was seventeen years old and going to St. Mary's School in Katonah, I worked odd jobs and one of the jobs was at the Grand Union after school. I'd get off the train and work from four to six earning fifty cents for the two hours. Regular employees got eighteen dollars a week. Some chain stores only paid fifteen dollars a week. On Saturday I worked at the butcher's department and had to be down there at 7a.m. I had a lunch period and a break in the evening. The store closed at 9 p.m. I averaged about $1.50 all that time. Bread cost 7 cents and chopped meat, three grades, was 19 cents a pound and up to 20 and 29 cents a pound for the best grade. Fresh milk was cheap – 10 cents a quart if you went to the farm. We had people like Burdick who would come around delivering vegetables, the old truck loaded with all kinds of produce.

The milk was delivered, and when you got up in the morning, the cream would be up at the top. It was not pasteurized. Nobody ever heard of homogenization. You'd better not get caught skimming off cream. Some guys would come to our farm and skim off the top of the cans, and when the dairy sent back the report on the milk, they'd want to know why the butterfat was coming down. I won't tell you who did it; they weren't people who worked at the farm. Everybody knew everybody else around here. There was a certain amount of trust, but it might not always work out that way. You might have some friends who liked the good thick cream in their coffee.

We had to be eighteen with our parent's signature to get into the Navy. So after graduating from St. Mary's in 1939, I figured I'd join. My father was in World War I, and I had two uncles in the Navy and one in the Coast Guard in World War II. I remember riding on the train where I liked to read the daily news. Well, inside the paper in the upper right hand corner of one page there was a very small notice. It said Roosevelt is looking for I think it was 50,000 volunteers to sign up for six years in the Navy. And it went on to say his two-ocean navy was becoming a reality which would eliminate the necessity of going from one coast to the other by way of the Panama Canal. The ships being built were being launched, and they needed crews to fill them. So I thought that looked pretty good. I worked all summer at odd jobs. After my birthday I was working at the Grand Union, and a couple of guys wanted to go deer hunting up in the Catskills in October before I went into the navy. So I went. On my return Dr. Cleaver sent me to Danbury Hospital to have my appendix removed, and I was home until after New Years.

Shortly after January 1940 I went to the recruiting office in White Plains. The officer talked to the chief as they were poking around my side asking me how I felt. After some routine eye tests I was told to go down to the Federal Building in New York. Other fellows were trying to get in also. I stayed down there all day while they went over us from head to toe. I thought that was the final physical. We went out to eat around the corner and had a good meal which we paid for. In the afternoon they got us all together and told us to go home. We would be notified within thirty days, and be told when to report. So I came back to Brewster. It was not more than two to two and a half weeks when I got a little white government card asking whether or not I would appear at seven o'clock in the morning at the Federal Building in New York. I checked it and sent it back. It was the end of January, and my father and I got up so I could take the first train out of Brewster at 4:14 a.m. It got us to Grand Central in time to get to the Federal Building by 7 a.m. I spent all day there going through the whole physical, the same thing I had gone through two weeks earlier - but they took us out to eat. We came back around three in the afternoon. It was time to be sworn in. An officer came in and told us once we swear allegiance and take the oath we would be in the Navy for six years. Then he said if anyone thinks he doesn't want to be in now is the time to speak up. There weren't too many of us, and no one raised his hand. They lined us up and marched us around the corner to the same restaurant. Around seven in the evening they marched us down to the waterfront where we were put on a day liner to Providence, R.I. overnight.

Another fellow and I were standing on the deck looking at the chunks of ice banging off the hull. We were on the way to the Navy. We got to Providence and were picked up by bus and taken to the Naval Training Station the very last day of January 1940. They took us into a big room with a lot of doctors where we stripped down and were given another physical examination. We were then assigned to a barracks and put in Company G. There were men from Boston, a couple from Vermont and New York, but the whole two months I was there we did not have a full company. I don't think we ever filled out a hundred men. It was dead of winter and bitter cold up along the Narragansett Bay. I was eighteen; some were a little older. We were assigned a chief petty officer. These chiefs were the head honchos and one had been in an Army National Guard outfit, but they were all right. They seemed to have a competition amongst themselves to see who could have the best outfit.

In the dead of winter we didn't go outside because there was so much snow. They had massive drill halls where we had physical training and were tested to qualify in swimming. I could swim very well because of all the swimming I did at Tonetta Lake.

In Newport we lived on the old sandwich ship at the end of training, and then we were put in the SEA detail waiting around to ship out. We never did have two companies – not even two hundred men. They sent us to Philadelphia where we were assigned to the *USS Dixie AD 14*, a brand new 9,000-ton Destroyer Tender built at Camden, New York Shipbuilders. The sister ship, the *USS Prairie* stayed on the east coast and burned in Argentia Bay, New Foundland while tied up to the pier.

Our ship was put in commission and stayed along side the pier while it was being loaded which took a good three weeks or more. I thought we would never get it filled up. A nice old gentleman (old to me) who was the representative of the N. Y. Shipbuilding Co. stayed aboard all the way to the west coast.

We went to Norfolk, Virginia and loaded up with ammunition and then to Newport, R.I to the naval torpedo station and loaded up with torpedoes. From there we went to Camden, Maine where they had a calm harbor and had it all set up with what they called the "measured mile". They wanted to see what the ship could do, so they would get the ship underway and build up speed; they would maneuver from port to starboard or forward to reverse. We stayed there a day or so, then came back to Boston. We went back to Norfolk and then to the Caribbean. July 4, 1940 we were in Guantanamo Bay, Cuba, where we made a landing force drill. It was really hot down there. We got underway on a shakedown to San Juan, Puerto Rico, Dominican Republic and eventually went through the Panama Canal. We went to San Diego, then to San Francisco and up to Mare Island Navy Yard above San Francisco. It was an old yard, and ships became too big for the dry dock there. They built good submarines and good small ships there at Mare Island.

We went back to San Francisco, where the Japanese were still able to get oil. It was summer, the latter part of July 1940. I looked around, and I said this place is loaded with Japanese merchant ships – oil tankers. We were moving slowly amongst these tankers, and I can remember up on the bridge I could see two officers who had white uniforms on. I thought for merchant marine they looked pretty spiffy. One guy had a pair of binoculars. They were busy. They couldn't stand still. I think they may have been more than merchant ships. One fellow had a big pair of binoculars and kept looking at us. The other one kept looking in the chart house bringing out an identification book. They may not have had anything about our ship because it was a brand new ship. They probably reported back and may have had someone else somewhere taking pictures. The place was filled up with Jap merchant ships.

We got underway and went to Pearl Harbor, Hawaii. When we arrived there, we got a place in the middle lock by the airfield and anchored. They would have two buoys, and we would hook up to the buoy off the stern and the bow. The port side was the working side. We'd have five destroyers on one side of us all the time, day and night. They'd come in from sea for three weeks for what they called tender time and get work done that wouldn't require them to go all the way over to the naval yard and tie up to dry-dock. We used to see them get underway back out in the channel. Then about eight in the morning you'd see another group coming in. They'd start coming alongside, and we would have another five ships. Whatever work they needed to have done, they'd have their people over for the various departments: gunnery, torpedoes, boilermaker, etc. I was a machinist mate.

We left September 1941 for Mare Island Navy Yard. They wanted to take a good look at our ship because it was the first of its class. So when we were there we were given 90 days yard time. We had people on leave all over the US. When Pearl Harbor was bombed on December 7, 1941 all the men on leave had to report back. After January 1942 we went down to a good-sized pier near San Francisco. Because of the threat of Japanese sub-marines entering our coastal waters and destroying our ships, torpedo nets were put behind the ships and the pier. Some destroyers came all the way from the east coast to have work done. We'd take them alongside and do whatever was necessary. In early April of 1942 we got underway for Pearl Harbor and tied up at our original spot. Some ships came in for repair, but most were out; it was during the battle of Midway in June. We went to general quarters and battle stations for quite a while until we got the word that everything was clear. They didn't know whether they were going to be able to hold them off, and the next stop would be Pearl. I might have ended up in a Japanese prison camp. With the amount of ships they had they could have steamed right in. If we hadn't gotten rid of those Jap aircraft carriers, it would have been a totally different story. I stayed there until July 1942.

They were looking for several firemen from our division to be sent to Naval Pier, Chicago for diesel school. From Pearl I went by transport to the west coast, then by train to Chicago. We were given seven days leave. The school was to be two to three months, but after a little over two months I was sent on July 14 to Miami. There was to be a new operation called SCTC or Sub Chaser Training Center - more training, swimming tests, etc. We were in a large downtown Miami hotel called Everglades Hotel. It had been cleaned out including the carpeting, and bunks had been installed. Later we went to a smaller hotel down near the Navy pier where they put all the engineers. They loaded us on a truck and took us to the Miami Police Department Firing Range for the day.

One day we were in the lobby of the hotel, and a chief who had a clipboard in his hand asked, "Do you want to go on a DE?" We didn't know what a DE was. It was a brand new type ship, a destroyer escort. We all signed right up. When we were organized we got on a train heading west, and it took eight or nine days pulling off on sidings as other trains went by. The food was good; we went first class. We arrived at the barracks on Mare Island November 1942 before the holidays. The ship was being built, so we were just hanging around. The ship was finished and commissioned the *USS Brennan DE 13*, destroyer escort. We went on a shakedown cruise to San Diego for six weeks of training, chasing old subs. From there we went through the Panama Canal to the Sub Chaser Training Center in Miami. Our ship was turned into a training ship for officers. We'd go out for most of a week, come back, take on a new group and go out for another several days. Our captain, chief engineer, chief quartermaster, machinist mate and I were sent to the Boston Navy Yard to put another DE in commission. It was the *USS Steele DE-8* named for a marine killed in the Pacific. We then went to Bermuda for a six week shakedown and training. From there we went to Boston, then down the east coast and through the Panama Canal and across the south Pacific to Bora Bora and to New Caledonia Naval Base to refuel.

We became part of a convoy headed for Guadalcanal and Tulagi in the Solomon Islands patrolling for submarines around the islands. We started to have trouble with the strut on the shaft on the port side; the weld on the hull didn't hold, and it started to leak; we had to bale out water. So we were transferred off the ship to go back to the Sub Chaser Training Center in Miami. In July 1944 we were to go to a newly commissioned ship at Mare Island Naval Yard, the *USS Connolly, DE 306.* From there we went back to Hawaii in January 1945 and joined a big convoy for the invasion of Iwo Jima. The DE's had long hulls, over 300 feet, 20 mm AA guns, three torpedo tubes and four 3-inch guns. Nobody liked them, because they didn't have enough power. We had to go down to the New Hebrides. There were a large number of DE's in that convoy, and we were tied up for about a week. The 27th Infantry Division was one group that boarded our ships. We proceeded to go north toward Guam, headed for Okinawa. One early morning going along by Guam and Saipan we saw ships coming down, and I heard my name called out over the load-speaker to go up on the bridge. And low and behold it was my brother Bobby's ship, an APH Hospital Evacuation Ship, the *USS* Rixey. He was a radioman, and he sent a message. One time both our ships were anchored together, and we were able to spend some time with each other.

We were to be at Okinawa D Day + 9 to bring reinforcements. Then we got assigned to the anti-sub station. There were air raids night after night with kamikaze's, hundreds of planes. The ship in the next station to us got hit. That was the day that Ernie Pyle got killed on the beach by a Japanese sniper on Ie Shima. Later they sent us into the China Sea. There were a lot of floating mines, so it was a bad place for ships. That's where we almost got it. We had heavier guns on our ship by then. We shot a plane down, and when it became light we came upon a raft. Those in it were waving, and when we got close we found they were Japanese aviators. Their raft was painted with rays so that from the air it looked like the rising sun. One of the men was dead; we took him aboard, they wrapped him up and put him on a board. The captain came down with a bible and read some prayers. He was buried in a dignified manner even if not in his own religion – he was treated better than many of our guys. The two others were alive. We took one aboard. Five men won awards for jumping down and taking them aboard. The commanding officer on the raft jumped off and just swam away. The old man wanted the raft, so they got it on board and stuck it away. I climbed up where I could see the man who had swum away from his raft. He would swim a little, then dive under, then swim and dive under. He finally went down for good.

We were sent to the Philippines and while there the war ended. Everyone was shooting from the ships. I got out of there; I didn't want to be hit after the war ended. There was a Japanese ship that had been intercepted; it appeared to be a hospital ship, but on investigation they found it was carrying other things like explosives on board. It was interned there.

We got underway and went to Pearl Harbor. There were DE's everywhere we looked. We went to Los Angeles, Santa Barbara, through the Panama Canal to Mississippi for Navy Day. We ended up in Charleston, SC at the Navy Yard where they decommissioned our ship. They had a three-section leave party; spare parts had to be labeled. The DE's were being cut apart and the metal and parts recycled for washing machines and other appliances. They removed the GM engines and took them back to General Motors to be rebuilt and resold as new.

I got 30 days leave in November 1945. Christmas night I had to go down to Brooklyn Navy Yard, because I still had a couple of months to put in. From there I was sent up on the Hudson, then to Staten Island for two or three weeks. On Long Island they had a mustering out station, so I went out there, and in 72 hours I was out.

On June 14, 1953 I married Veronica Vassak of Brewster. We had one child.[82]

Farrell Reed

My Brewster High School class was 1944; however I enlisted in the United States Navy on August 18, 1943. My father picked up my diploma for me, but I actually ended up with two war diplomas. Boot camp was in Newport, Rhode Island. From there I went to Norman, Oklahoma for 21 weeks Aviation School. When I graduated I went to Naval Aviation Gunnery School for five weeks in Purcell, Oklahoma. From there I was sent to Pee Vee Ventura Bomber School for five weeks, then two more weeks for Aviation Radar Operator OTU in Lake City, Florida and from there to Squadron 1-14 Fleet Air 14, Buford, South Carolina for five weeks Air Gunnery School. I learned to study in these schools. There we received our Combat Air Crew Wings. We formed an Operational Squadron for the South Atlantic and Caribbean sub patrol operation from Naval Air Station Boca Chica to Gipmo Naval Air Station, Cuba.

While in Florida I met Lt. Commander Sterling Geesman, our coach in Brewster High School. We had a great talk about football, sports and Brewster.

We were in a big gin mill in Nevada one night, and we ordered five drinks for the crew from the bartender. Our top gunner was Native American. The bartender served us four drinks and said, "he doesn't get one". We knew why. One of our crew stood up and asked, "any crewmen in here?" Everyone stood up. Then the bartender gave us the fifth drink. It was a great crew and pilot.

After sub patrol we were sent to North Island Naval Air Base in San Diego, California. A few days there, and we were sent to VPB 198 Operational Moffit Field, California Fleet Air-8. I met Tom Jones from Brewster in California, and we had a good time. From there I went to Woodbie Island Naval Air base en route to Hawaii and New Guinea. While in Hawaii I met Eddie and Jim Collins, and we had a ball. I then went to Port Morsby, New Guinea, also Naval Air Station Newina and Green Island. We flew patrol, bombing and strafing missions over the Carolinas and Gilberts, Nauru Islands, Truk and Rabaul in the North Solomon Islands from land bases. The twin-engine Ventura, King Baker was one of the best airplanes and the best bomber in the Navy. We patrolled every day looking for ships and submarines. Had good liberty in Darwin. I love those Aussies.

On May 7, 1946 I was back in Shoemaker, California, some happy. I received my Naval Air Combat Air Crew Wings. They count.

Back home I went to work for New York State Electric and Gas as a lineman – was sent to Boone College in New York. I retired as a Supervising Foreman of Districts in Pawling, New York and Bedford Hills, New York.

In 1946 I married June Jenkins of Brewster. We divorced in 1974. I married Marie Fournier of Au Sable Forks, N.Y on April 12, 1975. I have no children.

I was happy to serve in the United States Naval Air Arm as a Crew Chief, Air Gunner Amm 3/C, and would do it again.[83]

Peter A. Tavino

Peter was also known when he was young as Pietro, to distinguish him from his cousin. He enlisted in the Navy on October 25, 1943, took his boot training at Sampson Naval Base, N.Y. and was assigned to Landing Crafts, specifically an LSM, (Landing Ship Medium) which was smaller than an LST.

Peter took part in the landings of Iwo Jima, and he states that he was too young to know fear. War's end found him in San Francisco.

In 1951 he married Beryle Delage and had six children. For a time he was a chef, and then he went into real estate, buying and selling houses and apartments.[84]

James M. Terwilliger

Jim or "Twig", as his friends called him, grew up in Brewster and attended Brewster High School. When the announcement of the attack on Pearl Harbor came he was with his friends, the Palmer boys and the Murtha boys at the Palmer farm on Peaceable Hill.

On September 8, 1944 at the age of seventeen, he enlisted in the U.S. Navy and went to boot camp at Sampson Naval Base in New York State. While in boot camp he crossed paths with another Brewsterite, Joan Beal, who was beginning her service as a WAVE.

As Aviation Machinist Mate 3rd Class he maintained the PBY two engine Navy Flying Boats which patrolled the waters off the coast of Texas looking for enemy submarines. He went on patrol now and then.

Jim was in service from November 1, 1944 to August 5, 1946 when he was discharged at Lido Beach, L.I., N.Y. When the war ended he was at NAS Corpus Christi, Texas.

When Jim returned to Brewster, he worked for P.F. Beal & Sons, Inc., New York Central and spent thirty-five years with New York State Electric & Gas, retiring as Chief Lineman in 1985. On February 4, 1954 Jim married Bette Fournier of the Bronx who had spent many summers at Tonetta Lake. They have four daughters. They now live in Florida.[85]

Vincent Vanaria

My mother died in 1933, and in 1937 I had to leave school and went to work for Brewster Ford. My friends and I decided to drive to the 1939 World's Fair on Long Island in an International Truck. It was really an open passenger car with brass, gas headlights and with the shift on the steering wheel. Someone gave us license plates to use for that occasion, and people were taking pictures of us. It was quite a spectacular sight.

I left my job and joined the Navy as an apprentice seaman in October of 1941. Boot camp was in Rhode Island, after which I had a two-week leave. I was there on December 7th, Pearl Harbor Day, awaiting orders. On graduation day, if the Chief Petty Officer didn't get the honors for the best group, he'd be awfully mad. Five years in a row our CPO won. He was in the navy 20 years.

I was transferred to Ford Motor Co. in Detroit for schooling in aircraft engines and was there four months. I graduated as Third Class Petty Officer. After four months I was transferred to Puerto Rico Naval Airbase for seven months tower duty. I was then transferred to Hangar Deck, and my first job was to paint the admiral's airplane. So, I took a bunch of boys, and we painted the plane in blue here and gray there, camouflaged, as the admiral wanted it. An enlisted man piloted the admiral's twin engine Lockheed which carried about 25 to 30 people and had upholstered seats along the side. The admiral would go from one island to the other. The Chief Petty Officer told us if any of this paint flew off, we were in trouble. He gave us a little scare. It could happen because it was fresh paint, but we took it up and flew it around. It was fine.

Ten days later I was transferred to Class B School in Chicago for aviation engines about which I was already knowledgeable because of all the cars I had worked on. I married Patricia Hertha in February 1943 in Chicago. After three months I was transferred to a newly formed squadron VF-32 and was put in charge of nine torpedo bombers (TBF). Another fellow had charge of nine fighter planes. In June or July of 1943 we were ordered to Philadelphia and assigned to the *U.S.S. Langley* CVL27 which had been a cruiser converted to a flattop.

We went on a shakedown cruise to Trinidad. They flew the airplanes to and from a temporary field in the bushes. We went back to pick up supplies and had some repairs done on the ship; then we were headed for the Panama Canal and up the western seaboard. We picked up supplies in San Diego, picked up more supplies in San Francisco and then headed for Pearl Harbor, Hawaii to stock up on everything including fuel and ammunition. They were starting the push. Our Task Force included 2 aircraft carriers, 2 or 3 battleships, 2 or 3 cruisers and 2 or 3 destroyers grouped together. The first island our task force took was Kwajalein. We were there to bomb any enemy airplanes that were trying to interrupt our ships. There were 21 islands including Kwajalein, the Philippines, Truk Island Group, Iwo Jima and Okinawa. Our planes bombed during the day and our battleships bombed during the night. We had many interruptions by Japanese airplanes attacking us, but thank God we took care of them. My ship, the *U.S.S. Langley*, was the second ship with that name, the first having been blown up in the Battle of Guadalcanal. We had eighteen pilots who were great guys. They went through hell. One was killed. On the ship a scorecard was painted which showed how many planes were shot down, how many islands were bombed, etc. We were on the *Langley* for nine months never leaving the ship.

Our ships were being attacked by the kamikaze's; some were severely damaged, and some were lost. The guns weren't that accurate. The planes would be coming at us. First the destroyers, then the cruisers, and then the battleships would all try to get the planes. They would still be coming at us. Many days the Japanese observation planes would be flying above us at 12,000 feet checking the number of our ships, and we couldn't shoot them down. As we shot at them, the flak would be coming back at us. It was unbelievable. Thank God not too many reached the flattops.

The war proved one thing. We all got together and did the job no matter what the cost was. The whole country was behind us. It was a good experience.

I was honorably discharged as First Class AMM (Aviation Machinist Mate) on September 1945. I went back to work at Brewster Ford and stayed with them until 1957. I then went into business from 1957 – 1963 as V & S Service on Route 22, Brewster. In 1963 I sold the station and went to work for Brady Standard Motor Co. After five years I went into partnership opening a brand new building called Brewster Tire Co. I sold the business in 1986. After my wife died I returned to work until 1990 when I retired at age 70. I subsequently remarried. I have five children.[86]

Harvey J. Van Derlyn

The first day at Sampson Naval Base, Geneva, N.Y. we were just a bunch of kids and we were thrown around pretty much that day. Kids were away from home for the first time. Lights went out at 8:30 or 9:00 at night. We would lie there in the barracks, and you could hear sniffle, sniffle, sniffle. It was sad. The next morning we were out on the drill field at four or five, and out comes this World War I retread, a Chief Boson's Mate, Chief Petty Officer to be our instructor for that barracks. He was about 5 feet 7 inches tall, broad as tall and had a whiskey tenor voice. He had 25 or 30 years worth of hash marks up his sleeve. He said, "Yesterday you were home safe and sound in the bosom of your mother. But today your backside belongs to me. When I say jump, you say how high." He scared the life out of us. Here we were a bunch of 17-18 year old kids having for the first time in our lives come up against something like this. We didn't dare look cross-wise at that guy. He put the fear right into us - we came from gentle people. My father was a navy veteran and had put twelve years in, so I dared not go in any other branch of service but the navy.

My ship was the *U.S.S. Comet* (AP-166) which had carried marines for the initial assault of Saipan on June 15. A week later we sailed for Pearl Harbor to load troops for the invasion of Guam, July 1944. There was a Lieutenant Savage who received the Navy Cross for his handling of the troops during the invasions of Saipan and Guam. I got on the ship after those battles, and we went to Leyte, the Philippines. We had eight 20 mm guns - four on each side of the ship, 3 in. forward, 5-in. toward the back. We would take the troops to the point of landing. We had boats called LCVP's and LCM's, 40, 50, 60 personnel per boat. They would put the cargo nets over the side; the men would climb over the sides and down the nets into the boats. These boats would take the men into the beach while the battle was going on in full force. It was the only way to get the men in – and there was mortar fire, machine gun fire and everything on those boats. We would stay until after the invasion and then we pick up casualties. We saw many casualties come aboard. We had a small operating room and a small sick bay. The two or three doctors on board would take care of the wounded, and on the way back we would drop them off either at a hospital ship, or we would drop them off somewhere in back of the lines where they could be put into a hospital. We did that quite often. We did that every invasion I was in. One afternoon I watched frozen in my tracks as a Japanese torpedo bomber approached. The pilot spotted the cruiser *Honolulu* in an adjoining anchorage putting a large hole in its side, saving our ship. We went into the first invasion of the Philippines, which was at Leyte for the initial assault. The Battle of Leyte Gulf was a ship-of-the-line battle. These were battleships, cruisers and destroyers. This was where the Japanese navy was defeated. We were not part of that. We were told, "you people get out of the way, find yourself a safe harbor and wait until the battle is over." We could see the guns flashing and everything else.

I knew a fellow who was wounded twice in the battles from Utah Beach to the border of Germany. He had to pay for anything he got from the Red Cross, so he has no use for them. Brewster's Bertha Hall, an older citizen used to spend hours on the phone for the Red Cross contacting people, getting passages home for servicemen. She was very active. When we were able to have a movie, we would look down on the lower deck and see the officers bring young Red Cross workers aboard. When it became dark, one by one, they would disappear.

Bill Dwyer, a friend from Brewster was stationed in Honolulu in some type of communications. He knew where all the ships in the fleet were, and he would be there to meet me when my ship came in.

I was in New Caledonia off the coast of Australia, and I was standing way up on the bridge in the radio shack. I kept looking at this fellow for a couple of days because I felt I recognized him. I kept watching and watching. Finally, one day I went down to him, and I said, "Hey, soldier, where are you from?" He said, "White Plains." I told him I was from Brewster. It was Aldo Sagrati, and I said, "Why did you tell me White Plains?" He said, "Nobody ever heard of Brewster - it's such a small town." So, we introduced ourselves, and I asked him what I could do for him. He had been overseas at that time for three or four years. He had been through the whole nine yards down there. He said, "I could use some socks, some underwear, and some tee shirts." I said okay, went down to the ship's stores, and got whatever he needed, and I gave it to him.

When I came home in 1945 I was still in service, and that's when I got married. I was one of the first of our high school class to get married. I had a thirty day leave, and I went to see Mrs. Sagrati. I mentioned my visit with Al, and she had all of us up for a real Italian dinner. We had a good time. She said "You tell me about my Aldo."

Crossing the equator for the first time I was initiated into the brotherhood of Neptunus Rex. The initiation lasted a whole day. It was harsh. They had a king sitting up on a throne with a crown and robes. There was a canvas tunnel, and we had to go through the tunnel. At the end of it, they had a fire hose going full speed coming at us. As we came through they were beating us. We were soaking wet, and then they were hitting us with the electric prod. We then had to present ourselves to the king who had a big kettle of castor oil. He would take a big spoon, and we would either take it or else. After I went through it I did the same thing to others – I had my time. After going across the equator and through this initiation we were then considered a "shellback".

We went back and forth ferrying troops. We saw a lot of action, and our ship was pretty well beat up. There were some good times, some bad times. I got out of the Navy in 1945.

I spent several years as manager of the Grand Union Store in Beacon, N.Y. Subsequently I worked at the Metropolitan Life Insurance Company for thirty years, fifteen of those in management, retiring in 1983. I then became a Financial Consultant for Allmerica Financial spending ten years with them. From there I went with the Hudson Heritage Capital Management, Inc. in estate planning and money management and I work on a flexible basis to this day.

On April 29, 1945 I married Mary Emma Cessna from Bedford, Pa. We have two children.[87]

Ferdinand Vetare

In 1943 I took a test (V-12) to get into the Navy Officers' Training School. I think all of us senior boys took it, and it turned out that Phil Williams, the class brain, scored highest. As fate would have it, Phil did not pass the physical, so yours truly went as the alternate. Off I went to Middlebury College where, after three semesters I washed out. From there I went to boot camp at Great Lakes, radio school at Madison, Wisconsin, and then out to sea on the APA 188, a troop transport attack, sailing the blue Pacific and copying code from May of 1945 till April of 1946.

Most of the time we sailed alone, which meant for some nervous times as we sailed some areas popular with Japanese subs, but fortunately we never saw one, or more importantly, none of them ever saw us. The only brush with disaster that I'm aware of was a typhoon off Japan. I was sure the ship was going to break in half as it fell from peak to trough, but in time I realized Henry Kaiser had done a good job, so I watched from the bridge and enjoyed the scene.

Most of our trips back and forth to California ports involved picking up and dropping off troops. One thousand soldiers was a normal load, but on occasion we carried closer to two thousand, a real fiasco during rough seas. Some of our destinations included Manila, Tacloban, Guam, Lae, and eventually Tokyo and Amori in Japan. Mt. Fuji is beautiful. Yes, the house partitions were paper thin, and it gets very cold as early as September.

A few things I still remember: I was receiving at the radio when the message came through that we had dropped the atomic bomb. It seemed important at the time, but I did not realize until later what a moment in history it truly was. I remember being initiated into the shellback society when we crossed the equator, King Neptune and all his crew garbed in wild seaweeds and other costumes that made for an exciting time. I remember the bedraggled youngsters not more than six or seven years old offering to sell their sisters to American servicemen for a dollar or two. I remember meeting young men from backwater America not knowing how to read or write. I remember the blue water, smooth as a rolled carpet stretching in every direction to the horizon and broken only by the occasional flying fish leaping, flying a brief distance, then diving abruptly back into the tranquil blue. I remember a few of my shipmates, the few beers we shared, and relatively peaceful existence we knew aboard ship. I remember meeting Harvey Van Derlyn, the only Brewster contact I ever had in the service in the Pacific. It was a wonderful but short meeting.

Norm Donley (Merchant Marines) and I were good buddies in high school. On the day I was to leave home, Norm accompanied me along with my mother to the train station. Of course, my mother was in tears, so in his inimitable fashion Norm was determined to ease everyone's pain. "Don't worry, Mrs. Vetare," he said, "you have one less mouth to feed." I miss Norm and my mother and the people and places I used to know, but the experience of all those relationships is the fabric of my very existence.

In April of 1946 I was honorably discharged on Long Island grateful to have survived and proud that in my small way I had given a little of myself back to the American dream.

Note: Using the G.I. Bill Ferdinand Vetare went on to graduate from Middlebury College. In 1954 he married Lois Tyson. He taught English for 35 years - first at Culver Military Academy and then at Valhalla (N.Y.) High School. He was Village Trustee of Mount Kisco, N.Y. for six years and Mayor for four years. The Vetares have four daughters.

Ferd says of his military and community service: "You see, all very staple stuff and ordinary!"[88]

Left: Iola Dutcher Adam, Ernest Adam

Right: James P. Collins, Edward A. Collins

Robert B. Pitkat

Frederick W. Burdge

George J. Hinkley

Vincent Vanaria

Ferdinand Vetare

Farrell Reed

John Santorelli   Joan Beal

Home Front

Marjorie Lane Beal

In 1944-45 I worked for the O.P.A. (Office of Price Administration) and Rationing Board, which was located in the War Memorial Building in Carmel N. Y. People with "legitimate" needs for extra gas, tires or fuel oil would fill out applications for these. The fuel oil applications were submitted to a panel of volunteers who came in once a week to process them. We handled the rest, giving out stamps or coupons. These sheets or books were kept in an old vault in the post office at night. One morning, try as we may, we couldn't get it open, so we simply took the hinges off the left side of the door. (So much for security!).

Service men on leave were entitled to a few extra gas coupons. We always went out of our way to do as much as we could for them; so when one particular service man asked for more so he could visit distant relatives I said, "Yes, but we'll have to pretend your mother is in the hospital." His reply was, "But can you make it my grandmother? She's dead, and I don't want to jinx my mother."

In 1945 I married Malcolm T. Beal on his return from duty in the Aleutian Islands. We have four children.

In 1985 Malcolm's mother's house was sold. The wife had come from Germany as a young girl to work as a nanny and then stayed on. Her mother still lived in Germany and came over each year to visit. Once, while she was here, I was invited to lunch. There were a couple of other guests, but I was the only one who was American-born. As we sat there, all of a sudden the mother began to talk. She looked straight at me, and as she spoke in German, another guest translated. She went on at great length about the hardships they had endured in Germany during the war. She kept saying that they had nothing – the men were gone; they couldn't get anything repaired. There was an extreme scarcity of food, clothing, gas, fuel oil, etc. Then she said the bombing started, night after night.

As I sat listening, I was beginning to feel very disturbed. All I could think of was, "We didn't start that war!"

Then, the last words she spoke, when translated were, "And the worst of it was, we had no one to blame but ourselves."[89]

Jane Beal Blackwood

My early years were spent at the Brewster school, but I spent my junior and senior years at The Knox School from which I graduated in 1940. I attended Payne Hall to become a medical secretary and subsequently worked at Grasslands Hospital in Valhalla, N.Y. assisting the nurses in the Tuberculosis Department. When a patient told me I shouldn't work there because there was a chance I might develop TB, I decided to work elsewhere. That was when I started working at J. P. Stevens in N.Y.C. testing nylon for parachutes. My family was very interested when I brought some pieces of parachute nylon home and especially when I brought home my first pair of nylon stockings.

Since food was in short supply and the government had instituted rationing my mother decided on a plan to allot a small amount of sugar to each family member. There were my two sisters and little brother. When one sister started borrowing sugar from another sister's bowl because she had used up her allotment, starting a minor feud, my mother decided to discontinue her plan. Since she was always fair to each child I'm sure she came up with another solution.

Although he was older than draft age and had a family, my father Ross Beal went into the Army Engineer Corps. He went into Casablanca after the initial invasion, as it was his job along with his crew to drill wells providing water for our troops.

It was at J.P. Stevens that I met my first husband who soon after joined the U.S. Army Air Force. After my father had returned from Sicily and was stationed at Ft. Belvoir, Va. we had our wedding in the post chapel there. My sister Joan was in the WAVES stationed at Alameda Naval Hospital in California and came back east for my wedding. When she started on the trip, she was sick with a cold or flu, and when she arrived at Ft. Belvoir she had become more ill. After our marriage we went to Avon Park, Florida while my husband studied aviation navigation, and then he went to England. I wrote him often and regularly and awaited his return. When he came home, my father let us have the cottage at Tonetta Lake for the length of his furlough; it was there that he told me that he was in love with an English girl. After the shock, eventually I divorced him.

Someone in the armed forces came home from North Africa and when seeing our gas shortage said there was plenty of gasoline in North Africa. They even used gasoline to wash clothes.

I was taking drivers education when I met my future husband, Neil Blackwood who was the instructor; he was also teaching industrial arts at Brewster High School. It wasn't long before we started going out on dates. My sisters Joan and Dodie were great teasers, and when he would walk up the driveway passing our dining room window, I am sure he could hear them yelling, "Here comes Neil, here comes Neil". They became very fond of him. Like many veterans who had seen the worst of war Neil said very little about his experiences in the Battle of the Bulge, the senseless killings by Germans of innocent civilians at Malmedy and the hardships endured. Sometimes he would watch a war movie on TV, and although it was upsetting to him he said he wanted to know just where he fitted into the whole picture. Eventually he stopped watching movies that had to do with World War II.

We had one son and spent most of our married life at Tonetta Lake. After retirement we lived in Florida. [91]

Marie Destino Brady

My early school years were spent in a one or two room schoolhouse outside the village of Brewster. There weren't many children; we received lots of attention, and I felt very secure. When the war started I wasn't even in high school. When I moved from the little schoolhouse to the Brewster school it was very difficult for me as I had no friends there, and everyone had been going to that school from the beginning.

I didn't have family members going into service, and I didn't seem touched by the war. Harry Thorpe was a friend in high school who eventually was inducted. He was a good dancer and a very good singer, and we used to go to hear him sing at The Hotel Green in Danbury, Connecticut.

Our Brewster High School Class of 1946 couldn't go to Washington, D.C., as those class trips had been cancelled for the duration of World War II. We did have a day in New York City.

Anna Lottrechiano (Folchetti) and I worked in Hopes Drug Store, and Eddie Brady and Robert Folchetti used to come into the store. Sam Seiffert, the owner, was good to work for. I wasn't involved in Eddie's life at that time, as he was five years older than I. When Eddie graduated from high school I graduated from eighth grade; when I graduated from high school Eddie was in the Navy.

When there was roller-skating at Peach Lake, Mary Brady and I would go skating. But when Mary's brother Eddie was home on leave from the Navy we couldn't go anywhere. Our other form of entertainment was square dancing.

On September 5, 1948 Eddie and I were married; Brewster friends, Frank Vetare sang at our wedding and John Santorelli, Larry Enright and Robert Folchetti were our ushers.[92]

Alice Gorman Brandon

My family first came to Brewster in 1938, first to stay a short while with my aunt and the Caggiano family at Tonetta Lake. Our Long Island Beach had been wiped out by a hurricane, and the homes all along the water were taken. So we started to come to Brewster to visit – first a few weeks at a time, then we rented a bungalow, then buying a bungalow near Dodie Beal and her parents' summer home.

We had wonderful summers at Tonetta Lake getting to know everyone in town. Every night we walked to town for butterscotch marshmallow nut sundaes at Hopes Drug Store. And then we walked home. I undoubtedly earned the money hanging clothes on the line for a penny a sock.

My Aunt Nellie Caggiano had a Victory Garden at Tonetta Lake. Once the war began my two older brothers George and Bob were in service. Joe Caggiano was in the Navy and Charles (known as "Burp") was in the Army. I remember "Bunky" O Brien (who perished over Europe) coming up to the lake all the time. He would visit with my cousin Charles and the Pinckney boys, Earl and LaVerne. "Pop" Smith would chase the non-payers all over the place trying to collect the dime for swimming at the pavilion, and Mrs. Smith was like an eagle, spotting those who owed her even if they were out in the water.

When we first came up to the lake our new friends took us "snipe hunting". We were new people. The guys took us to the other side of the lake in a rowboat, and we had sticks. There were no houses, and animals would come down to the water. We called it cow beach. With sticks in hand we would start beating the bushes to get the snipes out, and the guys would take off with the boats and leave us. "Snitz" Snider was one of the culprits. Both boys and girls were taken "snipe hunting". There were no roads or houses in that area of Tonetta in those days, just woods. We had to make our way around the lake through the woods to get home.

I remember the Palmer's old icehouse well, not far from the pavilion near the lake. Everyone at some time used to play around that. There was straw inside used for storing the ice taken from the lake. It burned down and different boys were blamed, but we were not sure what caused it.

The fun we had at the pavilion was unmatched. There were arts and crafts; they would run watermelon races, three-legged races and running races. There was always dancing to the jukebox. My father used to take the boys hiking up Third Mountain.

Then the lake would "turn" in early July. I remember swimming to turtle rock. The people I remember whose families were at Tonetta were Ralph Snell (who died in medical school) and Dotty and Helen Shore.

All my brothers and I took swimming lessons there. My four brothers, George, Bob, Ken, Frank and I were all athletic and goal-oriented toward the Olympics. Frank became a Silver Medallist in the 1964 Tokyo Olympics. He learned to swim and dive at Tonetta Lake and did his practicing on the regulation competition three-meter diving board at the now defunct Clancy's Beach. Using this board helped him excel in diving. It was perhaps the only such board in the area. Frank received ten scholarships, graduated from Harvard, and then entered the Navy. From there he tried out and became an Olympian.

I did high jump, broad jump, tossed the discus and shot put – everything. I ran throughout the 1940's, competing in track and field all around the country through the German American Club in Queens. I was a member of the women's relay team. A woman wasn't permitted to run more than 220 yards, because they thought it would affect her childbearing. (I disproved that theory later having six daughters.) I tried out for the 1948 Olympics in Women's Track Relay Team. I was eliminated in the semi-finals because they took the fastest four women in the country rather than the fastest relay team.

I married Bernard Brandon, a World War II veteran of Brewster, whom I met at Tonetta Lake in 1949. We have lived in Brewster all those years.[93]

Janet Anita McNeill Burdge

My parents were Sarah and Newton McNeill, and my father was superintendent of the David Ball Estate on Mohecan Hill. David Ball was president of the Lorilard Tobacco Co. and lived in Mt. Vernon, worked in New York City and came to Brewster on weekends. He and his wife Daisy were wonderful, down to earth people and got me interested in nursing, because Daisy had been a nurse. David died in 1940, but we lived there until 1941 when the place was sold.

We moved to Poughkeepsie where Dad took a job making shells for the Navy at U.S. Hoffman Co. working 12-hour shifts. He often wondered if Fred would ever get one of the shells he helped make to fire from the *Mahan*. My mom worked there part time, as everyone at that time wanted to help in any way they could in defense work. Another reason they chose Poughkeepsie was because I had been accepted at Vassar Bros. Hospital for their three-year Nurses' Training Program. I can still hear the horns of the blackout drills. My mom would get up early and walk to the A & P to stand in line for rationed sugar; if it were my day I would do the same. Oleomargarine and gas were also rationed. I still have our ration books.

Vinnie Vanaria, a mutual Brewster friend, introduced me to Fred Burdge in 1937. He bet Fred a dollar that he couldn't get a date with me. In 1940 I graduated from Brewster High. Fred went into the Navy, and I wrote him every other day. My letters would arrive on the ship in large amounts because they didn't get mail from port or another ship that often. He would sort those letters by postmark to read them in order. His letters to me were censored before they left the ship; I still have his letters with cutouts. He tried to be clever one time saying he had bought a pair of alligator shoes so I'd know he had been in Australia, but it was cut out. Not until he was home did I know what it was that was cut out. One time he ended his letter saying, "I'd send you some kisses, but the censor might object". The censor must have had a sense of humor and made some X's and O's stating that they were put there by the censor for Fred. The strange thing was one present he sent to me and one for his parents. It was a jewelry box shaped like Australia – different colors of wood for their states. Inside was one of his white handkerchiefs filled with coins from different places he had been in the Pacific. It is a mystery! He had told us some places he had been which should have been censored.

November 1943 was our lucky day when he returned to Poughkeepsie to my parents' house in his fathers 1932 Chevy. I knew he was coming home but didn't know the exact date. I was working evenings on maternity floor, had come out of a patient's room with a bedpan, and there he was with my mom. I often wonder what I did with that bedpan. What a thrill to see him at last (hadn't seen him since Oct. 1940). We were engaged that Christmas and then off to Nevada he went. I finished training in February 1945. We married July 29, 1945. He was still home in August of 1945, so it was great to celebrate the end of the war. When he was discharged, I was able to be replaced at Vassar Bros. Hospital in September of 1945 and joined him in Nevada until his discharge in August of 1946.

We have many good memories of Brewster. We'll never forget spending so much time in winter ice-skating. Fred liked fishing and hunting. All came to a halt until after the war. Dad and Mom were active in the Argonne Post American Legion, so their parades and carnivals were fun. I enjoyed roller-skating at Brewster High School gymnasium until they replaced the floor. Movies at Brewster theatre were frequent because television came after the war. Fred and my dates often were movies and then ice cream sundaes at Charles Anderson's Drug Store. Newsreels at the movies didn't describe the war like our TV does today. I think there were more events for entertainment before the war – hill climbs for motorcycles at Croton Falls and talent shows at the Town Hall.

I still remember Dr. Cleaver, our family doctor. He treated everything, made house calls and a lot of times gave you pills from his office instead of the drug store. Fred worked one time at the Brewster Diner; he served Robert Montgomery (movie star) who had an estate in Towners. I remember the boys mixing chemicals in Mr. Truran's chemistry class, and we all had to exit the classroom because of the fumes. Memories of the First National Store – Mom took her grocery list, and as she stood at the counter the clerk brought items to her one by one from the shelves behind the counter. What a change now! Fred and I have a son and a daughter.[94]

Mary Palmer Cioccolanti

In 1941 I was in my freshman year in college at New Paltz. My mother and father were driving me back to school. We had the radio on in the car, and I think it was around Hopewell Junction that we heard the announcement that the Japanese had bombed Pearl Harbor. I didn't think about it then, but my father must have had terrible feelings about it because he had been a soldier in the first World War – and he had four sons.

In the little village of New Paltz in the Catskill Mountains we did have to learn to spot airplanes. We took courses and took a test on recognition of them. So, I was very sharp on identifying planes. We had air raid drills quite often. We had to be in our house at nine o'clock, but the senior citizens of New Paltz would be assigned different streets and if they saw any little light there would be a big knock on the door. The sororities would get into contests, so that they did a better job and nobody knocked on their doors. During one period I went to Stuart Airfield to a dance. During the fall, classes were cancelled so we could help with apple picking.

I worked three summers in Bridgeport, Connecticut at the G.E. factory inspecting the dynamo motors. I left Brewster at five a.m. with Everett Ballard who drove his car, a fellow by the name of Ellis and one by the name of Thompkins. Pat Durkin and Marie McGary rode with us; they worked year round. During my last summer I worked in a smaller G.E. plant in Danbury.

I can remember in school there were no fellows around. Many of my friends were working in defense plants making so much money and having much more interesting lives than I was having up in New Paltz. There was nothing very glamorous about learning. So one day I hitchhiked home with a boy. My father thought I was "wacko". He looked at me and said, "young lady, get yourself back where you came from – your mother has three sons that she is worried around the clock about (she would wait for the mailman to come). She doesn't need to worry about you." That was the end of that.

My father and his sister Mrs. O'Brien, Jackie's mother, were very close, and we were neighbors. It was very lonesome for them, because Jackie ("Bunky") was in the service and his sister Wiletta worked in

Manhattan for Time Magazine. Jackie had been stationed around St. Louis and was engaged. They would come up and would listen to Gabriel Heater '...it was a black night over....'because so many planes were going down. It was terrible because my mother was worried about her sons, and my aunt was worried about Jackie who was a gunner on a B-24. And of course Jackie was killed. I think it was my father and uncle who were notified and who told my aunt. Jackie's fiancée came to visit.

My brother Henry was in the Air Force over Burma delivering food packages and pamphlets all over Burma. We hardly ever saw Henry. His twin brother Ed was also was in the Air Force. In training he broke an eardrum and spent the whole time on the ground in Pecos, Texas. My oldest brother Bob was in the Eighth Infantry Division, 445th AAA battalion and went through Normandy and into Germany. John tried to get into the Army, but they found he had a hernia and couldn't be operated on without my parent's permission. He was told to go work in a defense position. He worked on the railroad, which was considered defense employment. After six months he was old enough to have the operation without my mother's approval and was then accepted in the Army. By then the war was over. He was assigned to the Philippines.

When V-E Day came I was with Joan Beal. I had a date with Lieutenant Bob Enright and Joan had a date with Lieutenant Donald Von Gal who was recently back from service in the Air Force. We had a grand time riding up and down in Don's convertible. It was a wild, wild time with everyone out having a great time.[95]

Note: Mary married Joseph Cioccolanti, a veteran from Brewster. They have four children. Mary's father Edward and his twin brother Henry were familiar to many people who lived in Brewster in the 1930's and 1940's, as they delivered ice in their open truck from which they would permit children to run up and grab a piece of ice to suck on. The brothers also operated a family farm on Peaceable Hill Road. Henry was Road Commissioner of the Town of Southeast for thirty-five years. He was the father of Francis C. Palmer, another Brewster veteran (class of 1944). Mary became a teacher and taught for many years in the Brewster schools.

Millie Buck Collins

I graduated from Brewster High School in 1939. Bobby Collins was president of our class. He was rather shy and at times when we were making plans for something he would ask me to take over for him. My best girlfriend was Helen Reynolds who married Fred Jenkins. Bob Palmer was in my class. I eloped with George Donley (son of H.H. Donley, B.H.S. principal) my childhood sweetheart who died six weeks later.

I worked for a while at the G.E. plant in Bridgeport and rode in the same car with Pat Durkin. George Fowkes also worked there. Lloyd Barber worked at the Sikorsky plant. My brother, Robert Buck, was a staff sergeant and on his way to Pearl Harbor when the Japanese bombed that base. He served in the Pacific.

The Red Cross held dances for the MP's at Greenhaven, and several of us went there to dance with them. Della Scolpino, Betty Waters, Mary Waters, Margaret Hart and I all went on different occasions. We also went to the Pawling Prep School which had been taken over by the Army Air Force as a rest center for their wounded and combat-weary personnel. There we would play pinochle or other games or just walk around the grounds with the servicemen.

I had one daughter when I married Jimmy Collins, twin brother to Edward Collins. We had three children. Their brother, Bob Collins, was killed in the battle of Guam Island.[96]

Andrew J. Durkin

In 1941 when Pearl Harbor was attacked I was thirteen years old. Being a Sunday, it was movie day. My friends and I were in front of Millar's Candy Store when we heard the news that the Japanese had bombed Pearl Harbor. I was in seventh grade at that time.

As many people did, my cousins worked in a defense factory in Bridgeport, Connecticut. The money was very good. Some men went to the defense plants hoping to be declared essential so they would not be drafted. Young girls and married women worked there also.

My father owned a coal and feed business in town, and it was affected by the priority system of that time making it very difficult to keep a supply of coal or feed. In 1942 there was a big fire in my fathers coal and feed warehouse on north Main Street. All the feed went up, and all the coal burned. The building was gone. Howard Kelly of Eaton, Kelly was very generous to my father offering him whatever coal he had and whatever feed he needed until he could get back on his feet. The business then started selling wood and coke which they didn't normally do.

I wasn't old enough to get my license at 13 or 14 years old, but I drove making deliveries for my father. Charlie Schafer, the police chief, looked the other way as long as I was working. He never said anything – whether he spoke to my father or not I don't know. Chief Schafer was in office a long time. He had a niece Ruth Orton who lived on Putnam Terrace not far from us. Ruth's brother drowned on the reservoir when the ice was too thin for a rescue. It was a sad thing. He was a teenager.

During the North African Campaign I used to write to Rooster (Don) Smith who lived just up the hill from me. He worked for my father for a short period of time and was a nice guy. His brother Ed Smith was killed in Alaska, and there was a wake at his home which I attended. I remember talking with LeRoy Barrett at the 100th Anniversary of P.F. Beal and Sons, and he told me that Ross Beal when he was in the Army Engineers and headed for North Africa was told he could choose two of his former employees who were in the Army, and they could join him in the work of drilling wells. He chose LeRoy Barrett and Art Ashby to go with him.

Marge Addis the editor and publisher of The Brewster Standard put a great deal in the newspaper about Brewster's servicemen; there were lots of pictures and news. Many servicemen came to school in uniform when I was a freshman. In an assembly program H.H. Donley who was the Principal talked about two men being drafted from school. Fred Weizenecker was drafted out of high school as well as Dick DeVall. Two Brewster High School students I remember being killed were Wilbert Nagle and Henry Alfke.

Still a kid, I got hold of a cigar wrapped in cellophane. I put it between my lips like a big shot and left it there until the cellophane broke and the tobacco juices leaked into my mouth. Eventually the juices made their way to my stomach, and I was so sick. It was the end of the war and everyone was celebrating and we went up to the Busy Bee, but I was too sick to get out of the car. I never put a piece of tobacco in my mouth after that.

On V-E Day or V-J Day Charlie Anderson, the druggist on Main Street, threw candy, gum, cigarettes and cigars out onto the street- an unusual act for Charlie, but it was not the usual day.

I graduated from high school in 1946 and went into service in 1950. On my return I joined the A.J. Durkin oil business and on April 16, 1955 I married Maureen Costello. We have seven children.[97]

Susan Foulk English

Of course, the reason for my "late arrival" in Brewster was that my father was called to be the Baptist minister in Brewster. It was a difficult move for me in the middle of my senior year (Class of 1944), especially since my mother had died in the midst of the move on December 28, 1943.

The girls were so kind to me and included me in many of their activities. Hank Alfke sat in front of me for homeroom, and I remember his visiting with me. He wasn't there very long before he enlisted in the service and never returned.

Hope's Drug Store, the movie theatre and the bowling alley were the centers of social activity. The bus trips to Pawling for dances with the soldiers there under the supervision of Mrs. Harold Beal were the highlights of the season.

I remember the girls talking about various boys who were already in the war theatres. They were just names to me. Several of the girls had boyfriends they wrote to in service and anxiously awaited their V-mail letters. Of course rationing was taken for granted – gasoline, shoes, sugar, tires and the little red and blue tokens for meat. We were all given to believe we were helping the war effort, and we were happy to go without these things.

The radio was always turned on at the hour for the news. No one dared talk during the broadcast so we could hear the latest from Lowell Thomas, Edward R. Murrow or Ernie Pyle about the war. Money was tight so there weren't many frills...what was it, 25 cents, 50 cents for the movies? There were always news and war pictures, and we all shuddered at the things we were seeing.

After school we would go to Hope's Drug Store for ice cream. They had Breyer's ice cream, and we were told to notice the little brown flecks in it that proved it was made with *real* vanilla beans!!

I married Paul English from Greene, N.Y. Phyllis Schutz, a Brewster resident, introduced us. We have four children.[98]

Beatrice D. Green

In 1935 I graduated from Brewster High School and then attended college for two years. I went to work on Fifth Avenue at the New York State League of Savings & Loans as a statistician. There was a secretary who worked in my office for the executive vice president; he was from Czechoslovakia. He knew people and had family there. When news came of the Nazi invasion of Czechoslovakia we all knew it. This man was very upset and worried. It worried all of us. At home I talked about this with my parents, and they thought nothing was going to happen to worry about. But it was the first time I started to think there might be a war. This was 1939-1940.

I married Kenneth Hopkins in September 1940. We weren't really aware of the looming war.

On December 7, 1941 we had been to dinner at the apartment of Elizabeth Schutz Hopkins and Clayton Hopkins. After dinner we were sitting listening to the radio. I was sitting on the floor. I remember exactly where I was sitting, and it came over the radio that Pearl Harbor was bombed. We just couldn't believe it.

In the spring of 1941 I wanted to stop commuting and left my job to work for my stepfather, Alvah D.Townsend who ran a lumber business in Brewster. He was a real father to me. He was finding that the bookkeeping was getting complicated. The government priority system made it difficult to get building supplies that he needed, and I thought I could be a big help to him. There were restrictions for everything. Kenny worked in a defense factory in Bridgeport and rode with George Fowkes in a carpool.

One day either Mr. Vought or Mr. Sikorsky came into the office. He was trying to get anyone who would, to invest in his company, which would make the helicopter known then as an autogiro. He was asking for a one hundred dollar donation. (The Vought Sikorsky defense plant was in Bridgeport, Ct.). This was sometime after 1941. It sounded like a Buck Rogers scheme, so we didn't give him a donation.

Rationing started for sugar, gas, shoes, meat and butter. We did a lot of walking. We lived on Allview Avenue, and I could walk to work. Kenny went into the Army in 1943. There wasn't anything to do. You couldn't go anywhere. You couldn't go to Danbury to the movies. Dad thought it would be a good idea to join the Grange because there would be activities there, and I could walk to the meetings. I was in my early twenties. So I joined the Grange, and they immediately put me on the ways and means committee with Frances Pinckney and Elizabeth Hopkins. So we decided since nobody could go anywhere that we would start square dancing. I had never square danced in my life, but the others had. So Joe Young who was married to Gladys Griffin, Ken Griffin's sister, knew a caller from Danbury. I think we had the dances every other Saturday. Everyone in town came, because there was no other place to go. We paid off the mortgage on the Grange Hall building. I learned to square dance, and we all had a good time.

After being inducted at Fort Dix Kenny went for basic training at Camp Croft in Spartanburg, N.C. He became an expert in marksmanship, and because of this he was offered additional training at O.C.S. He rejected it and within three weeks he was sent overseas. On a Sunday he got off the train somewhere and telephoned me. He said he had been issued very warm clothing, long, heavy underwear, and it was the middle of July. He couldn't figure out why. He went through North Africa and Anzio beachhead where Billy Cox was given a field commission. When Kenny got to the beach at Anzio it was very muddy and difficult running. As he stumbled along, a partial denture fell out of his mouth into the mud somewhere around his feet. Under gunfire he scrambled around feeling for his denture and eventually found it. He proceeded with his unit through Italy and up into Germany. He fought in the Battle of the Bulge.

He never came home until after the war. After the war Kenny and I were divorced. I later married Harold Green of Goldens Bridge, N.Y.[99]

Marjorie Wilkinson Hazzard

My great grand parents lived in Brewster, and my parents Mary Edna and Leo Wilkinson, having lived elsewhere, brought me to Brewster when I was about two years old. I attended the Brewster school and graduated in 1929 and married my classmate, Herbert Hazzard in 1931. My mother died when she was quite young, and in 1935 my father married Lillie Eberly who for several years ran a restaurant in the village.

I was living at 12 Putnam Avenue; Florence (Mrs. Ross) Beal, newly married at age 19 lived across the street, and I just loved her. When Jane was born she taught me everything about taking care of her. I was only twelve years old, and I loved caring for her. One time when Florence and Ross wanted to go out, she asked me if I could take young Jane to my parent's cottage at Peach Lake for the night. I knew Jane and her sister Joan much better than Dodie, because when she was born I was in high school and not as interested in babies.

Florence and Ross bought our house at 12 Putnam Avenue, and while we were building a house on Garden Street we moved into the house across the street, which they were leaving so they, being anxious to get into their new house, could move in. So we swapped.

When Pearl Harbor was struck, "Hap" (Herbert) and I were living on Center Street, and he was working for Metropolitan Life Insurance Company. We didn't think it was going to come to us, but he was drafted in 1943. At 34 years old, they were scraping the bottom of the barrel. He went into the Navy under "limited service" because of his less than perfect eyesight, spent time in Puerto Rico and then was reassigned to New York City. It was a difficult time with three little children, so it was of some help that he was near enough to get home on weekends. While he was in service I got part of his pay and also part of the commission on any insurance policy he had written. My aunt and uncle, Gabrielle and Earl Blockley who lived up on Hillside Terrace were wonderful to me.

Ruby McKenny, whose husband Bill was in the Naval service and Helen Owens, whose husband was in service, worked at the Barden Corp., a defense factory in Danbury. My dad Leo Wilkinson worked at the Grumman plant on Long Island. John Furst, for many years the Fire Chief, was married to Ruth Morehouse. He was in Civil Defense, as at that time all firemen were in Civil Defense. Florence Beal was in the Red Cross and worked at the Mt. Kisco Hospital as a Red Cross Nurse's Aide as well as at headquarters in Carmel. Dorothy Beal was a Gray Lady who arranged dances for servicemen. A bridge club, which I belonged to, decided as a group that we should be doing something for the war effort and decided to sew for the Red Cross. There were a couple of good seamstresses in the group, and Amelia Pigat, a professional seamstress, would come and help us. It was gratifying to know we were doing something.

Our eating habits changed due to rationing, and we didn't do much baking. It wasn't too bad, really. When Hap was back home and back in the insurance business, he had to make calls to customers but wouldn't have enough gas. So, some farmers in the area who were given more ration coupons gave him some of their coupons.

We were just glad the war was over. [100]

Irene Gaines Hinkley

Irene lived in Tilly Foster with her sister Ethel and her parents, James and Irene, just outside the Brewster village limits in a house which was built by her family in 1929. She looks back with love of her childhood, the simple life and the great place she knows it was:

"I went to a one-room schoolhouse in Tilly Foster and loved every minute of it. There were two teachers in the school – one was Mrs. Mary Adams for grades one through four. Mrs. Williams took over for my fifth grade through eighth. They were from Carmel and were super teachers.

Then on to Brewster High School in 1939, going there by taxi. Of course I was lost with changing classes and all those rooms – and so many teachers and kids. I was scared!! I met a lot of great kids. Some I still see and talk to by phone after all these years. I remember two very special teachers: Mr. Eugene Watson and Miss Kathryn Hubbard (Mrs. Bernard Waters). I remember 'Babe' Tuttle looking out for the kids crossing the street to get back to school. He was a nice man. I remember Charlie Schafer, the 'cop'. He always looked so stern. I was a little afraid of him, but I'm sure he was a great man. My dad said he was.

My dad worked for New York Electric & Gas in Brewster from when I was a year old until he retired in 1965.

I remember the Cameo Theatre where we saw all the new movies, and across the street we never missed going to get a Texas Hot Weiner. They were delicious. I tried to get Jimmy and Leo to give me their secret but of course was unsuccessful. Hopes Drug store and the Radler's 5 & 10 cent store were two favorite places to go, and of course Benny's.

Cheerleading was great, and I loved it. My most favorite time in Brewster High was meeting George Hinkley* – the love of my life. We were married June 1,1946 at St. Lawrence O'Toole in Brewster by Father Edward Dugan. We have a son and a daughter.

We get back to Brewster once in a while to visit old friends and relatives. I have many great memories of Brewster – the way it was and the kids I went to school with. It was a great place to grow up."

* Irene's husband, George Hinkley, is a Brewster veteran.[101]

Joan F. Larkin

Even before the Depression there were hoboes – men going to houses in Brewster for food. It was said that marks were put down indicating a friendly house where one could get a meal or coffee.

I was a teenager in high school during the depression and graduated from B.H.S. in 1934 at the age of sixteen. Oak Street where I lived growing up was a dirt road, and calcium chloride was put down every summer to keep the dust down. The Palmers came with their ice truck, and all the kids ran out to get a piece of ice. My father who was born in Mahopac started the Fenaughty Bottling Corp. on Oak Street in Brewster. They bottled all kinds of sodas (beer came in from elsewhere). They had a bottling machine, a capping machine and a washing machine. The syrup came down from the second floor and was mixed with the seltzer, then bottled.

On Washington's Birthday a horse sale was held. The farm horses would be brought from Frank O'Brien's freight office; they would be brought up Oak Street, then down to where there was a barn at Wells Pond passing our house on lower Oak Street.

There was a swinging, walking bridge across the Croton River about one quarter mile below the Borden milk factory bridge. I think the Snidero's built it so their kids could more easily walk to school.

Norma MacLean, Florence Beal's half-sister, was studying piano, and she made all the costumes for our dancing class. She might also have played for us. After the old wood school building burned down in 1923, classes were held on the second floor of the building across from the savings bank.

One day I had permission to clean the blackboards after school and had spilled the pan of water. I had cleaned it up; but even so I remember being upset about going to school the next day because of having spilled water. Then the school burned the next day. Harry Wells was in my class. The Kindergarten and first grades were held in the basement, and when the schoolhouse was burning Harry ran back into the building. He had forgotten to bring out his coat. Mary Connors, who was half-sister to Frank and Dick O'Brien, was in high school. She must have seen Harry run back into the school because she ran in after him and brought him out, saving his life.

My mother who was about fifty-five years old worked at Barden Corp. in Danbury during the war. There must not have been a bus at that time, because she went to work in a carpool with Ruby McKenny. She had to work; my dad was one to lend a lot of people money, and he wasn't always paid back. She also had my brother Tom to raise.

I graduated from Syracuse University where my mother had graduated. Ralph Palmer from Carmel was Commissioner of Social Services for Putnam County and a Republican. An old friend of my father, who was a Democrat, called and said there was going to be an opening in the Social Service Department. I was still in college studying to be a social service worker. So my sister, Marion ("Tot") took the job until I was out of college. She married Coach Sterling Geesman, and John ("Bunky") O'Brien was their best man and their son's godfather. ("Bunky" O'Brien was killed over Europe).

In June of 1940 I married John F. Larkin. I was at the Larkin's home when Pearl Harbor was attacked. Eddie Markel who married my sister-in-law, Ann Larkin, was employed by The Daily Mirror and called from New York to tell us about the attack.

Jack went into service in 1943, enlisting in the Marine Corps. Our son, John III, had been born. While Jack was at Lakehurst, New Jersey his sister Regina and I drove down to say good-bye to him, as he was on his way to California. On our return trip we were traveling through a N. Y. tunnel; the lane to our left was clear, so we pulled out of line to pass, and soon sirens were blasting and horns were blowing. We soon found out that passing was forbidden and got back in line. We had two women from the Bronx with us who had gone to New Jersey to see their sons off. We dropped them off on the west side at the foot of a stairway. I have often thought about that.

I remember, because of rationing, a grocery store might be out of butter or some other food. The grocer would put a sign in the window stating that he expected butter the next day, and the following day housewives would be in line to buy. While Jack was in service I took his job as a rural mail carrier. Jack and I lived in Brewster our entire lives, and I am still there.[102]

Louise Vanderburgh Nicolai

In the 1800's my grandfather spent many years in northern China as a medical missionary. From 1925 to 1927 my father was also a medical missionary and understood more than one dialect. He spoke, understood and read Mandarin, but he couldn't write the language. He could understand Cantonese. My parents were on the island of Hinan when I was born. My mother died when I was quite young, and my father eventually remarried. So I had a stepsister and eventually two brothers and another sister.

My father was one of Brewster's physicians, and during the depression before the war his patients couldn't afford to pay his fees. He did get paid in milk, eggs, butter, vegetables, meat and such, so we didn't suffer as some did. My mother's Scottish father was an architect and a proud man, and my grandmother did all sorts of things to save money. Nothing was ever thrown out – even paper plates were washed and re-used. Everyone had to eat everything on his plate, even the fat.

We had a barn behind our house that looked over to the family who had a bunch of little kids, and they were always dirty and very little on in the way of clothing – and no shoes. Their house was on Marvin Avenue. I used to think they could at least buy a bar of soap and wash the children. At some point I heard Marvin Avenue called "Slop Street", and being about twelve years old I used to think it was because of that family. I don't really know how the name came into use. Actually when you looked out across Marvin Avenue it was quite pretty with woods and a brook, quite rural. It was a cruel name. There was a gate to our property on Marvin Avenue that was never opened, and weeds grew all around it. I had a little playhouse down there, but my mother used to warn us about touching a flower nearby called deadly night shade because it is poisonous.

During the war my sister and brother were very much into victory gardening at the school. I wasn't involved in that. I did buy war stamps from Dodie Beal who sold them every Friday after school, and I did fill a stamp book and had a war bond or two.

My father had to close his medical practice because he was drafted. This was before Pearl Harbor and he was 45 years old with five children. Each medical society had to choose one physician and for some reason my father was taken rather than a younger one who was in that area.

We couldn't have a Junior Prom or a Senior Ball, and I think we ended up with a dance with the music of a record player which I ran. It wasn't a formal dance, but we had a committee to organize it. There weren't many boys there, and those who were there were two years younger. I believe since my father wasn't at home that my stepmother felt even more responsible for me in that she kept close watch on where I went and for how long I would be gone. She clamped down on me to make sure I did what I had to do during my teenage years. I liked to walk into town in the evening, and she would embellish what I was doing. And I was such an innocent kid. I probably thought my dad would have been more lenient.

Henry Alfke was a classmate who went into the Army in our senior year. He was killed shortly after being sent overseas to France. That brought the war home to us for certain. I hope somebody mentioned that loss at our commencement. Of course my dad wasn't home yet and so wasn't at my graduation when I sang a solo. I missed him very much.

That fall I went to Simmons College to start a four-year nursing program. After one year I transferred to Brooklyn Hospital School of Nursing enrolling in the last class of the U. S. Nurses Cadet Corps. graduating in 1948. My father had returned in time to see my capping ceremony. In September of 1948 I married Robert C. Nicolai, and we had five sons.[103]

John Palmer

I was not quite fifteen years old on that fatal day Dec. 7, 1941 - the day the Japanese bombed Pearl Harbor. I can remember precisely where I was, who I was with, when we heard the dreadful news of the bombing which took place twelve hours earlier that Sunday morning.

Being fifteen years old, a freshman in high school, seeing a lot of our classmates' fathers, brothers and sisters going into military service for the first time and moms getting jobs in defense plants didn't seem to matter. We were doing all this for the "war effort", but when we heard the news that some were missing, others were dead – they were fathers, brothers, cousins, classmates and friends – reality set in. Everything changed.

I can remember going to Farrell Reed's father's gas station on Rt. 22 with my father and brothers. The station became an Observation Post. Its' function was to spot enemy airplanes that could drop saboteurs who could damage our water supply or defense plants. We did this in shifts, four hours on, four hours off, mostly at night and weekends. We got quite familiar with the different German warplanes.

We all remember the rationing of sugar, gas, and meat. Just about everything was rationed. Our years in high school were somewhat limited. We were not allowed our class trip to Washington, D.C. because travel was somewhat restricted. Despite all this, my high school years were the greatest. You got to know everyone in school. Our teachers were the best. I have always regretted that I didn't find the time and make the effort to at least thank them. Most of the friends you made were for life. I can remember getting time off from school to harvest corn and pick apples for the farmers in the area.

I tried to enlist after high school, but it was found that I had a hernia. My parents would not give permission for the operation, and so I was told to go into defense work. After working on the railroad for six months I was old enough to have the operation. I went into service in March of 1946 and took my basic training at McClellan, Alabama, near Montgomery. We embarked to go overseas from New York, by way of the Panama Canal, to Pearl Harbor. Our final destination was Manila in the Philippine Islands. Our duty was mainly to oversee the Japanese prisoners, keeping them busy until they were sent home. Our other duties were guarding our military supplies that were abandoned after the war to see what could be salvaged and what was to be destroyed.

All in all it was a great experience. I was able to travel half way around the world. I can't say I enjoyed all of it, but I will say most of the time it was okay. The only soldier I met from Brewster was Francis Creighton. He was my drill sergeant in Basic Training. He was highly decorated for heroism in the defense of the Aleutian Islands. Quite a guy! I was discharged in Fort Lewis, Washington in April of 1947. I came home by train from Fort Lewis by way of the great northern route. It took about five days. All in all a great experience – the memory I've cherished my lifetime. I was in the plumbing business with my brother Henry for forty years. On June 14, 1952 I married Jane Dedde of Chappaqua. We have three children. [104102]

Rita O'Hara Rapp

"Only two are riding the trains today; times are getting better." I was in the class of 1943, and that's what Eugene Watson, our history teacher used to say about the hoboes on the New Haven line. He had quite a sense of humor. The hoboes had their little camping sites outside Brewster. We had a Brewster man who used to raid our garbage pail every week. He probably had money stashed away.

My father Henry O'Hara and Harry Reynolds were on the aircraft watch at the school. I went over sometimes, but I didn't have scheduled times. My father was on the Brewster Village Board and subsequently on the Southeast Town Board and then became Town Assessor.

I cannot remember where I was when Pearl Harbor was attacked. My brother Harding went into the Army Air Corps in 1942 and was doing combat missions over Europe in 1943. In the movie theatre I was watching the newsreel when it showed my brother's B-24 airplane. It had come down with one engine, having been shot up by flak and was full of holes. The name of his plane was "Sack Time", and I could see the name of the plane in the newsreel. I went home and told my mother I had seen Harding's plane. She wrote my brother, and of course, the letters being censored, all she was told was that now "we have Sack Time 2". The picture of his first airplane, full of holes was also in the newspaper.

My brother, a gunner on the B-24, was on a mission over Norway when he was shot down. He was first declared missing in action, eventually being declared dead, the date established being November 18, 1944. Within two weeks of receiving word that he was missing, my mother developed a white streak in her hair which ran back from her forehead.

In 1943 I was attending New York Institute of Photography. When I became engaged to Richard Rapp in 1947, he was still in the Army, but was discharged in February of that year. Dick's brother, Robert, a member of the 10th Mountain Division died in northern Italy while crossing the Po River in 1945.

We were married September 1, 1947. We have two sons.

I have spent most of my life in real estate management in the Brewster area.[105]

Muriel Pinckney Richards

A four-star flag hung in the window of our home because I had four brothers in service. Remington (Buddy), the eldest, went in the Army early on in the war; in fact I believe he went in before Pearl Harbor. He was a medic stationed in Hawaii and took care of the wounded that were sent back from various battles in the Pacific. He contracted dengue fever and lost all of his teeth and eventually got a medical discharge. Lafayette and LaVerne were twins. Lafayette was in the Army stationed in England, and LaVerne was in the Coast Guard on a Coast Guard Cutter. The actor, Victor Mature was on his ship, and Vern used to say he was the biggest baby. Rita O'Hara who was studying photography took a picture of me, and I sent it to LaVerne who showed it to Victor Mature. She had touched up the photo, and it turned out well. Victor Mature apparently made a remark that I looked pretty good, and of course, I lived on that for a long time. Earl, the youngest boy, was also in the Army and involved in the European campaign. Our house was always a gathering place for any fellows home on leave. They always felt comfortable in our house. Lindy Tranquilli was an only child, and he loved to come to visit. (Lindy Tranquilli was taken prisoner by the Germans).

We did some pretty stupid things when we were kids. One of them was when Dodie and I, spending the day together and walking toward the bridge near Carmel Avenue, were drawn down beside the railroad tracks. A little rivulet of water ran along the tracks, so we started floating sticks in the water. Being focused on the fun we were having we didn't hear a train coming, but when we looked up a train was backing up from the direction of the Brewster station going toward the roundhouse. Of course we never told our parents; we both agreed our mothers would have "killed" us. My father worked on the railroad.

Since the war was on the population of boys our age and older was considerably reduced. Therefore, many of us could be seen with younger boys. During my senior year we put on a play in which there were two young couples. I remember that Charlie Anderson, a younger student played opposite me, and we had to kiss. That caused a few giggles. He was a good guy though, and we all had a lot of fun.

We knew that the senior Washington trips had been cancelled as well as the Junior Proms and Senior Balls, but we were nevertheless busy and often made our own fun. One day Dodie and I cut a couple of classes to go visit a favorite history teacher, Mr. Watson, who was then teaching in Ossining. He was pretty surprised to see us. I don't remember any repercussions.

During our senior year a couple of us were sitting in English class near the window; we would flash reflections on the mirrors across the room. Our teacher got very excited and blamed a student, Henry Alfke who sat far from the window, in fact near the door. Henry was made to go to the principal's office for this, and he never "squealed" on us. He was such a gentleman. (Henry Alfke was in the Army and went into service either before graduation or just after. He was killed in battle shortly after arriving in Europe.)

We sometimes took advantage of teachers. In our senior year our English class was the first class of the day. One day our teacher, who was also our homeroom teacher, covered all the blackboards with passages from Shakespeare. When the teacher left for the day, Dodie and I were still in the building probably working on the school paper. When we went back to our homeroom we saw all the writing on the blackboards. We proceeded to selectively remove words and replace them in these passages with inappropriate, funny words. The next day when the teacher started class and she saw what had been done, she began replacing words with the proper ones. We had fun at the expense of the teacher, not understanding how it might have affected her.

I had a cousin I had never met who was in the Coast Guard, stationed on Staten Island. He would come to Brewster every weekend and stay with us. He was my cousin, but I really fell for him. He was to get a date for me, and since my cousin was a great guy, I said okay. We went down to the city, and the blind date who was supposed to come couldn't get out so my cousin grabbed someone else as my date. I knew he wasn't 4-F, but he was to me. That wasn't a very good experience.

Six of us went down to Times Square on New Year's Eve. It came time to go home, and we missed the last train to Brewster. I called my father and told him we would be on the next train. Rather upset he said that we wouldn't get into Brewster until eight in the morning. Betty Cleaver called her father. We had no money. The guys had no money. Dr. Cleaver told Betty to go to the Commodore

Hotel and to put our rooms on his bill - just the girls! The fellas were saying "throw us out a pillow; we'll probably have to sleep in the park!" The three guys ended up sleeping in some third-rate hotel; it was probably a facility for servicemen, since they were in uniform.

We pulled into Brewster, and we figured everybody knew about our adventure. It was New Year's Day. The girls had been wearing leg make-up the day before. When we showered of course all the leg make-up had washed off. So we arrived barelegged.

Rita O'Hara and I and others went to dances at the Pawling School, which was an R& R facility for the Air Force. We invited two young men to come to dinner at Rita's house the next weekend. While we were taking a walk I asked one of them, since I was quite taken by him, if he would like to come again the following weekend. He thanked me but said that his wife would be coming to visit him that weekend. So, that was the end of that.

After graduation I was working for the New York Central Railroad when Herman Donley, the principal of Brewster High School, came to me and offered me a job as secretary to begin September 1945. After the end of the European hostilities a ticker-tape parade was given to General Dwight David Eisenhower. I was still employed in the city and had the thrill of attending his parade. On June 22, 1947 I married Kenneth Richards who had been a co-pilot on a B-29 in the Pacific and was a teacher in Brewster High School where we met. We had four boys [106]

Ruth Godfrey Roth

During the Depression we were all "broke". We lived on a farm, so we had food. We all worked each one having chores. I even milked cows and brought in the hay. I was a farm girl. My father was very much ahead of his time. On the farm he wouldn't use anything but natural manure – no chemicals. He knew what plants to put next to other plants to keep the bugs away. He was an extremely intelligent man and a very, very good dad. Not everyone could have tolerated nine kids!

My 1943 class at Brewster High School was the first one that could not take a class trip to Washington, D.C. After I graduated I took a job at Chance Vought Aircraft in Bridgeport, Connecticut. They sent me to their school to learn riveting, welding and drilling, but I wasn't quite hefty enough to be a riveter, and I only did it occasionally; nevertheless, my family gave me the name "Rosie the Riveter".

Each day I rode to Bridgeport with five men from Croton Falls. They were all family men, and they were so good to me. They were great guys. They would tease me, but they would also protect me at the factory. A lot of men would come up to a young girl and say they could give her a nice weekend. That happened to me, and I went to one of the five men I commuted with, and he went over to the man and told him to leave me alone, not to go near me. They made me feel safe. My father trusted me, and he felt comfortable with my working there. I was only a kid. In those days we only did things with our fathers' permission. Those men would make my life fun. Once they teased me and took a picture of me holding on to me. They showed it to my father and told him they had control of me. They were a lot of fun. I worked very hard with very little time off and no life of my own. Toward the end of the war my father became worried about my health and wanted me to stop working at the war plant. He got me a job at the I.G.A. in Brewster where I worked in the vegetable department.

Eddie Roth and I had become engaged in 1943 just before he went overseas. We took a bus to Danbury, and he gave me my engagement ring on the bus. It was the only time we could be alone with nine kids in the house. When he was overseas I wrote to him every day and sent him packages.

My Uncle Ralph Smalley (my mother's brother) from Brewster who had been a New York State Trooper was a lieutenant in the U.S. Army, but never returned. It is assumed that he was killed in the terrible battles to take back France and to push the Germans back. We know that he was in the battle of Hurtgen Forest, south of Aachen, but there is no information about what division or company he was in. While fighting in Europe he disappeared and was never found.

My uncle was probably in that narrow area where infantrymen were fighting off attacks by the Germans. There was no food or water and only small amounts of ammunition were getting through. The area was under such constant fire that it was impossible to evacuate the wounded. Medical supplies were scarce making it impossible to properly care for the wounded, and a soaking rain covered everyone and everything. The snow covered foxholes and shell craters. This was the environment my uncle was fighting in and where he probably lost his life. Lieutenant Ralph Smalley's body was never recovered.

I worked for Guidepost Magazine for fifteen years in the Prayer Fellowship Dept. Edward Roth and I were married on September 30, 1945 and we had one child. [107]

Dolores Beal Stephens

My first memories of war clouds go back to 1938 when news came about Adolf Hitler and his Nazi army over-running Austria and Czechoslovakia in what was called the *Blitzkrieg*. Little attention was paid. Our country was not interested in war, as it had its own problems because of the Great Depression. Hoboes were encamped at the edge of our village near the New England Railroad tracks within sight of our school, and another was between the railroad tracks and the shore of Lake Tonetta. Occasionally, we were visited by a hobo to whom my mother would give whatever meal we were having and a large cup of coffee. She would keep us girls in the house, protecting us. The memory of the Lindberg baby's kidnapping was still fresh in every mother's mind. 1938 was also the year my brother Ross was born bringing great joy to the family, and I became the chief baby sitter.

In 1939 there was foreboding news in newspapers, radio and the movie newsreels. But I was a teenager and far more interested in the upcoming movie, *Gone With The Wind,* which my friend Charlotte Tuttle and I attended with great enjoyment. We were also excited about going to the New York World's Fair where Mr. Harold Knapp, our school director of music, had arranged for our school band to play several selections on the promenade.

The next country to be devoured by the Nazi army was Poland. The attack on Finland by the Russians is very vivid to me, as newsreels showed the courageous Finnish ski troopers in action. Winston Churchill became Prime Minister of England replacing Neville Chamberlain who preferred to appease the enemy rather than fight.

One summer two of my girlfriends and I arranged with three boys from the lake to get up about 4 a.m. and go fishing. Muriel Pinckney was one of the girls. Ray Shalvoy and Eddie McDermott were with us. We thought this was a lark. We arranged to meet on the lower road and sat on the road in the mist waiting for all to gather. We quietly walked between cottages toward the two rowboats and managed to get in without falling into the water. We couldn't have been serious about fishing. It was dark, but we rowed out. None of us wore life preservers in those days. There wasn't much to it, except that we were having great fun, trying not to laugh too loudly, doing something different, staying out until the sun rose. In those days the greatest teenage exclamations were "golly", "darn", "gee-wiz", and " swell". Anything stronger than those words was not tolerated in public or at home.

At some point I became aware that we had two students in our midst who had come from Czechoslovakia. Joseph Karaffa was in my class, and he had an older brother Michael who later entered military service for the United States. I later learned that his parents had brought them and their sister Anna to the United States in 1936. Even then I sensed that they had come for a better life, but little did I realize how very disastrously the lives of those eastern Europeans would be affected by the events of which only limited news was coming to us.

I remember fragments of news about Norway and the invasion of Denmark and in time the fall of Belgium, Luxembourg and France. Life went on in my town, in my family and in my school.

One day I came home from school and on walking into the dining room I saw six women sitting around our table that was covered by a four-inch stack of heavy woolen fabric. My mother explained that she had worked out an assembly line for making skirts: one person cut, one person basted, one stitched and so on until there was a completed skirt. The American Red Cross would send these skirts to England where there was a grave shortage of both food and clothing.

My freshman year was uneventful, except perhaps that I almost got myself killed. It was at the end of class with Miss McEnroe, a seasoned and fine teacher who once appeared with green hair from an error in her home dye recipe. At the end of class a couple of classmates got me into trouble. One of the students in our school having recently come from Italy was learning English. This day they were joking about saying something in Italian to our new classmate. Naive (or stupid) as I was but with no mal-intent I took up the challenge when given Italian words to say to him. After I said the words he immediately took out a knife and ran toward me. Down the hall I ran, into the auditorium balcony. There we came face to face with one another, and I guess at that moment he understood that I meant him no harm. We both retreated. From then on we were on good terms. A close call, but in those days it was pretty certain that this incident could only have ended as it did. That sort of thing simply did not happen in Brewster in those days. And to this day I cannot believe it occurred – and I never knew what words I spoke.

War had been declared by England, and there were conferences between the Prime Minister, Winston Churchill and President Roosevelt. England needed the help of the United States. Japan was in the news with its imperialistic army, and it looked as though our country would certainly become involved. Wellesley College educated, Madame Chiang Kai-shek visited our country raising money for her cause, China Relief. She was a beautiful and striking figure. Americans gave, not knowing the money was going into their personal treasury, not to the Chinese people.

On December 7, 1941 the news came over the radio about the Japanese attack on Pearl Harbor. Most people of Brewster were at home with the radio on, but many were at the Cameo Movie Theatre. The news spread quickly when it was announced. Already there were Brewster boys serving in the Army who had gone in under the early conscription for what they thought would be a year of service.

In late August 1942 I was fifteen years old and sitting with my jitterbug - dancing partner, Ray Shalvoy, on the lawn in front of our cottage at Tonetta Lake. My dad was indoors talking with my mother and showing her the uniforms he had just purchased in New York City. When I went indoors, the uniforms - olive drab blouse, pinks, Captain's bars and Engineer Corps. pins - were spread on the bed. He had tried to get into the Navy, but upon learning of his particular business background (water well drilling) he was told that the Army might be interested. Though he was well above draft age, they immediately accepted him for the planned North African invasion. Of course what he was told by the Army was top secret, and he could not divulge the location of the upcoming invasion. "A Slip of the Lip Could Sink a Ship" it said on posters. However, my parents had their signals, and my mother deduced that he would be heading for Africa. She was sure he would be landing at Dakar, which wasn't too far off, as I later found out some landings did take place there. (His story tells about his assignment.)

It was the end of the summer of 1942, and we moved from our Tonetta Lake cottage back to our home in Brewster. We thought that my dad would be leaving in late October. There is a feeling of sadness as I write this, because although I don't believe I could imagine what life would be like without my father, I know now what it was like. At about three o'clock in the morning he came to each of us and kissed us good-bye. He hated leaving his family, but he was proud to serve. He was in his new uniform already to perform his duty. He called my mother from somewhere near the New York piers. After that we heard nothing for weeks.

That fall I was in my junior year in Brewster High School, was on the basketball, field hockey and softball teams and played volleyball. I sang in Mr. Harold Knapp's school chorus and played the trumpet in the school band. I particularly loved Sousa marches and still do. I did not mind getting to school at eight in the morning to practice marching on the wet football field. We wore uniforms of our school colors, green and white and had a drum majorette, the first being Margaret Bradbury, followed by Marjorie Lane and later Wilma Truesdale. We had played at all the football games when Coach Geesman was there, when we had untied and undefeated teams with players like Henry Alfke, "Bunky" O'Brien, "Red" von Iderstein, Lucian Styne, Eddie Brady, Ferd Vetare, Tom Lottrechiano, Malcolm Beal and many others. "Bunky" O'Brien, Henry Alfke and Lucian Steyn would later be killed in action in the war. The others including Coach Geesman served their country in various branches of the military.

The war was on; young men still in school enlisted in the armed forces, many needing their parent's signature because they were underage. Ray Shalvoy was in the class of 1943, and he went into the Navy. I didn't see much of him after that, as we both went in our own directions. So, the paucity of high school junior and senior boys was noticeable. Our beloved football was no longer a sport at Brewster. Coach Geesman was a naval officer, and the school hired a coach who instituted soccer. Most boys objected, and the sport didn't bring the school together as football had.

Rationing was in full swing, and there were great shortages of meat, butter, sugar, leather goods, metal and rubber for tires. Since breakfast sausage was a rare item, my mother discovered a pork product called "Scrapple". It was sliced, browned in a pan and served with syrup. It didn't become a favorite, but wasn't bad once in a-while. We understood the rationed items were going to our military forces, to England and finally to liberated countries.

War surrounded us. Dr. Vanderburgh, the father of my good friend, Louise, was in the Medical Corps. serving in China; he spoke at least one Chinese dialect. Another good friend, Muriel Pinckney had four brothers in the service, some in the heat of battle. I don't remember sharing our fears and exchanging more than highlights of V-mail letters, but we were one in sharing like circumstances and we knew it. I did my best to keep my mind on my studies.

I was still a teenager, and my friends and our activities were an important part of my life. Our senior class Washington trip was cancelled. When our junior prom and senior ball were also dispensed with, because of the war, we organized a dance with records and refreshments. I was fortunate to have attended a prom and a ball previously with my childhood sweetheart, Eddie Collins, and driving to it with my cousin Malcolm in his father's car. My first formal dress was of aquamarine taffeta with puffed sleeves – so unsophisticated, and the second was somewhat better in blue. Styles were simple. It was one of my first dates, and that had to be exciting. Our senior class put on plays in which there were young couples. For one play we had to recruit a boy a class behind us who was younger. It was hard to accept having a younger boy, especially when he had to be kissed. It evoked giggles and snide remarks.

My mother was spending time at Red Cross headquarters in Carmel as well as two days a week as a Red Cross nurse's aide at the Mount Kisco Hospital. Nurses were scarce as they were then in military service, and these Red Cross nurse's aides were a great asset, replacing nurses at the hospital. Physicians were also scarce. She wore the uniform of the Red Cross Staff worker with its patches and the crisp uniform of the Red Cross nurses aide, which was a light blue cotton pinafore and white short-sleeve blouse with its patches, nurse's cap, white stockings and white shoes. My mother loved this work.

The first Christmas (1942) that my father was away was very hard for all of us. Perhaps there is more sadness in retelling because at the time there was more mystery – about where he was, how he was, was he lonely, has he gotten our letters and packages? We had received a Christmas package and eagerly awaited opening it to see what he had found for us in that strange land. I am not sure we knew he was in French Morocco at first, just that he was "somewhere in North Africa". His gifts were of tooled Moroccan leather, a colorful belt for me, a goatskin bag and etched bracelets. He sent each of us a maroon, Fez hat, which were worn by the Arabs. Innocently I initiated mine by wearing it to church. I know now on reflection that it wasn't the gifts that pleased us, but the thought that my dad had taken the time and trouble to find gifts for each of us. The gifts and letters were our contact with him until he returned.

After the invasion of Sicily we received word of my father's back injury due to a truck accident. He was soon on a stretcher awaiting evacuation back to North Africa and was eventually able to mail a letter to my mother. After finally reaching Atlantic City, he was able to get a leave. He was so happy to be home; it was a long awaited event for us all. Other families were to wait much longer.

Army convoys were a common sight throughout the nineteen forties with guards placed at strategic corners to direct the lead vehicle; then Army jeeps and trucks filled with young soldiers, waved as they went past villagers. There was a certain excitement to it all, but we had no idea of the dangers into which they were heading – nor could they have imagined the realistic horrors of war. Our blackout curtains were drawn at night.

In April 1944 on his third mission over Berlin "Bunky" O'Brien's plane was shot down. I had just seen him a few weeks before, when he gave me a ride home from basketball practice. Many of my schoolmates – Harvey Van Derlyn, Fred Weizenecker, Bill Macomber, George Schneider, Peter Tavino and Fran Palmer were in the Navy, Marines, Army, Air Force, Coast Guard and Merchant Marines. Others would soon go in service. Many saw combat and experienced inexplicable fear. They were far from home for long periods and witnessed injuries, death and devastation, often helping to create it. Regardless of horrendous experiences, most upon separation from the service were able to move on with their lives, have families and become productive citizens. I have great respect for them all.

At seventeen years of age I graduated in June 1944, and neither my friend Louise Vanderburgh's father nor my father were in the audience. She sang a solo, and I played Schubert's Serenade on my trumpet. My knees were shaking beneath my black robe, and I was certain everyone in the audience could see that. My classmate Henry Alfke was in the army and was killed soon after getting into combat in Europe. He was a gentleman and the only child of a minister's widow.

The day after graduation my mother, my brother and I left Brewster with our gas ration coupons in our car to drive to Columbus, Ohio where my father was on temporary assignment. On the way there we stopped and picked up a hitchhiker who was in the uniform of the Merchant Marine. He was about a year older than I and on his way home. No one in those days hesitated to do this. We spent two weeks at Columbus and then went to Marion, Ohio where we stayed in motels. From there my father was assigned to Fort Belvoir,

Virginia as Assistant Post Engineer, and was put in charge of the dump. Like many dumps all the debris was exposed. My father wanted to improve that condition and decided that a bulldozer should be brought in. All the trash was pushed to the periphery, leveling everything, daily covering up all fresh garbage – a considerably more sanitary situation. This is a common practice today.

Before we moved onto the Belvoir post we rented an apartment outside Alexandria. One day I walked down the dirt driveway and picked up our mail from the box, and in it was The Brewster Standard. It always had news of those in service, injuries and deaths, photos and addresses. This time I read about the death of Robert L. Collins, older brother of my friends Eddie and Jimmy Collins. Bob had died in combat on the island of Guam in the Mariana Islands in the Pacific. It made me sad.

We found out that my cousin Malcolm Beal was stationed at Fort Belvoir. My dad obtained permission to go out to where he was training to visit with him before he left for the Aleutian Islands. It was pouring rain. His sergeant advised my cousin that we were there to visit, and we eagerly awaited his appearance. Soon amongst the trees he appeared, very wet, and we walked toward him. It was so good to see him. I reached in my pocket and gave him a candy bar, only wishing I had a box to hand him. He eagerly took it.

We eventually moved to a little house on the new or temporary side of Fort Belvoir adjacent to the drill fields. Daily, troops would march past our house onto the drill field, and sometimes we would see my five-year old brother, Ross, in his fatigues and toy gun bring up the rear. Across the road were row upon row of barracks. My mother found out that my brother had made friends in the barracks – and the soldiers were good to him. They probably had little brothers back home. It is no wonder that he made the Army his career.

It was the summer of 1944 and a new life for my mother and me. I had left my friends behind; the boys I knew were in the war, and I was surrounded by Army barracks. We would go to the post movie theatre for twenty-five cents and have some meals at the Officers' Club. For a small town girl this was heady stuff.

One Sunday, my father dressed in his uniform, my mother, my brother and I were ready to go out the back door to the car and drive to church. My mother had homemade baked beans in the oven and had turned the oven off knowing that they would be perfectly done and warm when we arrived home. My father, who could never keep his nose out of the kitchen, decided that the beans needed a little more time baking and had turned the oven on again. We drove twelve miles south on Route 1 to the historic Pohick Church and were in the middle of the service when my father turned to me and whispered, "I smell smoke, do you?" Bewildered, but knowing my dad had been up to something, I asked, "why?" Then he told me that he had left the oven on with the beans inside. While driving home he explained to my mother with a boyish glint and regret what he had done. We could picture our little house in flames. My mother had certainly lost her beans and our Sunday supper. When we walked into the small kitchen, it definitely smelled like burned beans – they were black! Needless to say we all ended up going to the Officers' Club for our dinner.

My sister Jane had met a young man while working in a parachute nylon-testing laboratory in New York City. He joined the Air Force and their wedding took place at the post chapel. My sister Joan had joined the WAVES after my father's return, and after leaving St. Albans Naval Hospital on Long Island she was stationed at Alameda Naval Hospital in California. She came across the country by train to attend the wedding. When Jane's husband returned after flying missions from England over Europe, he told her he had fallen in love with an English girl. They eventually divorced – another casualty of war.

While my father was working, my mother, brother and I often spent the afternoon at the Officer's Club swimming pool. It was on the temporary post and not as elegant as the one on the permanent post, but closer to home. Besides, any pool was luxury for us. My mother sat on a chair on the long side of the pool, and I went to the end of the pool and sat on the edge in a wet bathing suit with my feet in the water. Soon I started to feel a sensation like a bite or burning on my derriere. I went over to my mother and told her about it. After removing my suit and rinsing off, the burning became worse and constant; it wasn't a bug bite. When my father came home for dinner, I told him about it, and brought my bathing suit to him to examine. It had two holes in the seat where I had been sitting. My mother and I were informed that the chlorinator for the pool, which my father was in charge of, had been out of commission for a long period of time, and he had spoken to the colonel trying to get it repaired. The soldier who worked at the pool had been mixing the chlorine solution by hand and tossing it into the water. Drops had spilled on the edge of the pool and dried. That is where I had sat. After looking at the suit, my father said, "You are going to have to go with me and show the colonel your burns." I knew my dad was kidding, and he did take my suit to show his commanding officer; this undoubtedly hastened the repair of the chlorinator. My dad said he was lucky a colonel's wife hadn't sat in the chlorine.

That fall I enrolled in Saint Agnes School in Alexandria, Virginia for a post-graduate year. I didn't know what direction I was going in. Attention hadn't been paid to my future, and I was struggling with my next step. I missed my town very much and the friends I had known all my life, but of course my friends were going their own ways too. I felt out of place in this school where the girls had been going for many years. Many of my schoolmates' fathers were colonels and admirals. But I couldn't have been more proud of the contribution my father, a captain, had made to the war effort.

The following year I entered Blackstone College, a junior college in Virginia. The first year I helped organize a formal dance with a good orchestra, which we all greatly enjoyed. I was on the student council the first year and president of the student council my second year. My sisters had gone into the city to work, but I decided to return to Brewster. I enjoyed my employment at P. F. Beal and Sons working for my father and cousin, Malcolm – and becoming reacquainted with local people. In Brewster I was president of the Women's Club in 1953-1954 and helped organize a formal dance, the Snow Ball which was an enjoyable event. We also had The Little Theatre Group in which many Brewster men and women participated.

In June of 1954 I married Mallory Stephens of Brewster. Our wedding took place a week after he graduated from Syracuse Medical School, and in early July he started his internship at Kings County Hospital in Brooklyn. After one year of residency program he was called to serve in the Army Medical Corps and spent two years at Fort Detrick, Md., the biological warfare center for the Army. I did not work but attended classes at Hood College in Frederick, Md. Back in New York I worked for an engineer/inventor until I became pregnant with our first child.

After moving to Mount Kisco our second child was born, and that was just after I lost my father. We lived there for thirty-six years, our two children Mallory, Jr. and Diana graduating from Horace Greeley High School in Chappaqua, N.Y. and Hamilton College. When our children were grown, I continued my studies at Pace University. My husband closed his practice of Rheumatology, and we moved to New Hampshire in 1998 where I continued my interest in sculpting and started to volunteer at the Wright Museum (WWII) near our home. Working at the museum and speaking with veterans was surely the catalyst for collecting the stories of the Brewster veterans.[108]

Mallory Stephens

Once the war in Europe started, Hitler's armies marched through eastern Europe, then western Europe, followed by north Africa and finally deep into Russia. It seemed nothing could stop the German army's *Blitzkrieg*. I can remember looking at a map in the newspaper showing how much land Germany occupied and thinking perhaps Hitler may fulfill his dream of conquering the world and wondering what it might be like to live under Nazi rule. At about that time I had nightmares of *SS Troopers* knocking on the front door and demanding to enter and search our home.

I remember hearing about the new German battleships *Bismarck* and *Graf Spee*. They were the largest and most powerful vessels afloat, posing a real threat to the English navy, which at that time was supposedly the most powerful in the world. Fortunately, the *Bismarck* was disabled by the British shortly after it entered the North Atlantic Ocean, but more exciting to me was the fight between two British cruisers and a destroyer and the *Graf Spee*. Most interesting was the day-by-day reporting of the chase after the *Graf Spee*, which ended in the "neutral" harbor at Montevideo where the German commander ordered his own ship scuttled.

But in spite of the exciting events, life on the home front remained basically unchanged. We went to school every day as usual and played afterwards. Except for football, the basketball, track and baseball events were scheduled and performed as before. With our winning coach Sterling Geesman in service, we now played soccer, which was not embraced by the students as football had been.

On Sunday morning, December 7, 1941, the heating system in St. Andrew's Church was not functioning. Sunday school, which many of us attended regularly, was cancelled, and the eleven o'clock service was shortened to thirty minutes. After our noontime dinner my family took a trip to pick up a new dog, which was to be a gift for my cousin, Helen Hine (Marvin). For some reason the dog wasn't there, and we came home. On our return, I turned on the radio and the announcer was excitedly describing the surprise attack on Pearl Harbor. My father and mother came into the room and listened intently as the announcer described one battleship after another and cruisers which had been sunk. After hearing this I felt as if Japanese airplanes had sunk our entire navy.

After the war had been under way, several Army vehicles, usually jeeps and trucks, started traveling through Brewster on Route 6 heading east toward Danbury. In the beginning on several occasions, after crossing the bridge over the railroad tracks, the drivers, instead of bearing right and proceeding south into the village, would go straight up "Day's Hill" and end up on Garden Street near the school and my house. The Army soon learned to station a guard at the foot of "Day's Hill", so their vehicles would remain on Route 6. Then convoys became longer and longer lasting one hour to most of the day. Before long people would bring food and beverages to the guard directing traffic. As children we loved to see all the men (usually 8 – 10 in the back of a truck) going by and cheer them on.

Another exciting event was to see the freight trains loaded with tanks, jeeps, half - tracks and even parts of airplanes traveling east on the New Haven Railroad. These became longer and longer as the war continued, some of them requiring two engines in front and occasionally even a third engine pushing in the back. It was more fun watching these convoys through the window from the schoolroom than paying attention in class. At least once I counted over one hundred freight and flat cars in one train.

According to my diary, on Friday January 2, 1942 a two and one half hour talk and exhibition were given in the schoolyard about incendiary bombs and how to extinguish them. This was undoubtedly a response to the assault on British civilians in 1940 and 1941. The Red Cross taught First Aid courses, and my father and I attended one later the same month.

Civil Defense was instituted and everyone had to either shut off their lights or cover the windows of their homes and businesses as part of the "blackout" for the eastern seaboard. A "lookout" tower was built in front of the school to spot airplanes and report their movement by telephone to a central office. Volunteers, two at a time, staffed it around the clock with four-hour shifts. Perhaps because our home was next to the tower, I was assigned the 12 – 4 A.M. period. After several weeks it soon became obvious this was too much for a twelve-year old, so my time was changed to 4 – 8 A.M. until the threat was over. The partner I served with more than any other was Norman Donley. With his jokes and amusing stories he was fun to be with. Towards the end of the war when it was obvious we were not going to be bombed, he enjoyed sleeping in and let me sit it out alone. Norm later joined the Merchant Marines.

The Boy Scouts met infrequently but on at least several occasions we helped collect scrap metal. Everyone remembers gas rationing – ineffective in the beginning, because people with X cards could get all the gas they wanted. When the government instituted the A, B, C coupon program, gas rationing was more effective. But throughout the war there was always the "black market" for gasoline and meat. Of course, gutta-percha, most of which came from Japanese-controlled Malaysia was in short supply, so tires were scarce. Meat, butter, coffee and sugar were rationed, but fortunately many other foods were in adequate supply so that we didn't suffer as those in Europe did. Victory gardens helped out in this regard.

To me the most significant feature of World War II was how it changed the people. Everyone wanted to help the country win the war. At first a few young men and later young women enlisted in the armed forces. Conscription came, later followed by the draft. Except for those medically rejected, young men eighteen years old were inducted into the army. Many young men enlisted in the services rather than wait for their draft notice. My brother, Willis H. Stephens, was in the Army Air Corps. Our family followed his career movements with interest as many "washed out" of aviation school. We were very proud of him when he earned his "wings", and when he became an instructor in an aviation school in Arizona.

The most difficult part of the war for everyone was learning that one of our young men died. When Henry Alfke whom I liked so much was killed, I felt deeply saddened and somewhat bewildered. Each time a service man we knew died, my family and I felt sadness and concern for the family left behind; Harding O'Hara, Robert Collins, "Bunky" O'Brien, Wilbert Nagle and Edward Smith still remain in my memory clearly.

In 1950 I graduated from Hamilton College. In 1954 Dolores Beal and I were married in St. Andrew's Church, Brewster the same week I graduated from Syracuse Medical School. We lived in New York City (except for two years in the U.S. Army, 1956-1958) where I did my internship at Kings County Hospital, residency in medicine and fellowship in rheumatology at Albert Einstein School of Medicine and medical research at The Rockefeller University until 1963 when we moved to Mount Kisco, N.Y. There I practiced internal medicine and rheumatology for thirty-three years until my retirement. We now live near Wolfeboro, New Hampshire. Our son Mallory Jr. was born while we lived in New York City, and our daughter Diana was born shortly after moving to Mount Kisco.[109]

Charlotte Tuttle

In 1939 "Dodie" and I were invited for dinner by the elderly couple that lived in the apartment of her parents house. We were twelve years old, and this was a new experience for us. I can remember she served as a first course broiled grapefruit. I had never had that before.

One of the simple pleasures we had in our teen years was going sleigh riding (sledding) at night after dinner. There was an occasion when the boys joined us, and one of the boys said something unseemly. I was impressed with Willis Stephens, because he didn't join in. He was a real gentleman.

There were two fellows who were several years older than Dodie and I, and we only knew them as upper-classmen. They were friendly, and for some reason whenever we passed them on the street, they would start singing, "You Are My Lucky Star." It was funny.

When we were seniors the Washington trips were cancelled, so instead of going to Washington as previous classes had, we arranged a trip into New York City. We didn't all go to the same place. Some went to Jack Dempsey's. My friends Muriel Pinckney (Richards) and "Dodie Beal (Stephens) went together, but I don't remember what I did. Instead of Washington for a week it was New York City for a day.

During our senior year a group of us decided to go to the Hollywood Café. After all, we were now about to graduate (1944), and you might say it was a right of passage to go where we knew most people went to drink. Most of us didn't drink, or were just trying it out ordering rum and cokes or mostly cokes. The next day I told my father I didn't go. But in the current issue of our local paper, The Brewster Standard, there it was in print - it said that I was there along with the other names. (My father worked for the paper as a typesetter). I don't know who put it in the paper. Of course my father was death on booze.[110]

Frank Vetare

After being out on Sunday afternoon we sat in the kitchen waiting for hot chocolate and crackers. The radio was on, but as I recall no one was listening very closely when suddenly one of the commentators broke through and told of the Japanese bombing Pearl Harbor with no warning. I was twelve and remember asking my Mother, "Will the Japanese bomb us here in Brewster?" She assured me that they would not, and so began my not-so-normal growing up. The years following this Sunday night in Brewster marked me for the rest of my life, as it did many millions of people around the world.

It took some time to notice, but Brewster was soon without young men, except for those of us still continuing our education at Brewster High School high atop Garden Street. The draft took care of calling up all eligible young men and left the town to those of us who were too young to serve. Because we were not of draft age did not mean that we were not involved with wartime activities.

In the shop where we learned to use a hammer, screwdriver and pliers each of us sawed, carved and painted wood models of aircraft, both American and German. These were silhouetted against a backdrop for learning and identifying them as we stood watch in the aircraft tower adjacent to the school. We would spend much time there scanning the skies for enemy aircraft that never came. We were very serious about our duties watching for these airplanes and kept a detailed log of any planes flying over and identifying them. At thirteen and fourteen this was serious business and made me very proud to help save the country from the Axis forces.

Other things that involved those of us staying home were rationing, canceling of sports programs, blackouts and seriousness about all activities encountered. The rationing made us aware of the need to conserve products such as meat, butter, gasoline, tires and of course autos which were no longer manufactured for civilian use.

In spite of these "hardships" for young students, we managed to have some fun. I can remember very clearly getting together with Bobby Donley and Billy Ives, and with one gasoline coupon I supplied (21/2 gallons) going over to Peach Lake to roller skate or to a dance. Usually on the way home we would run out of gas and have to push that big, old Buick touring car the rest of the way home. It was not only big and old but very, very heavy. It was the way things were, and we fully expected to run out of gas - just another sacrifice for the boys doing the fighting for us.

Sports were severely curtailed because of the war, since traveling from town to town for these events was not only expensive but also difficult with all the rationing in force. We did play baseball locally, and I can remember playing on the team with Hank Alfke who was a senior. Hank was as big and strong as he was a handsome young man, - the kind of upper classman we all looked up to – and we were proud to be his teammate. After graduation (or maybe before) Hank was drafted into the Army and sent to training. Within 60 days after playing baseball with Hank, we got word that he was killed in action somewhere in Europe. It would be hard to recall exactly how we felt hearing this news, but I do remember how close we came to the war because of this tragic event. Hank was, of course, not the only loss Brewster suffered during World War II. Every war death hit close to home because we knew everyone.

In spite of the difficulties of growing up during the war we all survived quite well. However, there was never a time when some type of guilt didn't follow me, because I was not old enough to be in uniform and therefore safe and sound in school. I can remember a time when my mother took me to Danbury to get fitted for a new suit. A woman watching me try on a couple of jackets remarked to my mother that I should be in uniform, and how come I wasn't. I was fifteen in 1944 and looked very mature, but it did affect me and added to the guilt. Teachers in Brewster High (Miss McEnroe, Miss Fitzmorris, Miss Harwood, Mr. Watson and others reminded us often of how lucky we were not to have to go to war. And, of course, our Pastor, Father Heany did it in a much more heated way. He reminded us that we should be grateful and better Catholics because of the sacrifices our boys in uniform were making for us. Joan and I laugh now, because we consider ourselves the "Guilt Generation".

I celebrated V-E Day with John Gavaghan and Joanie Tabor, and V-J Day alone. It was, even at my young age of sixteen, momentous, and I shall never forget each of these days.

On April 18, 1946 I celebrated my 17th birthday, graduated from BHS in June, and on July 5th reported to the Merchant Marine Academy in San Mateo, California. As a Cadet-Midshipman I had marvelous experiences for one year. I wasn't doing well in a couple of classes, missed home and Julie, and did not care to think of myself as a career Naval Officer, so resigned my commission. I was thinking more of a career in music or physical education, but neither turned out.

One year after returning to Brewster I had my draft call, so traveled to Danbury and joined the Navy as an Aviation Recruit and spent four years (1948-1952) in the Navy as an Aviation Photographer (AF2). In 1952 I was discharged and went to the Rochester Institute of Technology and earned a BS in Photographic Science.

After graduation I was hired by Kodak where I spent 22 years.

In 1955 I married Joan Cropper from Berlin, MD. We have four children. We presently reside in Berlin, Md.

Brewster was a great town to grow up in, and thanks to my father and mother we were able to grow up quite well...As you well know, our generation was not one to discuss our experiences, ...especially those who went into service during World War II and subsequent wars. We are the *quiet generation*, as we were taught not to boast or brag and not to complain.[111]

Virginia Dutcher Ward

Our home was on Carmel Avenue when I was born; we later moved to East Main Street. I always thought Brewster's Main Street was so great – the bank in the middle of the street and good sidewalks on both sides of the village.

My father worked on the New York Central Railroad and was called a Leader Inspector. He worked at the roundhouse unless he was called to work on a wreck, which could have occurred anywhere on the line. He would direct the clean-up operations of the crane which had to pick up one piece of debris at a time at the site of the wreck. The wrecks were sometimes derailments. One Brewster resident told me if Lou Dutcher inspects a car, it is inspected. I remember one bad train accident which my father was not involved in, because it was on the CNE or New Haven line at the edge of Brewster on the trestle over Route 6 near the old Love's Restaurant.

We had a large school orchestra under the direction of Harold Knapp. I played the violin, and one of the other violinists was Louie Diamond whose father was a tailor on Railroad Avenue. Louie played the violin beautifully.

Sterling Geesman was the coach at B.H.S. when I was in high school. That was when we had a powerhouse of a team and beat Danbury High School more than once. Sometimes there were night games, but I think they were at Danbury. Eddie Von Iderstyne and Kenny Butler were two of our football players that I remember. Kenny got an appointment to West Point. Some of the members of my class were Bill Cox, Gerald Brearton, Alfred O'Hara, Francis Pinckney and Beatrice Denton. I graduated from B.H.S. in 1935.

Politics was very important in our house, whether local, national or international. My father talked about Alf Landon when he was running for president. The country was *first* in our house; my father was very patriotic. He wasn't in WWI but had expected to be called when the war ended.

One of our favorite places was Diehl's Bakery or Brewster Bakery. In its heyday it was a beautiful place with marble counters and beautiful yellow glass chandeliers, a large mirror and tables in the back through an archway. School students used to like to gather there for ice cream sodas and talk. Their bakery was excellent. They made charlotte russe, ladyfingers, cinnamon buns, and beautiful cupcakes. Their special pink and white wintergreen and mint candies were my father's favorites. I used to pay attention to all the details of what was going on, and if my father wanted to know something, he would say, ask the Philadelphia lawyer.

We did a lot of roller-skating in the high school, when I was out of school. Emerson and Alec Addis who were very large men would go skating, and if one of them fell he couldn't get up from the floor. He would be laughing, and we would all be standing around laughing as he would try to get the wheels under him but couldn't. Everyone in town went skating before the new gymnasium floor was installed.

My mother ran a "tourist house" called Red Brick Tourist House. One of her guests was a personal beautician at the Commodore Hotel who would be sent to guest rooms to do her work. We became good friends, and she influenced me to go into hair dressing. After high school I went to beauty school in White Plains. After that I took a course in New York City to learn to do facials. For experience I worked in shops in Katonah and Bedford and did facials there. Eventually I opened my own business in my mother's house. I didn't do many facials there, but I was otherwise very busy. My classmate Iris Lawson was undecided about going to business school, and she was influenced by my going to beauty school and decided to do the same. Iris married a Brewster boy, Bob Brearton. Mary Gorilli, another classmate also had a beauty parlor in Brewster.

My niece Gail Adam was a camper at the Pietsch Lake Day Camp sponsored by the Brewster Lions' Club. She remembers that Dodie Beal (Stephens) was a counselor at the camp. Then Gail went to Coach Santore's camp in Sodom district with young Ross Beal. One of their activities was horseback riding.

I would go to the city quite often attending the show at the Paramount Theatre. I would sit in the first row, and when the stage rose I was about six feet from the entertainer. Jane Froeman was one of the entertainers I saw. I remember the thick eye make-up she was wearing for her appearance as she went up on the moving stage. One time I took my niece to the Danbury Fair. There were some kind of races, and when she found out that Elizabeth Taylor, the actress, was there in a box seat she bought two box seat tickets for us. We sat right behind her.

My sister, Pearl Dutcher married Ozzie Martel who worked for our assemblyman, D. Mallory Stephens for a long time working both in New York City and in Albany. He loved working for him and he loved his kids. The feeling was mutual.

Bobby Collins (KIA) introduced me to Robert M. Ward who was a New York State Trooper attached to Troop K, having been transferred from Troop B. When Trooper Ward asked Bobby if he thought I would be interested in dating him, he said he was sure I would be. We married in 1940 and lived in Brewster until 1968 when we went to New Hampshire. We had a son and a daughter.

On Sunday, December 7, 1941 I was driving over to Fishkill to meet my husband and was about at the causeway on Route 6 between Brewster and Carmel when I heard on the radio about the attack on Pearl Harbor. I was so shocked and upset – and angry. My brother-in-law Ernie Adam was the projectionist at the Cameo Theatre where many people learned about the attack. When the old Ritz movie theatre had undergone reconstruction, there was space next door for a shop. The former chauffeur for Mayor Harry Wells, George Snyder and his wife Helen opened a dress shop there which was very successful.

During WWII my husband was a member of the Civil Defense. When convoys would go through Brewster, we would wave as they passed, and many of them would throw out postal cards which they had written to family members, hoping we would mail them – and of course we did.

Numerous Brewster people worked in the defense factories in Bridgeport, Connecticut. My sister worked at Chance-Vought. Others who commuted to work in defense were Della Holder (Scolpino), Marie McGary, and Mrs. Raymond Shalvoy. Butter and sugar being rationed, were like diamonds. A customer was lucky if she was in the First National Store when a shipment of either one came in. My mother would combine oleomargarine with the butter and stretch it until the next available supply. Shipments didn't seem very frequent. We respected every rule and regulation and also bought many bonds.

I didn't stay in hairdressing, but worked part-time at Guide Post Magazine in Carmel for fifteen years.[112]

Family Picture sent to Wm. Ross Beal
Standing: Norma Jane Beal – Left
　　　　　Dolores "Dodie" Beal – Center
　　　　　Joan Ross Beal – Right

Lower: Ross Beal, Jr. hiding his left arm, which he had broken.

Seated: Florence L.S. Beal

Dolores "Dodie" Beal reading news about the war.

Charlotte Tuttle
Susan Foulk
Muriel Pinckney

Left: Muriel Pinckney
Right: John Palmer

Killed In Action – World War II

Town of Southeast, Putnam County, New York

Francis J. Adams
Henry Alfke
William Burke
Donald W. Card
Robert L. Collins, Jr.
James G. Duignan
Emery C. Hynard
Lloyd W. Knapp
Frances F. Lynch
Ernest R. Marasco, Jr.
Wilbert F. Nagle
John R. O'Brien
Henry Harding O'Hara
Robert C. Rapp
Ralph Smalley
Edward F. Smith, Jr.
Lucian Steyn

World War II Honor Roll

Brewster/Southeast, New York

1939-1945

Adam, Ernest J.
Adams, Francis J.
Adams, Thomas J.
Adams, Viviane W.
Adrain, Richard N.
Alexander, William
Adrian, Joseph M. III
Adrian, Richard A.
Alfke, Henry
Anderson, Charles R.
Anderson, Philip F.
Ashby, Arthur T.
Ashby, Joseph
Ashby, Louis F.
Auguston, Oscar E.
Bahr, Jerome F.
Ballard, Clifford H.
Ballard, Everett
Ballard, Kenneth R.
Banks, Clarence R.
Barbour, Charles T.
Barbour, David A.
Barrett, Arthur J.
Barrett, Dalton
Barrett, Donald S.
Barrett, Grange H.
Barrett, Leroy A.
Barrowcliff, Frederick
Bartram, Oscar F.
Beal, Joan R.
Beal, Malcolm T.
Beal, Maurice M.
Beal, Philip F. III
Beal, Wm. Ross

Bell, William H.
Bennett, Hillyer
Bettcher, Clayton F.
Bettcher, Edward M.
Bettcher, George T.
Bettcher, Rankin
Blanco, Miles P.
Blaney, Charles D.
Blaney, Eugene E.
Blaney, George
Blaney, Robert F.
Bolan, Cecil
Boland, Thomas J.
Booth, Frederick
Booth, Harry E.
Bouie, John R.
Bove, Anthony J.
Bowes, Martin E.
Brady, Edward J.
Brady, James J. Jr.
Brady, John E.
Brady, Patrick J.
Brady, Robert F.
Brady, Robert P.
Brandon, Bernard P.
Brandon, Daniel A.
Brearton, Gerald C.
Brennan, Emmett
Brennan, Joseph G.
Brennan, Kenneth J.
Brennan, Leo
Brewer, Bernard H.
Brown, Harold S.
Brown, Lewis M. Jr.

Bruen, George R.
Bruen, James M.
Bruen, Robert E.
Bruns, Bowling J.
Bryant, Walter R.
Buck, Robert G.
Buckstine, Ernest R.
Budzienski, Stanley C.
Burdge, Frederick W.
Burdick, Caprice F.
Burdick, Robert F. Jr.
Burdick, Roland
Burke, John J.
Burke, William
Butler, Edward
Butler, George M.
Butler, Lee
Butler, Leonard
Butler, Robert J.
Butler, Kenneth
Cable, Charles E.
Cable, Clarence R.
Caggiano, Charles
Cain, Theodore
Card, Donald W
Carlone, George, J.
Carlone, Patrick M.
Carollo, Ann A.
Carollo, Anthony J.
Carollo, Archimedes
Carollo, Charles
Carollo, Joseph
Carollo, Victor M.
Carr, Dale J.

Carr, Vane F.
Carroll, Francis
Caroll, Richard
Caruso, Mario F.
Castle, Eddie H.
Ceasrine, Dominic
Cioccolanti, Joseph J.
Cipriani, Antonio
Cipriani, Camillo H.
Clasgens, Al
Cleaver, Robert S. Jr.
Clough, George R.
Clough, William S.
Cole, Charles
Cole, John
Collins, Edward A.
Collins, James P.
Collins, Robert L. Jr.
Cornell, Kenneth R.
Coughlin, John J.
Cox, William S.
Creighton, Edward
Creighton, Francis
Creighton, James
Cunningham, Jerome L.
Cunningham, Leo J.
Cunningham, Patrick P.
Cunningham, Richard
Cunningham, Thomas
Curran, Kenneth J.
Dahm, Alfred N.
Daley, William R.
Davis, George
Delury, Michael
Devall, Raymond A.
Devall, Richard E.
Diamond, Louis
Dickinson, Fred A.
Dickinson, James F.
Dingee, Howard E.
Donley, Norman
Donley, Richard A.
Dorman, Carl Jr.
Dubois, G.D.
Duckworth, Leonard A.
Duignan, James G.
Dunford, Francis W.
Dunn, Edward D.

Durgie, Douglas R.
Durkin, Thomas H.
Dwyer, Donald
Dwyer, Gladys C.
Dwyer, William J. Jr.
Eakin, Arthur
Eastwood, William H.
Eaton, Arthur
Eaton, Ernest R.
Eckert, Raymond G.
Ekstrom, Frank H.
Elliott, Arthur Jr.
Ellis, Charles B.
Ellis, Gerald R.
Enright, George L.
Enright, James L.
Enright, Robert J.
Ercole, Patrick
Ernest, Delbert
Ernest, Robert J.
Ernest, William H.
Falconer, James
Farrell, James A.
Farrell, Leonard G.
Ferguson, Gerald W.
Finch, Edwin F.
Fineberg, Louis W.
Fish, Cortland
Fisher, Frank Jr.
Fisher, Matthew J.
Fitch, John C.
Fitzgerald, Raymond F.
Flanagan, John T.
Flanagan, Joseph T.
Flanagan, Philip J.
Folchetti, Robert
Foley, William Jr.
Foley, William G.
Fortenese, Alfred J.
Fosowitz, Martin
Fosowitz, Max
Fosowitz, Milton
Foster, Clayton
Foster, James R.
Foster, John J.
Foster, Joseph
Foster, Raymond
Foster, Thomas J.

Fowkes, George F.
Fratticelli, Anthony
Freda, Luigi A.
Fredette, Reginald G.
French, Clark
French, May E.
Furco, Anthony J.
Gallagher, Richard E.
Furst, John C.
Garnsey, Leon L.
Garnsey, LeRoy C.
Gatling, Norborne P, Jr.
Gavaghan, James L. Jr.
Gavaghan, John E.
Gebing, Howard
Geesman, Sterling A.
Genovese, Frank R.
Gilstad, Robert C.
Gladwin, William
Goossen, Behrend M
Goossen, Frederick L.
Gould, William H.
Green, Francis T.
Green, John J.
Green, Michael J.
Greene, Mearl H.
Greene, Michael J.
Gregory, Peter C.
Gregory, William
Hampton, William
Hancock, Harold T.
Hancock, LeRoy C.
Hanna, Edward A.
Hansen, Robert B. Sr.
Harmon, Frederick F.
Harmon, Richard J.
Hazzard, Herbert E.
Heinen, Robert
Heinen, Theodore B.
Heinchon, Robert E.
Heinchon, Raymond Jr.
Heller, Edward Jr.
Hinkley, George
Hoffman, Raymond F.
Hopkins, Kenneth C.
Horton, William C.
Hoyt, Philip D. Jr.
Huber, Walter S.

Hughes, Frank
Hughes, Herbert J.
Hughes, Joseph C.
Hutchings, Warren
Hyatt, George W.
Hynard, Emery C.
Irving, John W.
Ives, William Jr.
Jackson, Theodore
Jenkins, Arthur D.
Jenkins, Fred A. Jr.
Johnson, Edward
Johnson, George B. Jr.
Johnson, Lawrence
Johnson, Thomas Jr.
Johnson, Vincent L.
Jones, Paul
Jones, Thomas S.
Jones, William Reese
Junkin, Joseph
Junkin, Peter D.
Karaffa, Michael J.
Kautzman, James E.
Keiper, John
Kellogg, John A. Jr.
Kelly, John J.
Kenney, Norman E.
Kenney, Robert
Kent, Dan
Kilcoyne, Robert J.
Killarney, Francis
Killarney, James
Killarney, Lawrence E.
Killarney, Thomas
Killarney, Walter K.
Killory, Francis J.
King, Bertha E.
Knapp, Lloyd W.
Krueger, Fred T.
Lally, Rosemary
LaMere, Everett
Lane, Harrison
Larkin, John F. Jr.
Larkin, William H.
Laurens, Samuel
Law, Mortimer H.
Ledley, John J.
Lee, Coleman E.

Lee, Ronald
Light, Roy T.
Lord, Ralph
Lotrecchiano, Gaetano T.
Lovallo, Nicholas F.
Lucas, Malcolm C.
Ludington, George W.
Lynch, Francis F.
Lynch, James A.
MacFarlane, Peter
MacKenzie, Allen
Mackey, Douglas F.
Macomber, Harry T.
Macomber, Myron
Macomber, William A.
Magnuson, Frederick E.
Magnuson, James A.
Makenny, William R.
Mallory, William
Manes, Louis G.
Marasco, Ernest R. Jr.
Markowski, Stephen
Maroney, David C.
Martin, Harold W.
Martin, John W.
Matrin, Joseph S.
Mathews, Henderson
McCabe, Spaulding
McGarrity, Patrick W.
McGarry, Vincent J.
McInerney, John C.
McLagan, Donald B.
McNulty, John J. Jr.
McQuaid, James J.
Melody, John J.
Michell, Joseph
Michell, Ralph W.
Miller, Oscar F.
Miller, Ralph W.
Miller, Stanley B.
Mitchell, Benjamin F.
Monte, Henry E.
Moore, Robert N.
Morey, George E.
Morgan, George W.
Mullarkey, James W.
Murphy, James E.
Murphy, John T.

Murphy, Richard
Murtha, Bernard J.
Murtha, Edward J.
Murtha, William H.
Mygan, Thomas M.
Nagle, Wilbert F.
Nelson, Albert S.
Nelson, Carl A.
Nelson, Ernest
Newcomb, Kenneth T.
Newman, Edward W.
Newman, James T.
Newman, Joseph
O'Brien, Francis
O'Brien, John R.
O'Connor, Eugene Jr.
O'Grady, James E.
O'Hara, Haines
O'Hara, H. Harding
O'Hara, John F. Jr.
O'Neill, Kiernan, J.
Owens, Alfred L.
Owens, John A.
Owens, Robert L.
Paddock, John R.
Palmer, Edward F.
Palmer, Francis C.
Palmer, Henry J.
Palmer, John T.
Palmer, Kenneth G.
Palmer, Robert E.
Pappas, George F.
Parish, Preston S.
Parish, Richard L. Jr.
Penny, Edward H.
Penny, William A.
Perlini, Fred
Petersen, Frederick
Petersen, George A.
Petersen, Rudolf W.
Phillips, John W. Jr.
Platt, Felix
Piazza, August L.
Piazza, Frank J.
Piazza, John V.
Piazza, Salvatore
Pinckney, Earl
Pinckney, Lafayette

Pinckney, LaVerne
Pinckney, Remington, Jr.
Piersall, Clinton
Piersall, Wallace
Pitkat, Robert
Pitkat, William C. Jr.
Platt , Felix
Platt, Stanley
Princepe, John J.
Prisco, Louis R.
Purdy, Leon W.
Quigley, William M.
Rapp, Robert C.
Reardon, George J.
Reardon, James J.
Reardon, John J.
Rechen, Behrend J.
Rechen, Henry J.
Reed, Francis Farrell
Reed, John B.
Reed, Martin E.
Relyea, Charles
Relyea, Chester
Relyea, Douglas L.
Relyea, Marjorie G.
Relyea, Ralph B.
Relyea, Victor F.
Repp, Walter P.
Ricci, Mariano
Richardson, Frank
Rigdon, Beryl E.
Riley, Francis W.
Roach, William E.
Robinson, Frank E.
Rohacik, Michael P.
Rose, Louis F.
Rosenberg, Benjamin
Ross, Harvey D.
Ross, John
Roth, Edward G.
Ruffles, Clark W.
Russell, Arthur H.
Russell, Ernest
Rutherford, James L.
Ryan, Philip J.
Ryan, Thomas
Sagratti, Aldo J.
Salvia, Anthony P.

Salvia, Salvatore
Santorelli, Anthony A.
Santorelli, John B.
Schaefer, Harold
Schaniel, George Jr.
Schneider, Francis S.
Schneider, George W.
Schoonmaker, E.H. Jr.
Scolpino, Robert J.
Shalvoy, Raymond Jr.
Sheehan, John L.
Sheppard, William A. Jr.
Sheridan, Philip J.
Sherwood, Clifford M. Jr.
Slack, George W.
Sloan, John M. Jr.
Smalley, Asbury E.
Smalley, Chester L.
Smalley, Everett R.
Smalley, Grant
Smalley, Harold L.
Smalley, Ralph
Smith, Caleb F.
Smith, Donald J.
Smith, Edward F. Jr.
Smith, Harold
Smith, Herbert C.
Smith, Howard L.
Smith, John E.
Smith, Paul H.
Smith, Robert J.
Smith, Robert V.
Smith, Rodney L.
Smith, Thomas B.
Smith, William F.
Snidero, Margaret G.
Sniffen, Harold A.
Sniffen, Thomas E.
Sottile, Anthony I.
Sprague, Albert W.
Sprague, Robert T.
Sprague, Samuel.
Stefanic, Charles P.
Stephens, Willis H.
Stevens, George E.,
Stevens, Harry R.
Steyn, Lucian
Stokes, Daniel

Stokes, John P.
Strang, Carrel
Strang, Francis C.
Strobel, Arthur F.
Strobel, Edward R.
Struss, Francis T.
Susnitzky, Leo C.
Swenson, Robert F.
Tacchino, Louis
Tavino, Peter A.
Tavino, Peter J.
Taylor, Warren M.
Terwilliger, James M.
Thompson, Alphonse L.
Thompson, William J.
Thorpe, Harry
Thorson, William A.
Thompkins, George C.
Tranquilli, Ulindo
Travis, Albro S.
Truran, Edward
Truran, John R.
Turene, Charles W.
Turnrose, Raymond F.
Turnrose, Theodore H.
Tuttle, Earle
Tuttle, Edward S.
Tuttle, John L.
Tuttle, Mary F.
Tuttle, Nelson P.
Utter, Douglas E.
Utter, Harold R.
VanDerlyn, Harvey J.
VanScoy, Benjamin
Vanaria, Anthony, J.
Vanaria, Vincent
Vanderburgh, Alexander
VanVlack, Isaac E. Jr.
Vetare, Ferdinand
Vichi, Edward A.
VonGal, Donald R.
VonGal, George E. Jr.
VonGal, Herbert V.
VonGal, John C.
Vores, Alfred D. III
Vreeland, Dirck
Vreeland, Everett W.
Vreeland, Harold H. III

Vreeland, Harold H. Jr.
Vreeland, Jack
Vreeland, James F. Jr.
Vreeland, Somers R.
Vreeland, T.R. Jr.
Wallace, Francis
Walsh, Edward T.
Ward, Raymond D.
Waters, Bernard J.
Waters, John J.
Waters, Richard R.
Watts, Harold
Watts, Lester

Weill, Malcolm
Weizenecker, Edwin
Weizenecker, Emil Jr.
Weizenecker, Richard
Weizenecker, Frederick A.
Weizenecker, William
Welch, Francis M.
Welch, Joseph E.
Welch, Timothy P.
Welch, William M.
Wells, H. Crosby
Wells, Henry H. Jr.
Wells, Tomlinson

White, Leslie H.
Whitlock, Charles
Whitlock, Walter B.
Widman, John
Williams, Ernest J.
Williams, John C.
Williams, Phillip H.
Williams, Roger F.
Williams, Wallace
Wilson, Walter S.
Wolfe, Felix
Zecher, Ralph W.

292

Bibliography

Copyright © 1990 *Unsung Sailors,* by Justin F. Gleichauf, with permission of Naval Institute Press, U.S. Naval Institute, Annapolis, MD.

Copyright © 1994 *Before the First Wave,* by Larry L.Woodard. Reprinted with permission of Sunflower University Press, P.O. Box 1009, 1531 Yuma, Manhattan, Kansas 66505-1009

Retirement Speech:
Commodore Lewis E. Angelo's remarks at Captain Daniel Brandon's Retirement on Front Steps, Naval Hospital, Bethesda, Md. May 17,1984.

Interview with Captain Daniel A. Brandon, MSC, USN (Ret.), conducted by Jan K. Herman, BUMED Historian, Darnestown, Md. 1 July 1992.

---

[1]The interview for Malcolm Beal's story took place in Englewood, Florida in February 2001.

[2]Capt. Wm. Ross Beal's history was written by his daughter, Dolores Beal Stephens and taken from letters he had written home, from the diary written while in Sicily and from her recollections.

[3]Taken from the declassified document entitled, "History of the 401st Engineer Battalion (Water Supply) From Activation (April 1941 to 1 August 1944)."

[4]Emmett Brennan's story was written by his widow, Gertrude and sent to the compiler of these memoirs.

[5]Joseph Brennan's story was sent by Joseph's brother Leo on October 6, 2000.

[6]Leo Brennan sent the story which he wrote on October 6, 2000.

[7]Interview took place at Bernard Brewer's home in North Salem, N.Y. on May 31, 2001.

[8]Written by Ernest R. Buckstine's son, Ernest R. Buckstine III and sent June 5, 2002 with contributions from Elizabeth D. Buckstine who kept a scrapbook during the time she and her husband were at the camps in the U.S. Elizabeth's sister Beatrice Denton Green also contributed some information.

[9]George Carlone sent his story through E-mailings and telephone conversations. He also sent copies of Brewster Standard news clippings and photos from the war years.

[10]Patrick Carlone sent his story written on December 27, 2000.

[11]Anthony Carollo's widow, Dorothy, wrote her husband's story on September 27, 2001.

[12]Joseph Carollo's history was written on January 17, 2001 and mailed.

[13]The interview for Joseph Cioccolanti's story was on November 27, 2000 at his home in Brewster.

[14]Robert Folchetti's history was provided by his wife Anna Lotrecchiano Folchetti (Brewster), received October 19, 2001. In April of 2002 some details were added.

[15]Behrend Goossen's story was written by Chloe Goossen Morris for her father and sent on February 24, 2002.

[16]Frederick Goossen wrote his own story and added details in a letter of September 4, 2001.

[17]Interview with Nicolas Lavallo on September 10, 2001 at the VFW hall in Brewster.

[18]This history was written on February 6, 2001 by the daughter of Louis Manes with her father. She told me that he wanted to see his name on the Honor Roll list, and I promptly mailed it to him in Arizona.

[19]On February 26, 2001, David Maroney wrote the story on his military service.

[20]The first interview with Robert Palmer was on November 29, 2000 at his home, Another meeting on September 10 at his home was followed by an appreciated lunch with Bob and his wife Jean. We met again on November 18, 2001, and had numerous telephone conversations.

[21]Interview on June 26, 2001 at the home of Frank Piazza in Pawling, N.Y. where I also interviewed Vincent Vanaria. This was after a delicious luncheon served by their wives.

[22]Earl Pinckney sent some information in a letter in May of 2000 followed by a more detailed account of his experiences.

[23]Fred Rapp wrote November 19, 2001 and gave me information about his military service.

[24]On September 12, 2001 Richard Rapp related his own experiences in the Army. We met at the VFW hall in Brewster. At this meeting Dick provided me with copies of letters from the War Dept. (1945) and Headquarters, 10th Mtn. Div. (1945) pertaining to his brother Robert's death.

[25]Interview with Robert Rapp's brother Richard on September 12, 2001 at the VFW hall in Brewster. Fred Rapp also wrote about his brother in a letter dated November 19, 2001.

[26]The interview with Benny Rosenberg took place on June 26, 2001 where he works at the Southeast Community Center at the north end of Tonetta Lake.

[27]The interview with Ruth Godfrey Roth took place on September 10, 2001 at the VFW hall in Brewster.

[28]Interview took place on May 30 at Aldo Sagrati's home on Carmel Avenue, Brewster, and we became reacquainted. I was so sorry to learn of his death before publication of the book.

[29]Sam Salvia wrote his story and sent it to me in May of 2001.

[30]Donald Smith's separation papers stated,"GUNNER ANTIAIRCRAFT: Operated a range finder (pecker stick) on a .40 MM antiaircraft gun to make it easier for layers and cannoneers to get a lead on the plane. At various times filled in as a cannoneer, loader, and firer".

[31]Interview on May 29, 2001 at Donald Smith's home on Putnam Terrace.

[32]Thomas Smith's interview took place at the VFW hall in Brewster on September 10, 2001.

[33]Peter J. Tavino's story was related to me on November 29, 2000 after a class of 1944 luncheon at Sciortino's Restaurant in Brewster.

[34]Anthony Vanaria was interviewed on May 31, 2001 at his home in Brewster.

[35]Dr. Vanderburgh's story was given during an interview with his daughter, Louise Vanderburgh Nicolai on July 31, 2001 at our home in New Hampshire.

[36]The story of Isaac VanVlack was written by his widow, Jeanne Jenkins Van Vlack, and was received February 23, 2002. Jeanne was a Brewster girl, and her brother, Arthur, served in the Army Air Corps.

[37]The interview for Bernard Water's story took place at his home in Brewster on May 31, 2001.

[38]Richard Weizenecker's story was related to me on September 10, 2001 at the VFW hall in Brewster.

[39]Crosby Wells mailed his story to me in October, 2001 and is in his own words. Some details were added in a letter of May 26, 2002.

[40] Note: Crosby's father, Henry H. Wells, Sr. was the beloved Mayor of Brewster for many years and served as Chairman of the Selective Service Board of Putnam County throughout the WWII years, faithfully seeing off the recruits as they left home to serve in the military.

[41]Interview took place at the home of Bernard Brandon in Brewster on June 27, 2001.

[42]Arthur Jenkin's story was gathered by Arthur's fifteen year-old grandson, Brett, written and mailed to me. His wife Jeanette also provided information. Arthur talked with me about his experiences while visiting on October 2,2001 at the WWII Wright Museum in Wolfeboro, N.H. where I volunteer. Unfortunately Arthur passed away before publication of book. F.C. Sigmond, Vice Consul of the United States of America, at Stockholm, Sweden, signed the document proving U.S. citizenship.

[43]Harrison Lane's story was sent by his widow, Arlie Mae, in September of 2001. His sister Marjorie Lane Beal also contributed some information verbally in February 2001 in Florida.

[44]Bill Macomber's interview was in Brewster on both Nov. 29, 2000 and on May 30, 2001, the former after a Class of 1944 luncheon at Sciortino's Restaurant and the latter at Benvenute's Restaurant after a Class of 1944 luncheon. He also sent information and gave me some details which I requested over the telephone. I greatly appreciated Bill's resurrecting the painful memories.

[45]Donald McLagan wrote his story in the summer of 2001.

[46]This story is from an interview on September 11, 2001 with Wiletta O 'Brien Bruen at her home near the house in which she and her brother John R. O'Brien grew up. She gave me her written account of her brother's history, copies of the newspaper article about the battle over Berlin and copies of the letter from which I took the quotation. She also told me that in the 1930 's she saw Italian Air Force airplanes fly over her house and up over Hine's ridge. She could clearly see them. She said they flew from New York. The only other person I could locate who remembered this was her cousin Robert Palmer who lived in the same area with a view of the same ridge. Other people have thought it was at the time of the World's Fair in New York.

[47]Interview on September 12 at the VFW hall in Brewster with Rita O 'Hara Rapp, sister of Henry Harding O'Hara. Some information came from news clippings from

The Brewster Standard of that time and possibly The Danbury News Times and other papers provided by Rita O'Hara Rapp.

[48]1945 letter to Mr. and Mrs. Henry O'Hara from the War Dept., Washington, D.C.

[49]Lafayette Pinckney wrote his recollections and mailed them in June 2001. He and his wife, Geneva also visited us at our home in N.H. in the fall of 2000 at which time I took them through the Wright Museum (WWII). Copies of clippings from The Brewster Standard provided by George Carlone, stated that Lafayette's twin brother LaVerne was a Seaman first class in the Coast Guard and Remington "was aboard a Coast Guard LST that landed troops on the Okinawa group five days before official invasion was to begin".

[50]George Schneider wrote his story and sent it to me in April 2001

[51]Charles Stefanic sent his history in September of 2001.

[52]The interview with Willis H. Stephens took place in March, 2001 in Florida.

[53]Edward Vichi's story was provided by his wife Doris Johnson Vichi who acquired the information from her husband. This was received in September of 2001.

[54]From the Military Record of Headquarters Ninth Air Force – Awards of the Distinguished Flying Cross.

[55]Donald von Gal's story was related to me by Lizette von Gal on September 10, 2001 at the VFW hall in Brewster. Some information was taken from the Military Record and Report of Separation provided by their son Reed von Gal.

[56]On October 19, 2001 Frank Genovese wrote a short version of his story. It was clear that many experiences were left unsaid, so I wrote to Frank and asked him if he would be willing to add more. He graciously complied, and in April of 2002 I received more details.

[57]From news clipping of The Brewster Standard – story written by a USCG correspondent at the time.

[58]Recent information about U-boat attack was taken from copy of LST Scuttlebutt Nov/Dec 2000.

[59]Interview at John Santorelli's home in Brewster on May 30, 2001.

[60]The Kenneth Brennan history was taken from The Brewster Standard, the local newspaper.

[61] Information for Robert Collin's story provided by Millie Buck Collins at her home in Brewster on May 29, 2001. She also provided copies for documents quoted.

[62] Larry L. Woodard, Before the First Wave: The Third Amphibious Tractor *Battalion – Peleliu and Okinawa* (Manhattan, Kansas ©1994): Sunflower University Press.

[63] John F. Larkin Jr.'s story was related on September 11th 2001 at the VFW hall.

[64] The Prisco family was well known to all of Brewster, having run the Prisco Bros. Taxi business as well as operating the Brewster school buses. Louis lives in Brewster but was unable to meet with me there; however he sent me his story in November of 2001.

[65] Ernest Adam's daughter Gail Manente wrote her father's story on Sept. 21st, 2001. She stated that her father was in the Oxford, NY Veteran's Home and was soon to be transferred to the VA Hospital at Montrose NY.

[66] Philip F. Beal's story was received by letters, written on May 23, 2000 and also June 30, 2002.

[68] The interview with Edward Brady's widow took place at the home of Alice and Bernard Brandon in Brewster on June 27, 2001. I received from her a copy of her husbands separation papers as well as information which she had received from Edward's friend and shipmate, Henry Harris. Marie Brady having acquired copies of her husband's service records from the Navy Department sent me some information from those. The information about meeting his friend comes from John Santorelli's own story.

[69] This story was taken from "Commodore Lewis E. Angelo's Remarks at Captain Daniel Brandon's Retirement on Front Steps, Naval Hospital, Bethesda".

[70] Interview with Capt. Daniel A. Brandon, MSC, USN (Ret.), conducted by Jan Herman, BUMED Historian, Darnestown, MD. I July 1992 and from further information, all sent on 27 July, 2001.

[71] Frederick Burdge told this story to his wife Janet McNeill Burdge (Brewster) who wrote it and sent to me September 2001.

[72] The story of Eddie and Jimmy Collins was given during an interview with Millie Buck Collins, Jimmy's widow on May 29, 2001 at her home in Brewster. A few lines are provided by the compiler of these stories who was a childhood friend of the Collins twins.

[73] Interview with Cecelia Harmon, widow of Richard J. Harmon took place at the VFW hall in Brewster on September 10, 2001.

[74]Interview with Marjorie Wilkinson Hazzard, widow of Herbert Hazzard took place on September 12, 2001 at her home in Brewster.

[75]This story was written by Robert Heinchon and given to me at the interview conducted at his home at Tonetta Lake Park on November 28, 2000 when we went over the story and made some additions.

[76]The story of George Hinkley was mailed in two increments in September of 2001. As I had known George and his wife Irene many years ago as teenagers, we also had several pleasant and informative telephone conversations.

[77]Unsung Sailors – The Naval Armed Guard in World War II (Copyright © 1990) by Justin F. Gleichauf.

[78]On June 28, 2001 Tom Lottrecchiano took me to lunch at Sciotino's Restaurant in Brewster where we conducted our interview.

[79]Interview with Fran Palmer took place on September 11, 2001 at the VFW hall in Brewster.

[80]Joan Beal Peckham's story was written by her sister, Dolores Beal Stephens.

[81]All the historical information on the U.S.S. Rixey comes from the History of the U.S.S. Rixey-APH-3 in the Dictionary of American Naval Fighting Ships, Naval History Division, Dept. of the Navy, Washington, 1976, sent to me by Robert B. Pitkat who had received it at a reunion of his naval buddies.

[82]Letters of Robert B. Pitkat dated February 27, 2001 and March 12, 2001 enclosing his history and other information.

[83]Interviews with William Pitkat at his home in Brewster on May 30 and June 2, 2001.

[84]From letters written to the author by Farrell Reed on June 25 and July 21, 2001.

[85]Peter A. Tavino sent information on April 12, 2001. Even though he was in the bloody landings of Iwo Jima, he said, "I don't have any great stories of the war".

[86]James Terwilliger's history was sent to me using a form provided and was received October 27, 2001.

[87]Interview took place on June 26, 2001 at the home of Frank and Bobby Piazza where I enjoyed having lunch with the Piazzas and the Vincent Vanarias.

[88]Interview took place in November 28, 2000 at Harvey Van Derlyn's home in Brewster.

[89]Ferdinand Vetare wrote his story and mailed it to me in January of 2001.

[90]Marjorie Lane Beal's story was written by her and given to me in February 2001 in Florida.

[91] Dolores Stephens interviewed her sister, Jane Beal Blackwood for her recollections in Florida in March of 2001 as well as by subsequent mail.

[92] The interview for Marie Destino Brady's recollections took place at the home of Alice and Bernard Brandon in Brewster on June 27, 2001.

[93] The interview for Alice Gorman Brandon's story took place at her home in Brewster on June 27, 2001. Although Alice was not a year-round resident of Brewster, she and her brothers were so much a part of the summer activities, especially at Tonetta Lake, that I felt the book would be enhanced by her inclusion

[94] Janet McNeill Burdge's recollections were sent to me in October of 2001.

[95] Interview on November 27, 2000 at the home of Joseph and Mary Cioccolanti in Brewster.

[96] Interview on May 29, 2001 at the home of Millie Collins in Brewster.

[97] Interview at the home of Andrew J. Durkin on May 29, 2001.

[98] Susan Foulk English wrote her recollections in a letter dated November 28, 2000 and another May 1, 2002. About the Brewster High School 50th year reunion, Sue said. "I did so enjoy our 50th reunion – meeting 'old' classmates for the first time. (Those names without faces back in 1944)." She hadn't met those classmates, because they had already left school and were in the service.

[99] Interview with Beatrice Denton Green in April of 2001 at Daytona Beach, Florida.

[100] Interview took place at Marjorie Hazzard's home in Brewster on September 12, 2001. This interview was very much on a personal basis, since Marjorie obviously had fond memories of Florence and Ross Beal.

[101] Irene Gaines Hinkley wrote her recollections in a letter on September 1, 2000.

[102] Interview with Joan Larkin took place on September 11, 2001 at the VFW hall in Brewster.

[103] The interview with Louise Vanderburgh Nicolai took place at the Stephens home in New Hampshire on July 31, 2001.

[104] Interview with John Palmer took place at the VFW hall in Brewster on September 12, 2001.

[105] Interview with Rita O'Hara Rapp took place at the VFW hall in Brewster on September 12, 2001.

[106] Interview with Muriel Pinckney Richards took place on October 14, 2000 at the Stephens home in New Hampshire.

[107] Ruth Godfrey Roth related her story at the VFW hall in Brewster on September 10, 2001.

[108] Dolores Beal Stephens wrote her story at different times in 2001 and 2002.

[109] Mallory finally wrote his story as the deadline approached – March 2002.

[110] Charlotte Tuttle's recollections were from a conversation over lunch in May 29, 2001.

[111] Frank Vetare's written reminiscences were sent on February 12, 2001.

[112] On October 30, 2001 Virginia Dutcher Ward drove to the author's home from her home in Andover, New Hampshire so that I could tape, and we could talk about Brewster in the 30's and 40's and to visit over lunch. She was very impressed with the Wright Museum (WWII) in Wolfeboro, N.H., the home-front section especially fascinating her.

About the Author

Dolores Beal Stephens remembers so vividly walking hand-in-hand with her mother in the Decoration Day parades in Brewster, N.Y. — the veterans of WWI walking proudly, some limping — and several marching bands playing, including the Brewster High School band which she joined in the sixth grade. A few years later she was learning about Hitler's Blitzkrieg, the blitz of London, England, and before long her friends were "joining up." War makes a great impression on young people, as it did Dolores. She graduated in 1944, a year before the end of WWII.

So, it is no wonder that as this great generation grew old, she reflected back on her youth and the people who so nobly served our country.

When she moved to New Hampshire, she thought she was going to continue more seriously her interest in sculpting, but soon found herself pushing the soapstone aside replacing it with a laptop and writing to the veterans of Brewster wherever they were. The WWII Wright Museum where she volunteers was surely a catalyst for this book. That and talking with visiting veterans enhanced the work on the manuscript. It was an exciting project made heart-warming by the interest and cooperation of all who contributed to the contents of *Those Who Served, Those Who Waited.*

3577591

Made in the USA